The Anxieties of Mobility

Migration and Tourism in

the Indonesian Borderlands

JOHAN A. LINDQUIST

UNIVERSITY OF HAWAI'I PRESS   *Honolulu*

Library of Congress Cataloging-in-Publication Data

Lindquist, Johan A.

The anxieties of mobility : migration and tourism in the
Indonesian borderlands / Johan A. Lindquist.

   p. cm.—(Southeast Asia—politics, meaning, and memory)

   Includes bibliographical references and index.

   ISBN 978-0-8248-3201-8 (hard cover : alk. paper)—
ISBN 978-0-8248-3315-2 (pbk. : alk. paper)

   1. Migrant labor—Indonesia—Batam Island. 2. Women migrant
labor—Indonesia—Batam Island. 3. Marginality, Social—Indonesia—
Batam Island. 4. Globalization—Economic aspects—Indonesia—
Batam Island. 5. Globalization—Social aspects—Indonesia—Batam Island.
I. Title. II. Title: Migration and tourism in the Indonesian borderlands.

   HD5855.I5L56 2009

   331.5'4409598192—dc22

                                        2008028725

Series designed by Richard Hendel

Printed by The Maple-Vail Book Manufacturing Group

CONTENTS

ACKNOWLEDGMENTS

I have always been attracted to reading acknowledgments, in part because they begin to describe the sociology of the book and its author. As I find myself in the situation of needing to write my own acknowledgments, however, it is proving very difficult to do so. The reason, of course, is that over the years there have been countless people who have offered support, even in the briefest of encounters. Recalling each of them and deciding who to include seems an impossible task, and, like so many other things, I feel like I should have started thinking about this earlier. But the impossibility of adequately acknowledging also reminds me that I have been very fortunate to meet an incredible array of people from around the world. For that I am truly grateful.

Victor Alneng, Matthew Amster, Tom Boellstorff, Clara Han, Johanna Gullberg, James Hoesterey, Sandra Hyde, Jennifer Mack, Kathy Quick, Maple Razsa, Natasha Schull, James Siegel, Karen Strassler, Eric Tagliacozzo, and Mats Utas all read and offered valuable comments on parts of earlier versions of the book. I am particularly indebted to Joshua Barker, who read the whole thing, and Mattias Viktorin, who did so several times. Rita Kipp and David Chandler, the series editors, and an anonymous reviewer for the University of Hawai'i Press offered helpful comments that allowed me to strengthen my argument considerably. I thank the editors at the press, Pamela Kelley and Cheri Dunn, for turning my manuscript into a book, and Susan Biggs Corrado for her careful copyediting.

The Department of Social Anthropology at Stockholm University has been my base since I started graduate school. I remain grateful to all the students, staff, and faculty, particularly Ulf Hannerz, who was my adviser for the doctoral dissertation upon which this book is based. He remains a model for intellectual inquiry. Patricia Spyer was the external reader for the dissertation, and her comments pushed me in the right direction. Others who have offered support in different ways include Tim Bunnell, Yosef Djakababa, Chris Dole, Mary Jo Delvecchio Good, Byron Good, Carla Jones, Alan Klima, Abidin Kusno, Ann Marie Leskowich, John MacDougall, Aihwa Ong, Susan Rodgers, James Sidaway, Mary Steedly, and Riwanto Tirtosudarmo.

The Swedish School for Advanced Asia Pacific Studies offered time and generous financial support as I was given the rare freedom to continue to explore and develop new ideas. I am particularly grateful to the coordinator of the school, Thommy Svensson, for his energy and vision. The Southeast Asia Program at Cornell University hosted me for a year. I thank the director, Thak Chaloemtiarana, as well as Jocean Bowler, Mercedes Chavez Ponzanelli, Deirdre de la Cruz, Erik Harms, Christian Lammerts, Christian Lentz, Adriane Lentz-Smith, Christophe Roberts, Loren Ryter, Lisa Todzia, and Benny Widyono for their friendship during my stay in Ithaca. James Siegel lent me his office to write, but it didn't help, since his questions had already moved me in new directions.

Together with Pelle Eriksson and Liam Dalzell I made a documentary film, *B.A.T.A.M.,* based on my fieldwork, which has helped me think through and subsequently improve my written work. I am very grateful to Pelle and Liam for our collaboration and Documentary Educational Resources for distributing the film.

I have been traveling to the Indonesian island of Batam for more than a decade now, but I have lost track of most of the people I came to know. This is the nature of a place where nobody quite belongs. A handful have remained. Socrates no longer rides around on his motorcycle, but has become the editor in chief of *Batam Pos,* while Lola Wagner and Husaini Tarmizi continue to work at YMKK, one of the island's few nongovernmental organizations. To them and to those who have departed I remain indebted. LIPI (Lembaga Ilmu Pengetahuan Indonesia), the Indonesian Institute of Sciences, made my fieldwork possible by granting me permission to conduct research on Batam.

Finally, in the last few years Johanna Gullberg, Aron Lindquist Gullberg, and even a dog named Sasha have made the world a better place for me. Having them in my life and finishing the book with this final sentence, I am reminded that I am quite a lucky man.

The Anxieties
of Mobility

A billboard advertisement for Hong Kong Bank. Photo by author.

Introduction

Before dawn Chandra has already showered and is ready to take his bag and leave. Left behind are a thin mattress and two cardboard boxes that function as storage space. The photos of Indonesian and Western pop and movie stars, cut from old newspapers, cover the wall but are barely visible from the light of the single bulb that dangles from the ceiling. Chandra knows that his girlfriend, with whom he has been living for the past three months, will be devastated when she returns in a few days from a short trip to her village. However, he feels ashamed (*malu*) to be living off the salary of a woman while he has nothing to offer. Without a good job or some savings, he cannot afford to send money to his mother in Aceh, much less marry his girlfriend or even return home from *merantau,* the process of migration. Therefore, he reasons, it is better to move on.

With 300 Singapore dollars (175 U.S. dollars)[1] and a passport in his front pocket, he leaves his room and walks through Belakang Sony, or Behind Sony, the squatter community where he has lived for over six months, named after the factory it abuts. These squats are identified by the government as illegal *rumah liar,* literally "wild houses." As Chandra follows the path that leads out of the woods and onto the main road, the sun is slowly rising over the Batamindo Industrial Park, the flagship of economic development on the Indonesian island of Batam.

During the 1980s the "Pacific Rim" emerged as the economic region of the future—a region that would connect Asia with the United States (Dirlik 1993). "Globalization" became the key term of reference. As Japanese business guru Kenichi Ohmae (1995) put it, this was the era of a new "borderless world," and the nation-state was becoming increasingly obsolete. People, goods, and capital were to flow freely, as economic complementarity and comparative advantages became the dominant tropes. In East and Southeast Asia, transborder and regional initiatives were planned and implemented in conjunction with this ethos (Sparke et al. 2004, 485), and in the 1990s regionalization took a particular idealized, geometrical form in Asia as "Growth Triangles" embodied hopes for the future. The most successful of these were centered on the region's emerging global cities, Hong Kong and Singapore. As Hong Kong was incorporated into China, however, the Indonesia-Malaysia-Singapore Growth Triangle, which ideally connects Batam, the Malaysian province of Johor, and Singapore, became the most widely featured and discussed transnational economic project in East and Southeast Asia.[2] In practice, however, the critical relationship has been between Batam and Singapore, with Johor remaining peripheral to the Growth Triangle project.[3]

As Singapore has been transformed from an export-processing zone for the global electronics industry into a knowledge-based financial center, factories have increasingly been moved to offshore sites of inexpensive land and labor such as Batam, where environmental and labor protection have remained lax and local ownership and tax laws have been changed in order to facilitate foreign direct investment. The Batamindo Industrial Park exemplifies this process. It houses approximately one hundred multinational corporations, such as Sony and Siemens, and employs seventy thousand workers, most of them young women. Until one month earlier, when he was laid off, Chandra worked in one of the factories. Convinced he will not be able to find a better job on Batam, he has decided to join a friend and attempt to enter Singapore to work illegally. "Anyway," he says, "even when I had a job I could never save any money since it is so expensive here."

Chandra has seen Singapore only from Batam's Stress Beach (Pantai Stres), a patchwork of *liar* bars and housing inhabited by migrants from across Indonesia—a place and a name that embodies the ironies and emotional anxieties that characterize everyday life on the island. Chandra occasionally goes there with friends to stare at the Singapore skyline, a constant reminder of what Batam's planners imagine that the island will become, but also an incentive for migrants to cross the Straits of Malacca into Singapore or Malaysia, located only twenty and twenty-five kilometers away, respectively, in search of higher wages.

Global cities that act as financial centers have become increasingly important as nodes in the new global economy (e.g., Sassen 1991; Brenner and Keil 2006). Unlike London, New York, and Tokyo, which are part

Map of Batam and the surrounding region. Reprinted with permission from IIAS Newsletter (see Lindquist 2006).

of larger political entities, Singapore—just over 700 square kilometers in size and with a population of 4.5 million—is a global city that is also a nation-state, meaning that the boundaries of the city converge with those of the state. The distance to offshore locations such as Batam is much closer compared with other major cities, literally compressing the space between center and periphery. The Singaporean state thus has the ability to regulate the movement of unskilled migrants in and out of the city in ways that are impossible in other global cities. Much like the borderland areas that divide the United States from Mexico and Hong Kong from China, the borderless world remains characterized by inequality—literally dividing the "developed" from the "developing" world—and demands a border to keep unskilled labor in place. The transformation of Singapore and the growing ease by which Singaporeans can travel to Indonesia—the fourth most populous and the most populous Muslim-majority country in the world—has thus been matched by intensifying immigration controls, making it increasingly difficult for Indonesian citizens to enter Singapore.

Chandra's friend Guntur, who is already waiting at the side of the road as he steps out of the woods from Belakang Sony, has worked illegally in Singapore before and knows the way. Together, they walk toward the gate of the industrial park to catch a shared taxi to one of the island's ferry terminals, where they will take the forty-minute ride to Singapore. Just over four hundred square kilometers in size, Batam has a distinct frontier-town atmosphere. Golf courses, marinas, and gated communities coexist with factories, squatter communities, karaoke bars, and brothels, while large parts of the island remain covered by jungle. Facilitated by an efficient ferry system, Batam serves as a destination for inexpensive shopping and leisure activities—most notably sex tourism—for Singaporeans and Malaysians, many of whom cross the border to escape the "stress" of everyday life. An economy of the day and one of the night have thus developed together, both depending primarily on the labor of young women, leading to the marginalization of men like Chandra from the labor market.

The island's transformation from a backwater into a large-scale development project has coincided with striking demographic changes: by 2005 more than 700,000 people were living on the island—compared with 3,000 in the late 1960s—as unskilled migrants such as Chandra poured into the area from across Indonesia, lured by rumors of a booming economy.[4] During the same period, Batam became one of the main points of tourist entry to Indonesia, as the number of arrivals increased from 60,000 in 1985 to 580,000 in 1990, peaking at over 1.5 million in 2005.

As Chandra and Guntur drive across the island on the newly paved roads, they pass rows of *liar* squatter housing hidden behind the trees that line the roadside, dilapidated housing estates built for Singaporeans and wealthy Indonesians but never finished, and a new "mega mall" announcing its grand opening. Empty lots and half-built structures that appear and disappear along the road suggest rapid change but reveal little of the past or what the future has in store. Boom and bust appear to coincide. At the last intersection before the terminal, a large billboard advertisement for Hong Kong Bank declares, "Batam is no longer an island," suggesting that Batam is no longer peripheral, but located squarely at the center of a new borderless economy.

After disembarking at the terminal, Chandra and Guntur "rent" money from an illegal broker in the entrance hall before purchasing their tickets: money that will be shown to immigration officers in Singapore as "proof" that they are not impoverished and looking for work, then returned after their passports have been stamped. The money does not, however, guarantee entrance into Singapore. Particularly since the Asian economic crisis that began in 1997, it has become increasingly difficult for Indonesian citizens to cross the border as the Singaporean and Malaysian authorities have become restrictive with visas.

Entrance to the half-finished housing estate Palm Spring. Photo by author.

In this particular case, Chandra and Guntur are turned back at immigration despite carrying 1,000 Singapore dollars each. Back on Batam all they can do is take a taxi back to their squatter houses, 500,000 rupiah poorer (about 55 U.S. dollars) after having bought the ferry ticket and rented the money. The anticipation of entering Singapore for a few weeks to work illegally, making eight times the salary that they could on Batam, is effectively disrupted. Chandra returns to his house in the afternoon, empties his bag, and resumes his life in the shadows of economic development, having told almost no one that he was leaving.

MOBILITY, IDENTITY, AND EMOTIONS IN THE "BORDERLESS WORLD"

Batam is exemplary in contemporary debates concerning globalization. While some observers view the creation of economic zones such as Batam as a route to development and improved welfare, others insist that such zones facilitate new forms of inequality that allow multinational corporations to profit at the expense of vulnerable workers. Both perspectives view Batam as a case in support of a broader argument. In similar terms, anthropologists, human geographers, and political scientists have taken Batam and the Growth Triangle as an ideal point from which to consider transforming forms of economy and sovereignty.[5] Most of these studies understand the development of Batam as an effect of changes in Singapore and ultimately the global economy. Macleod and McGee (1996, 430) state this most clearly: the *"key to understanding the Growth Triangle lies in the restructuring of the Singaporean economy"* [emphasis in original].

This book shifts perspectives by taking as its starting point not the restructuring of the Singaporean economy, but rather the experiences of Indonesian migrants such as Chandra. Chandra's mobility reveals a structure of indeterminacy that can be reduced neither to his actual intentions nor to the Singaporean economy, as necessity and contingency converge. His story evokes a world in which human mobility is not only intensifying and increasingly regulated, but also driven by desires and emotions. In much theorizing concerning globalization, however, "movement" is taken for granted, a black box subsumed within universalizing discourses in which either poverty "pushes" and economic development "pulls" migrants, or diasporas are understood as imagined transnational communities.[6] Limited attention has been paid to how particular channels facilitate, organize, and constrain movement (Tsing 2000, 337), and there is little specificity concerning how circuits of human mobility "are configured in particular places, for particular groups of people, and to what particular ends" (Freeman 2001, 1009).

In response, *The Anxieties of Mobility* uses three Indonesian concepts introduced in Chandra's story—*merantau, liar,* and *malu,* meaning roughly "migration," "wild," and "shame," respectively—in order to construct an analytical model that emerges through the process of fieldwork. This highlights the importance of ethnography as a mode of knowledge production. If ethnography makes room for the unpredictable (Strathern 2000, 286), Batam thus becomes a place where it is possible to ask questions and offer responses that cannot be posed before one has been there.[7] *Merantau* means "circular migration" and includes the explicit demand to return home. *Liar* literally translates as "wild" but also connotes "unlicensed" or "undomesticated." It is a term used throughout Indonesia, but it is most clearly articulated on Batam, both by the state and popularly in everyday life. Most conspicuously, squatter settlements are identified as "wild houses" (*rumah liar*) and premarital cohabitation as "wild marriages" (*pernikahan liar*); prostitutes who work on a freelance basis outside a designated location, such as karaoke bars or brothels, are also *liar.* Finally, *malu*—the dominant emotional trope for migrants on Batam—means, approximately, "shame," "embarrassment," and "shyness," but also "restraint" and "propriety" (Goddard 1996, 432; Peletz 1996, 228).[8] Each of these concepts deals with the problem of belonging. *Merantau* is about the relationship with home; *liar* is about not belonging, about being out of place; and *malu* is about the feeling of not living up to the standards of "home," meaning the hopes and ideals that define the self.

Together these concepts suggest a particular mode of temporality, namely the *belum,* or "not yet," which characterizes life on Batam and, in effect, the open-ended mode of analysis employed in this book.[9] Those who are on *merantau* have not yet returned home, the *liar* is not yet developed, and migrants who have not yet succeeded are *malu.* More generally, Indonesian authorities recognize that Batam is not yet completed as a development project and therefore not yet at the center of the regional economy, as the completion of the island's master plan has repeatedly been deferred to the future. *Belum* thus characterizes both the material and existential basis of everyday life on Batam.

In *The Culture of the New Capitalism,* Richard Sennett (2006, 53) makes a helpful distinction between "anxiety" and "dread." While the latter is well defined and "attaches to what one knows will happen," the former "arises in ill-defined conditions" and "attaches to what might happen." *The Anxieties of Mobility* attempts to evoke this sense of temporal insecurity and open-endedness. On the one hand, Indonesian migrants express these anxieties most vividly as they transform Batam's place name into various forms of acronyms, of which the following are two of the most common.

> *Bila Anda Tiba Akan Menyesal* – When You Arrive You Will Regret It
> *Bila Anda Tabah Akan Menang* – If You Endure You Will Succeed

On the other hand, these anxieties are expressed most pervasively in moral terms through *malu,* which forms the basis for an emotional economy that connects the *kampung,* the village or home, and the *rantau,* the space of migration.[10] By "emotional economy" I do not mean the direct exchange of emotions, but rather migrants' emotional debt to home, which gains a particular valence in the migratory process with the intensifying temporal burden that characterizes the return of the gift.[11] *Malu*—not the global economy—thus becomes the force that drives the *rantau,* as the demands of what it means to be a moral person haunt the migrant, keeping him or her on the move and from returning home.

By using *merantau, liar,* and *malu* to organize the ethnographic description, this book explicitly avoids taking concepts such as "globalization" or the "Singaporean economy" as a starting point for analysis. This allows us to understand Batam not strictly as a place that is "offshore" in relation to Singapore, as part of the Growth Triangle, or even as a case study for export processing zones, but rather as a node in a system of human mobility that is territorially and culturally unbounded and that draws together Indonesian factory workers (chap. 2) and prostitutes (chap. 3), Singaporean working-class tourists on Batam (chap. 4), and Indonesian migrant workers in Singapore and Malaysia (chap. 5).

The framework is thus neither defined primarily by geopolitical boundaries between nation-states nor the changing regional economy, but by the experiences of migrants and tourists themselves, thereby placing human mobility, gender, identity, and emotion in a landscape of capitalist expansion and state formation. In an important sense, therefore, *The Anxieties of Mobility* is an attempt to write an ethnography of globalization not as a series of impersonal transactions, but rather in terms of relationships that bind individuals together over large distances. More generally, this positions anthropology in a world that can be reduced neither to dichotomies between the "local" and the "global," nor to concepts such as "global culture" or "political economy." Instead, the book develops a mode of analysis within an open system, providing "orientation, without determining where the system itself, or those who use it, go" (Fortun 2003, 186).[12]

PUTTING MOBILITY IN ITS PLACE

I conducted fieldwork on Batam at the height of the Asian economic crisis for thirteen months between 1998 and 1999 and five further visits between 2000 and 2007. I had initially planned to investigate the politics of HIV prevention in the Growth Triangle, but my interests shifted as Batam was affected by the crisis. While migrants arrived from across Indonesia in search of work or from Malaysia after a wave of deportations, Singaporean tourists crossed the Straits of Malacca as the Indonesian rupiah dropped to as low as one-fifth of its previous value against the Singapore dollar. During this period I rented a house in a lower middle-class area on the outskirts of the main commercial district of Nagoya,[13] but most of my attention was focused on other places and people around the island. Because of the nature of my Indonesian research visa, and like the majority of my informants, I was not allowed to cross the border to Singapore or Malaysia. Much of my time was instead spent shuttling around Batam on a motorbike together with my research assistant trying to make sense of what was happening during the economic and political crisis.

During fieldwork, many of my informants were more mobile than I was. Batam is a node in the circulation of both capital and people, where both can suddenly appear, only to vanish days, months, or years later. Indonesian migrants I knew would suddenly leave for Malaysia and I would never see them again, or a couple of Singaporean men whom I met at one of Batam's discos would take the first ferry to Singapore the next morning. Rather than following these circuits, however, staying in place gave me a sense of the complexity and variation of human mobility in the region.

This distinction between following informants and staying in place can suggestively be compared with that between a train and a train station. On the one hand, by taking a train from, say, Kuala Lumpur in Malaysia to Singapore, it is possible to learn something about the kinds of people who travel this route, or the nature of the landscape between these places, and most certainly the time-consuming experience of crossing the border between the two countries. The train station, on the other hand, is an ideal place to consider not only who is traveling where, but also, for instance, what particular routes are available, who is selling tickets, how the local pickpockets work, and what the police are doing about it. Studying mobility by remaining in place, so to speak, thus offers a type of perspective that is concerned more with the social organization of mobility than with particular circuits, more with a system than a place of origin or a specific destination.

From a similar perspective, Saskia Sassen argues that certain types of places, namely global cities, illuminate the various economies and cultures in which the global economy is situated, thereby allowing us "to recover the concrete, localized processes through which globalization exists" (1998, ix–xx) and situating the channels, circuits, and flows that globalization theorists constantly grapple with.[14] *The Anxieties of Mobility* shows how a concern with places like Batam, located at the periphery of the global city, offers further methodological incentives by allowing us to consider the social organization of human mobility from the vantage point of the spatial and temporal border between the "developing" and the "developed" worlds, thus highlighting both the unevenness of global economic development and human mobility.

Although ethnographically situated on Batam, this study is thus not limited to one place.[15] Paying attention to the stories of migrants like Chandra suggests a series of links between different places—for instance, a small town in Aceh, a squatter village on Batam, and the Singaporean global city. From this perspective, the stories that people tell, and the consciousnesses they embody, articulate links, both explicitly and implicitly, to various overlapping political, cultural, economic, political, and religious systems. My concern has been to identify how particular forms of knowingness about—and practical engagement with—these systems are articulated with regard to the more specific multilocal systems in which subjects are entangled, and through this process to create an analytical space for description (Marcus 1995, 111; see also Spyer 2000). More broadly, this is a form of "post-ethnographic anthropological writing" that uses "local knowledge" but refuses "the bounds of conveniently sized localities through venturing to speak about regional relations and histories" (Thomas 1991, 316–317).

THE MOBILE SUBJECT

In 1963 anthropologist Hildred Geertz considered the position of an emerging unskilled and illiterate "urban proletariat," as migrants moved from the villages into the rapidly expanding urban areas. Indonesia had entered the postcolonial era less than twenty years before, and Geertz claimed that a "metropolitan superculture" was developing that transcended the regional cultures of the colonial era. This new national culture—produced in cities like Jakarta—was the culture of bureaucrats and skilled workers, while the proletariat retained their links and allegiances to the villages. Little was known, she pointed out, about this much larger group of Indonesians, subjects who had not yet been transformed into citizens (H. Geertz 1963, 37–38).[16] More than forty years later, it is evident that the urban proletariat has grown substantially in Indonesia but arguably still has not achieved citizenship, while continuing to be of limited concern to contemporary anthropologists.[17]

Historically, *merantau* was "essentially a male business" (Mrázek 1994, 11) associated with particular ethnic groups. Today, however, there have been two significant changes. First, *merantau* has become a pan-Indonesian phenomenon as increasing numbers of Indonesians have been transformed into migrants in search of new forms of life and labor. Most people who pass through Batam are on *merantau* and ideally hope to gain access to the economy of development before returning home successfully. Second, unmarried women are increasingly going on *merantau.* This is particularly noteworthy on Batam, where migrant women have become the main sources of labor in both the electronics and prostitution industries. On the other side of the border, in Singapore and Malaysia, similar processes are evident as Indonesian women work as domestic servants for the expanding middle class, while men work illegally in plantations or construction sites.[18]

Phrased most strongly, *The Anxieties of Mobility* argues that during the postcolonial era *merantau* has become homogenized as a national cultural form; it is no longer a heterogeneous "culture of the fringes" (Mrázek 1994, 17). This becomes particularly evident if one focuses attention on the contemporary Indonesian migrants, most of whom are part of Geertz's urban proletariat. Becoming a *perantau,* or migrant, in Indonesia today appears to offer a route from the village into the economy of development and particular forms of modernity. The migrants with whom I am concerned dream of becoming part of the privileged site of the nation—the middle class—but are most often denied, as what is initially imagined as a rite of passage does not necessarily lead to a resolution (cf. Van Gennep 1960; V. Turner 1970). Instead, Batam is a place where one learns to become a particular kind of Indonesian, one who is part of the underclass. This book thus highlights commonalities between Indonesian migrants rather than primarily addressing ethnic distinctions. This perspective is not "an apologia for the nation," but rather an attempt "to open a space from which to imagine new geographies of identification" (Boellstorff 2002, 38). In other words, I am not concerned with describing a shift from one identity to another—from the local or ethnic to the national or global—but rather with the formation of experiences that in an important sense are lacking in closure and thus rife with uncertainty and anxiety.

THE ANXIETIES OF MOBILITY

I was surprised. People lived in houses that looked like chicken coops with roofs made out of rubber. "Why do the houses look like that? Why do people live like this?" I asked. My friend answered, "Because these *ruli, rumah liar* ["wild houses"; *ruli* is an acronym for *rumah liar*] will be razed soon, because they were built without permission from the government.

    Chandra (describing his initial arrival on Batam)

The Indonesian government's identification of the *liar*—most notably squatter housing, premarital cohabitation, and certain types of prostitution—is by no means random, but reflects concerns with the production of legible environments (Scott 1998). In this context, *liar* spaces and identities come to inhabit a particular temporal space, namely the *belum,* or "not yet" developed or ordered. This does not mean, however, that the *liar* is disorganized or merely an excess of the development process. It is rather structured by alternative forms of ordering, inhabited not only by Indonesian migrants, but also by Singaporean tourists—mainly working-class men marginalized in the new economy—who travel to Batam not in search of the developed sites of tourism, but rather recreational drugs, which are banned in Singapore, or gambling and prostitution, which are heavily regulated.[19] While many of these men develop sustained *liar* relationships with Indonesian women, others come to live in *liar* squatter communities on Batam, which are reminiscent of the village life that has been destroyed in Singapore. The *liar* thus becomes not only a transnational counterpoint to the Singaporean modernity project, but also a "contact zone" (Pratt 1992; see chap. 3) for different groups of circulating populations.

Upon arrival, migrants such as Chandra expect development but encounter the *liar*. This is the "shock of modernity" (Watts 1992b). The *liar,* however, is not necessarily a space or identity that migrants can or wish to avoid. Squatter housing can be a site of community formation, premarital cohabitation can be considered a legitimate relationship, working as a prostitute can be a way of gaining access to the economy of development, and engaging in drug use or extramarital sex can be desired. But from the perspective of the migrant, there is usually a sense of instability or anxiety with regards to the *liar;* squatter housing runs the risk of being razed, prostitutes run the risk of being detained by state authorities, Islam forbids drug use and extramarital sex. Inhabiting the *liar* is often a temporary condition threatened by violence and associated with the underclass;[20] there is thus generally a desire to move out of the *liar* toward the middle class or for *liar* communities to mimic the structure of the state in order to gain legitimacy (cf. Barker 1998). To recognize oneself as permanently—as opposed to temporarily—*liar* is to be peripheral to the Indonesian nation.

It is precisely through this process of self-recognition that *malu* gains its force. Generally, men are expected to respond aggressively to the experience of *malu,* while women are supposed to withdraw, thereby recognizing their subordinate position (Collins and Bahar 2000, 48).[21] This book problematizes this understanding of *malu* and, more generally, any understanding of emotions that precedes experience (Boellstorff and Lindquist 2004). In contrast, I emphasize that *malu* gains particular forms of valence as migrants engage in new forms of social interaction and moral boundaries become ambiguous. The classic studies of "shame-embarrassment" in Southeast Asia by Clifford Geertz (1973) and Michelle Rosaldo (1983, 1984) argued that emotions could not be analyzed outside of the social and cultural contexts in which they were experienced, understood, and talked about. However, both grounded their ideas in ethnographic contexts in which culture, ethnicity, and language were relatively isomorphic, and in which translocal economic systems were of limited relevance. In contrast, in the world I will describe, everyday life is constituted within the framework of the nation, and in tension with a transnational economy that utilizes female labor, rather than in the context of a local community where culture, place, and language appear more easily to correspond.

It is thus significant that in the *rantau* it is not "shame-embarrassment" in other Indonesian languages, such as the Balinese word *lek*—famously translated by Geertz (1973, 402) as "stagefright"—or the Javanese word *isin* that have become key emotional tropes, but rather *malu*, a Malay word that exists in other Indonesian languages, but more important in this context, part of the Indonesian lingua franca. This suggests the importance of moving beyond a false dichotomy between a local moral economy and a global impersonal economy, and instead highlights an analytical form that in a sense is national but also spatially unbounded. *Malu* thus appears as an emotion (and opens up a space of analysis) that describes the failures to live up to the ideals of the nation. It offers migrants an experiential trope as *Indonesians* in the shadows of the promises of *Indonesian* economic development (cf. Siegel 1997; Boellstorff 2005).[22]

Although economic failure is the main source of *malu* on Batam, for women, in particular, anxieties concerning sexuality are equally prevalent—for factory workers in relation to premarital sexuality, and for prostitutes with regard to selling sex for money. The large number of young women on Batam who control their own wages and move in public spaces generates rumors and gossip in the media and everyday talk.[23] As Murray (1991, 127) puts it bluntly, "Sexuality is used to judge women's morality but not men's." It is from this perspective that the gendered relationship between *malu,* sexuality, and Islam become especially pertinent.[24] On Batam, it is said, people "forget religion" (*lupa agama*). It is a place as full of danger as much as it is of possibilities; a place where one can either "destroy" (*hancur*) or "develop" (*maju*) oneself. While destruction—understood primarily in religious terms—comes through premarital sex, drug use, or prostitution, personal development is associated with making money or particular forms of religious engagements.

It is from this perspective that it is possible to understand how migrant women sometimes wear the Muslim veil or take the drug Ecstasy in the same places and for the same reasons—reasons that are both comprehensible and explicitly moral. On Batam migrant women use these technologies in order to deal with *malu.*[25] While veiling reinforces moral boundaries associated with *malu,* Ecstasy use facilitates the transgression of those same boundaries. Wearing the veil, or *jilbab,* appears to offer an identity that protects against the dangers of social interaction in the context of migration, while Ecstasy use allows female prostitutes to more easily engage in morally ambiguous forms of transactions. Both activities, however, can be transformed into legitimate models of personal development (*kemajuan*), which may displace *malu* upon return home—one as a sign of religious insight, the other as a means for creating economic value.

Veiling and Ecstasy use are therefore both directly connected with the demands of home and the expectations of migration. In this context, it is the experience of *malu*, or of being identified as someone who should be *malu*, that becomes an organizing principle for social action and the management of appearances. Although I am by no means equating the two acts, veiling and the use of Ecstasy both facilitate survival in the "situation of duress under which gender performance always and variously occurs" (Butler 1990, 139). More generally, the following chapters will illuminate how various forms of technologies—ranging from clothing to recreational drugs—are used by migrants in a wide variety of circumstances in order to function effectively in the tension between the region's shifting political economy and the emotional economy of the *rantau*. Although there are certainly varying degrees of reflexivity involved in these acts, in all situations the primary problem is not self-identity, but rather avoiding being identified as someone who does not belong.

In relation to these processes, a series of recognizable figures have emerged—and appear throughout this book—giving these anxieties a particular cultural form. In the Batamindo Industrial Park, the woman wearing the *jilbab* (the Muslim headscarf) offers a ubiquitous representation of the female worker in the official economy (chap. 2). Even in the late 1990s, as the recent wave of Islamization was spreading throughout the country, more than 50 percent of the women working at Batamindo wore the *jilbab*, a remarkable figure at the time by any standard in Indonesia.[26] While government officials and factory managers have viewed this as an effect of successful religious programs, many other people on Batam understand it as a sign of deceit, a facade masking immoral behavior, rather than as a sign of piety. In contrast, the *lontong*,[27] or prostitute, flaunts her body on the main streets of Nagoya wearing platform shoes, tight clothing, and heavy makeup, literally embodying Batam as an "island of sin" (chap. 3). Moving in the shadows of these worlds is the *bronces*, the long-haired and tattooed man who subsists on the money of women (chap. 3). Reminiscent of the *preman* (e.g., Ryter 1998), or thug, who is more frequently associated with crime, the *bronces* is a predator who brings to light the particular *gendered* anxieties of Batam, where women support men financially and engage in sex outside the context of the family. The *Singaporean man* who travels to Batam to gamble and buy sex and drugs makes explicit the island's ambiguous position in relation to a larger world (chap. 4). Representing either unambiguous chastity or unbridled sexuality, the *jilbab*-wearing woman, the *lontong*, the *bronces*, and the *Singaporean man* should be understood in relation to the feminization of labor in the *rantau*. In Batam's moral landscape, these figures become sites for allocating responsibility (cf. White 2000, 62). Finally, travelling in the opposite direction—toward Malaysia or Singapore—the *Indonesian transnational migrant* further illuminates the gendered organization of migrant labor throughout the region and the various channels that become available in an economy of border crossing (chap. 5).

MOVING BEYOND CRISIS

The Asian economic crisis of 1997 initiated a period of dramatic transformation in Indonesia and Southeast Asia. After the initial collapse of the Thai baht, the Indonesian rupiah followed during the latter half of 1997. The ensuing economic crisis in Indonesia led President Suharto to step down in May 1998, thereby formally ending the authoritarian New Order regime that had ruled for over thirty years and setting the stage for a proliferating political landscape characterized not only by *reformasi* (democratization) and political decentralization, but also by spectacular forms of violence, including religious warfare in the Maluku Islands, the Ninja killings in East Java, and the Bali bombings.[28] These changes have had profound effects both in Indonesia and on scholarship dealing with Indonesia. In the post-9/11 security environment, a concern with violent events and radical Islam, personified by cleric Abu Bakar Bashir and the organization Jemaah Islamiyah, has come to dominate public discourse throughout Southeast Asia, despite the limited support that the acts and ideals associated with them have among the vast majority of the populations in these countries.

This book argues that these terms of debate risk displacing enduring problems for the vast majority of Indonesians, who continue to struggle as they did during the Suharto era.[29] For these groups—who ultimately are the historical agents of this book—the expansion of radical Islam and the forms of violence associated with it are spectacles primarily experienced through the mass media, literally at a distance. Together with informants on Batam, I watched many of these events unfold on television. Although there was often a degree of awe with the effects of the bombs in Jakarta and Bali, or the power of the charismatic Abu Bakar Bashir, there was more noticeably incomprehension rather than identification with the perpetrators.

This is not to deny that the economic crisis, in particular, affected Batam (see chap. 1), primarily through a dramatic increase in migrants who were lured by rumors of employment. Arguably, however, these processes did not create a radical historical disjuncture, but rather accentuated the importance of the concepts this book is concerned with, namely *merantau, liar,* and *malu.* On Batam economic and political crises led to increasing flows of *perantau,* or migrants, the dramatic expansion of *liar* housing and prostitution, and intensifying feelings of *malu* for migrants who struggled to survive in a context of extreme competition. Thus like the economic development of Batam, the crisis and its aftereffects have clarified particular processes already at work.

In writing this book, I have struggled with closure and attempts at generating a kind of coherence in an area and era characterized by dramatic change. In the end I settle for an "ethic of openness" (Fortun 2003) in which *merantau, malu,* and *liar* form a conceptual framework. This allows one to consider how the landscape of human mobility is organized throughout the region. The concepts do not neatly overlap, since they identify significantly different forms: movement, identity, place, and emotion. But considering them in relation to one another creates the possibility of describing, analyzing, and writing about processes and landscapes that become evident through Batam. *The Anxieties of Mobility* thus attempts to create an alternative topography of Southeast Asia that is defined primarily by the mobility of Indonesian migrants and Singaporean tourists, rather than the force of the global economy.

Chapter 1 sets the stage for the chapters that follow via a description of the historical trajectory through which Batam has been transformed from an obscure island located "between" different centers of commerce and power into a major development project and part of a transnational economic zone. In turn, the chapter maps the changing regional forms of mobility and the transformation of space on Batam, thus beginning to describe the place that the migrants and tourists who are the subjects of this book come to inhabit for a period of time.

Chapter 2 takes as its starting point the Batamindo Industrial Park, a quintessential example of a spatial and economic global type—the development enclave—and the *liar* squatter communities that surround it. Moving between the factory floor and the squatter communities, and by focusing on the gendered relationship between *merantau, liar,* and *malu,* the chapter shows how the enclave is "diluted" and best understood in relation to the social world that it inhabits. It thus begins to map a broader emotional economy of *merantau* that takes further shape in the coming chapters.

Chapter 3 shifts ethnographic attention to Ozon and a different example of a transnational space—the disco. Centered on *liar,* or freelance Indonesian female prostitutes without pimps, the chapter moves from women's engagement with the drug Ecstasy and Singaporean clients in the disco to their relationships with boyfriends, children, and other family members. Highlighting the tensions between a short-term engagement with the *liar* and the long-term demands of *merantau,* the chapter describes the common emotional economy of the factory workers and prostitutes, one that places them between the demands of home and the promises of development.

Chapter 4 returns to Ozon, shifting focus to the Singaporean working-class men who travel to Batam not to visit the official tourist sites, but rather to spaces and relationships that are identified by the Indonesian state as *liar.* These men lead various forms of lives, some partake of recreational drugs and sex, others engage in long-term relationships with Indonesian women, and a few live in *liar* housing that appears reminiscent of a village life that has been destroyed in Singapore. This chapter shows how these men, increasingly marginalized in Singapore's knowledge-based economy, travel to Batam in order engage in a world of "fantasy"—as one of the men puts it—that remains beyond their reach in Singapore.

Chapter 5 shifts attention to a different form of cross-border mobility through an emphasis on the "immigration industry" that facilitates the movement of Indonesian migrants across the border to Malaysia and Singapore in a context of intensifying state regulation. These forms of circulation highlight the ambiguous boundaries between "legality" and "illegality" and, in particular, the exchangeability of female labor within the Growth Triangle. It is in this context that *The Anxieties of Mobility* becomes most explicit, as the tensions between the demands of *merantau* and state regulation lead to intensifying forms of violence.

Finally, chapter 6 offers not so much closure as a way forward. Taking as its starting point an ambiguous structure being built on Batam's Stress

Beach in 2003—a structure suggesting both boom and bust—this conclusion highlights the form of temporality—the *belum,* or "not yet"—and the related open-ended circuits of mobility that have formed the trajectory for description throughout this book. In so doing, *The Anxieties of Mobility* reaffirms the critical importance of ethnography as a method that reduces the gap between description and theory in studies of globalization and social life, more generally, thus positioning anthropology as a discipline at the center of social inquiry.

I

Borderland Formations

The lights from the Singapore skyline are still visible in the background when Pak Padil takes me out in his motorboat at dawn. In his broad Malay dialect he begins a lament that he obviously has spoken before. "When I was young," he tells me, "there were fish everywhere. It was easy to make a living. Now the water is polluted and the fish are gone." Born in the early 1920s on a small island just off the coast of Batam, Pak Padil was a fisherman for a large part of his life, but these days he has become connected to the new economy, guiding weekend tourists from Singapore on boat trips along Batam's coast. As a child he would sometimes take the three-hour boat trip to Singapore—even then a bustling cosmopolitan center of trade, a dramatic contrast to the quiet village life on Batam—to visit his father who worked there. In the years before World War II he moved there, running errands in a large store owned by a Chinese entrepreneur from Java, before returning to Batam when Japanese forces captured Singapore. After the war and Indonesian independence, Pak Padil worked for a few years at the Royal Dutch Shell oil refinery just off the coast of Batam but would frequently take the ferry to buy goods in Singapore's markets. "There were no markets on Batam then. We depended on Singapore." This changed, however, with the Konfrontasi, an armed conflict in 1963 between Indonesia and Malaysia (of which Singapore was a part) that initiated a period intensifying border regulation. "After that, I never returned to Singapore again."

Pak Awang Ali, another elderly Malay man who lives in one of the few remaining fishing villages on Batam, came with his parents from Singapore in the mid-1930s, leaving behind increasing land scarcity and competition among fishermen. At the time, he recalled, there were only a few villages and a Japanese rubber plantation along the coastal area where he lived. His father and other villagers would catch fish that they sold or bartered in

Singapore. They saw little point in living or working in Singapore; it was easier to survive on Batam.

But things have changed. When I talked with Pak Padil, Pak Awang Ali, and other elderly Malay fishermen on Batam about their lives before World War II, most became nostalgic and remembered what they had lost, often pointing out their own marginalization in relation to the development of Batam. "Now," Pak Awang Ali told me,

> even though I am Malay, and Singapore is part of the Malay World (Taman Melayu), I have to use a passport to travel to Singapore because they tell me that I am Indonesian. Even with a passport, it is not certain that the immigration authorities will let me across the border. Maybe they think that I want to work illegally: an old man like me! Who knows? And now, BIDA [Batam Industrial Development Authority] tells me that I live in a wild house (*rumah liar*) that has to be razed (*digusur*), even though it was built twenty years before they arrived!

This chapter begins with Pak Awang Ali and Pak Padil, not in order to reproduce a nostalgic lament of an era that has passed, but rather to suggest an opening for considering the historical transformations that have shaped channels of human mobility in the "Malay world," a region that

View of the Singapore skyline from Batam. Photo by author.

encompasses contemporary Malaysia, Singapore, and large parts of Indonesia. While the precolonial Malay world was characterized by powerful centers and unclear political boundaries, the Dutch and English colonial empires divided this world between them, forming the territorial basis for what after World War II became Indonesia, Malaysia, and Singapore. Each of these periods can be distinguished by different (overlapping) patterns of human mobility. In the precolonial era, migration was turbulent, as men easily shifted their allegiances between different hubs of power. In the colonial period, capitalist expansion led to the extensive import of pan-Asian coolies who labored in the tin mines and rubber plantations that fueled industrialization in Europe and the United States. In the postcolonial period, new regimes of citizenship and the regulation of borders within and between nation-states have made documents such as passports and identity cards critical instruments for most forms of human mobility, including migration and tourism.

Of particular significance in these processes is the regulation of the mobility of people such as Pak Awang Ali and Pak Padil, who are supposed to remain in their "proper" places on the Indonesian side of the border.[1] These men are not the ideal citizens of the Growth Triangle, and indeed they find themselves being caught up in an age to which they do not belong. In an important sense their stories illustrate how the production of borders has become critical in the formation of a transnational "borderless world."

The concern with state borders was initially a colonial project but became increasingly important during the postcolonial era as territory came to define the limits of the new nation-states, thereby creating the possibility of identifying Batam as a site of Indonesian *national* development. Pak Awang Ali and Pak Padil have thus been redefined as Indonesian citizens, while their livelihoods and homes have been positioned outside of the project of development, in the *liar* spaces associated with the Indonesian underclass. State formation coupled with capitalist expansion have thus produced new peripheries and spaces of exclusion—of which the *liar* is the most obvious example—as uneven development has taken a specific form. This chapter tracks the history of these transformations, thereby setting the stage for the following chapters, which will describe how contemporary Indonesian migrants and Singaporean tourists engage with life on and beyond Batam.

THE ENTREPÔT ECONOMY

In the early nineteenth century Sir Stamford Raffles and the English East Indies Company combed the Straits of Malacca—a narrow stretch of water linking the Indian and Pacific oceans—for a port that could handle the growing trade between India and China. After the Napoleonic wars England became the dominant power in Europe and expanded its influence throughout Southeast Asia at the expense of the Dutch, and in 1819 Raffles finally claimed the area that was to become Singapore, just across the straits from Dutch-controlled Riau (today the town of Tanjung Pinang on Bintan, located adjacent to Batam in Indonesia). Within a decade Singapore displaced Riau as the dominant port in the region, thereby allowing the English to gain control over one of the most important waterways in the world.[2]

The founding of Singapore led to a series of agreements designed to resolve economic and political tensions between the Dutch and the English. The 1824 Treaty of London literally divided large parts of Southeast Asia—including Riau and Singapore—between them. Although only allowing the right to make agreements with local rulers, not the right of governance or possession, the treaty dramatically changed the regional political dynamics in the region. Created in the boardrooms of London, it in no way reflected the existing cultural and economic reality of the region, effectively forming the cartographic framework for the Malaysian, Singaporean, and Indonesian nation-states in the mid-twentieth century (Trocki 1979; Tagliacozzo 2005).

Singapore became part of the English Straits in 1826 and was named a British Crown Colony in 1867. The opening of the Suez Canal two years later, the dramatic expansion of tin mining in the 1880s, and rubber production in the early twentieth century quickly positioned Singapore as a hub in an economy of mines and plantations that stretched throughout the Malay Peninsula and across the border to the Dutch East Indies, fueling industrialization in Europe, Japan, and the United States.[3]

Singapore succeeded because it mimicked earlier entrepôts in the region (Trocki 1979). Trade in the coastal area between the Riau Archipelago and the Malay Peninsula had for centuries centered on a series of ports that depended on cooperation with vassal states in the periphery.[4] Low population density throughout precolonial Southeast Asia meant that the control of population was more important than the control of land. In contrast to contemporary forms of state formation, outer territorial boundaries were unclear and the power of the center was crucial in the reproduction of the polity (Milner 1982; Scott 1998, 185).[5] Singapore's use of an indigenous state model allowed for expansive economies that transgressed the territorial limitations created by the colonial border and thereby bound large parts of the region to its markets. In other words, Singapore was based on a political economy that ultimately did not respect the border that the colonial powers themselves had created.

Singapore developed into a meeting place for Chinese and Europeans—the former offering labor, the latter capital—as the traditional Malay communities and states were increasingly marginalized (Trocki 1990, 4).[6] In this process, Singapore became a major destination and transit point for labor as migrants from China, in particular, labored on both sides of the colonial border. The broader structure of labor mobility during the colonial era varied in form from free migration to debt bondage and outright slavery, including not only Chinese, but also Tamils from India and Javanese from the Dutch East Indies (Tagliacozzo 2005, 236–244). The import of migrant labor over great distances—rather than the use of local populations—was a general pattern in the development of capitalist enclaves across Asian colonial regimes throughout the nineteenth century.[7] While alleviating labor shortages, this also allowed capitalists and state administrators to keep wages low and facilitated the control of migrants, who had no alternative means of local livelihood or support (Breman 1990, 15–19). It was not until the twentieth century that the trade in human labor was increasingly regulated and new forms of migration began to take shape.[8]

POSTCOLONIAL BORDERLANDS

Tagliacozzo (2005) has shown that while in 1865 the border between the Dutch and English was a "work in progress," by 1915 it had taken the form that it has today. During the late colonial and early postcolonial period, however, authorities on both sides of the border had limited resources in controlling the movement of people or goods, and islands like Batam and Bintan remained closely integrated with the Singapore economy. Even by the early 1960s, nearly twenty years after Indonesian independence, the national currency, the rupiah, was rarely used in Riau, and Indonesian civil servants continued to be paid in Singapore dollars.

This changed in 1963 when the Indonesian president Sukarno initiated an armed conflict, Konfrontasi, in reaction to Malaysia's creation as a state (which initially came to include Singapore) after gaining independence from England. Although the official reason for Konfrontasi was anti-imperialism—Sukarno saw Malaysia as a neocolonial plot—he had earlier expounded a vision of a great "Pan-Indonesia" that would bind Indonesia, Malaya, and the Philippines. In this scenario, the control of both sides of the Straits of Malacca was considered crucial for Indonesia to become strong and secure. Konfrontasi was thus directly connected to the search for a new pattern of international relations in the postcolonial era, as the control of territorial borders became increasingly significant (Mackie 1974).

Along with military intervention, there were other technologies for nationalizing the border area. The Singapore dollar was banned through a policy of *dedollarisasi,* and markets opened on Batam.[9] Whereas Riau's inhabitants earlier had generally traveled to Singapore, increasingly goods in the area were imported from the Indonesian capital, Jakarta. New immigration controls were also installed, making it more difficult for inhabitants of the Riau Archipelago, now redefined as Indonesian citizens, to cross the border. Although it did not make it impossible, many of my elderly informants such as Pak Padil and Pak Awang Ali never crossed the straits to Singapore again.

As an armed conflict, Konfrontasi was a minor historical event, but more important, it was a period of re-imagining the outer contours of the Indonesian geo-body (cf. Winichakul 1994) not only in the province of Riau, which Jakarta had neglected for the first twenty years of independence, but also along the Malay-Indonesian border in Borneo (Bala 2000), and in the conflict with the Dutch over West Papua (Rutherford 2002). After the Japanese surrender ended World War II and set the stage for independence, the new Indonesian leaders simply assumed that the borders of the new state would coincide with the borders of the Dutch East Indies, but the new constitution never made this explicit (Mackie 1974, 21). Thus, in effect, the nation preceded the state, forming the basis for the intensifying concern with the control of territory and population in the border regions.

It took five years for the Indonesian state to reclaim the Riau Archipelago from the Dutch and bring it under its own administration. The central government in Jakarta remained suspicious of Riau, however, with its high proportion of ethnic Chinese and their potential allegiances to foreign powers,[10] and in the early 1960s the provincial capital, which the Dutch earlier had located in the port town of Tanjung Pinang (formerly Riau), was moved to the booming oil town of Pekanbaru on the Sumatran mainland. Discrimination against ethnic Chinese, identified as "foreigners," was increasingly institutionalized after Indonesian independence. In 1959 Chinese-owned retail stores were banned from rural areas throughout the country,[11] which led many ethnic Chinese to leave the smaller islands in the Riau Archipelago for Chinese-dominated Singapore or Tanjung Pinang.[12] The Chinese groups that had originally made up the majority of the labor force that fueled nineteenth- and early twentieth-century capitalist growth in Singapore and Riau were thus increasingly compartmentalized with the expansion of the Indonesian state.

Through the 1960s and 1970s the structure of population mobility began to change and intensify as Riau became both a destination and transit area to Malaysia and Singapore for migrants from around Indonesia. The shifting political economy, increasingly centered on national development projects in urbanizing areas, together with a "veritable revolution" (Hugo 1985, 62) in transportation, set the stage for increasing voluntary migration from across Indonesia, in contrast to the import of labor common during the colonial regimes. As the *rantau,* the space of migration, became a site of engagement with new processes of identity formation, these migrants increasingly came to recognize themselves as Indonesian citizens. The following account begins to describe this process.

NATIONALIZING MOBILITY

Muhamad Radjab's autobiography, set in a West Sumatran village in the 1920s, describes his wish to leave home and head into the *rantau.*

> Sooner or later, of course, I had to leave the village! To follow Father's wishes and stay there forever, to share the fate of the majority of villagers who never journeyed more than fifteen kilometers from Sumpur from the time of their birth till their death—for me that would have been an

absolute impossibility. This would have meant killing off my sturdily developed longings and damping down the aspirations burning inside me. (Radjab 1995, 309)

Continuing his account, as he grows older, Radjab's desire to *merantau* merely intensifies, but his father refuses to grant him permission to leave the village. The stories of returning migrants never cease to fuel Radjab's imagination.

> The bigger I got, the harder I worked at interrogating people who'd just come back from the *rantau*. I'd do this till late at night and not get drowsy: I'd be totally absorbed in listening to and taking in each and every word they uttered. Everything that they portrayed with their stories was pictured with great clarity in my thoughts. Sometimes I would ask myself in my heart, why couldn't my body just fly off over there so I could witness all this for myself. (1995, 310)

One by one, Radjab's friends departed from the village, and he was left alone to contemplate his future. It became obvious that having been in the *rantau* was not only about gaining experience, but was also a criterion for increasing in status in the village or a rite of passage for becoming a man. Former friends and acquaintances who returned from the *rantau* no longer paid attention to him, and they married the women he loved. The attitudes and styles of the men and the signs of success that they flaunted made it all the harder to bear.

> His cigarettes would be Westminsters, from a can. Or he'd be smoking a cigar with a beautiful ring around it and a fragrant smell. One with a gold watch would pull it out of his pocket every ten minutes or so to check the time repeatedly, as if he had an appointment or something was rushing him, as if his time was very valuable. . . . Half of them had gold teeth. Every few moments they'd laugh. Sometimes, when there was no reason to laugh, they'd laugh; just so long as their lips would part and the gleaming gold teeth would appear. (1995, 317)

At last, his father allows to him to go to the *rantau,* if only to the nearby city of Padang. At this point his feelings are mixed; he feels torn between his hopes for the future and the longing (*rindu*) he knows he will have for the village and his family. But this sadness is transcended by his strikingly modern attitude.

> I knew these ties to the village were just bonds of feeling, and that sooner or later these would be snapped by my relentless, heedless life desires. And I simply could *not* base my character and life outlook on feelings alone, if I did not wish to become a mere ball in a game between nature and the world around me. (1995, 320)

Radjab self-consciously juxtaposes "feeling" with "desire," the former being associated with the village and tradition, the latter with the city and modernity.[13] He understands himself as being driven by the force of his own desires and believes that the feelings that bind him to home can and should be transcended in order to become a new kind of individual who is not a passive actor, "a mere ball" in the world. These tensions between the demands of home and hopes for the future describe the beginnings of an emotional economy that has characterized Indonesian migration since and will become more evident in the coming chapters.

I was first struck by Radjab's story not only because it reminded me of so many of the dreams and stories that I had heard from migrants on Batam, but also because of what it did not reveal. While I recognized the forms of desire that led people away from the *kampung*—the description of listening to stories of those who had returned home and the proof of success through the presentation of commodities and money—what was missing was equally conspicuous: stories of migrants who had failed, or the suspicion that the cigarettes and gold watches might be facades to conceal actual failure.

For the migrants whom I met on Batam at the end of the twentieth and beginning of the twenty-first centuries, this structure of (mis)communication survives, reinforced by the media representations of the island as a place of rapid development, located close to Singapore. The tales of surprise—and even shock—upon arrival make it evident that most stories that circulate from the *rantau* to villages throughout Indonesia do not primarily speak of disappointment.

The final lines in Radjab's story anticipate his own success, mimicking that of the returning migrants whom he witnessed in the *kampung*: "Life in the rumbling world was beginning to call to me; its voice was blurred, like softly rumbling thunder, audible from afar. Tomorrow I would begin, and attack this life" (1995, 320). Radjab's words suggest a novel intertwining of mobility, modernity, and agency, and his eventual path to becoming a successful journalist in Jakarta describes the beginnings of an Indonesian middle class. This account does not, however, compare with the experiences of most *perantau,* or migrants. For the majority, hopes of monetary gain and success in the new economy and a triumphant return to the home village inevitably do not match earlier expectations, and the feelings from which they try to break free come back to haunt them. This is the failure of modernity, the impossibility of leaving the *kampung,* and associated feelings of *malu* (shame and embarrassment) behind. Radjab's story is of a man who has succeeded, and it would most likely not have been written otherwise.

During the early twentieth century, *merantau* was a heterogeneous cultural form associated with ethnic groups such as the Minangkabau and Acehenese, and the Baweanese.[14] In Aceh, for instance, men came and went. "Like a guest, husbands can outstay their welcome and usually do. When their money is gone, wives urge them to return to the East" (Siegel 1969, 179).[15] In other words, *merantau* did not necessarily lead to a change in status; it was merely a way of earning a livelihood (Siegel 1969, 54). In contrast, among the Minangkabau, *merantau* was best described as a rite of passage (Kato 1982, 196), as exemplified by Radjab's story above. Throughout Indonesia, however, for those who entered the *rantau,* kinship and locality were still the main sources of identity (Siegel 1969, 56; Naim 1973, 292), and it was very bad for the *perantau* to become "destitute in *rantau*" (*melarat di rantau*), to be lost in *rantau,* forgotten by those staying home (Mrázek 1994, 10–11).

Beginning in the nineteenth century, the expansion of capitalist markets throughout Southeast Asia facilitated the *rantau* but continued to be associated with groups such as the Minangkabau. Prior to European rule, the "Malay world" was bound together not by political order, but rather by a common language and religion, Malay and Islam. With its lack of territorial boundaries and fluid political allegiances to individual rajas, or kings, the region was characterized by relatively disorganized forms of migration and demographic change (Milner 1982, 8).

By the early twentieth century, however, an emergent modern subject—evident in Radjab's autobiography—begins to appear. For some, the *rantau* became a way to learn about the world; for others it was a way of engaging with progressive political forces; and for still others it was an escape from the burden of culture in a matrilineal society in which men were guests.[16] "The *rantau* was as much an experience as it was a geographic destination" (Graves 1981, 19).

Benedict Anderson (1991) has famously described how print technology—the novel and the newspaper, in particular—was critical in the formation of the nation as a sovereign and geographically limited "imagined community." The national consciousness that developed during the first quarter of the twentieth century in the Dutch East Indies was based on the mobility of individuals from different ethnic groups, drawn together within the structure of the colonial educational system, who began to imagine themselves as belonging to the same national community.[17] In the 1930s Hamka, the influential West Sumatran novelist and scholar, described Medan, the capital of the East Sumatran plantation economy, as a mulitethnic city where a new Indonesian—not bound to any particular regional culture—was developing (1962).[18] These were the kinds of urban spaces that allowed for a particular form of nationalist consciousness to emerge through the production of difference.

The type of mobility that Hamka, Radjab, and others describe, however, was to a large degree bound to the world of an emerging elite, far removed from the experiences of Javanese coolies who labored in the East Sumatran plantations outside of Medan or the "urban proletariat" who were beginning to transform the demography of Jakarta. By the time of Suharto's rise to power in the 1960s and the expansion of an export-oriented economy based on wage labor, migration increased across Indonesia, only to further intensify with rising oil prices and high rates of economic growth since the mid-1970s. In this process, *merantau* was unmoored from particular ethnic groups, becoming widely used throughout Indonesia and associated primarily with the new underclass rather than the country's elite (cf. Waterson 1997, 230–231).

The form of *merantau* with which this book is concerned is thus not that of the urban elite—today generally understood as the middle class—but rather of unskilled migrants such as Chandra (see introduction) who hope to become part of a larger world beyond the village, but who experience constraints that they had not previously imagined. In this process they, much as Hamka before them, learn to become a particular kind of Indonesian, but ones who belong to the underclass, outside the promises of the nation. As the following chapters will clearly illustrate, Batam is an ideal place to consider these processes.

DEVELOPING BATAM

At some point during the Konfrontasi, General Suharto, who two years later would take power in a bloody coup and rule the Indonesian New Order until 1998, visited Batam, which had become a strategic base for the Indonesian military. Many years later Suharto would recount in a speech how it was then that he had the idea that Batam should be developed to take the place of Singapore as a regional economic hub. Indonesia was at the time extremely dependent on Singapore, which handled most of the region's imports and exports, and was a center for oil exploration and refining. While it is unclear if it actually was Suharto who first imagined Batam as a competitor to Singapore, it was at that precise historical moment that the development of Batam as *national* project first became imaginable and thereby possible.[19]

While the border that came to divide Indonesia from Malaysia and Singapore was initially a colonial artifact, it was first during the postcolonial era in the 1960s that it increasingly became recognized in daily practice. The regional economy—integrated for centuries—was divided, reclassified, and nationalized. This process allows us to understand how an island like Batam, which for 150 years had been located between two colonial entrepôts (Riau and Singapore), could be redefined as a space for national development, a tabula rasa for high modernist planning. The dramatic speed of change, however, cannot be understood strictly in national terms, but must be situated in relation to changes in the Singaporean and global economy described in the introduction. The intensification of foreign direct investment and dramatic increase in migration forged an environment that is best described as a frontier zone.

In the years following Konfrontasi, the Batam Industrial Development Authority (BIDA) was created by presidential decree and was largely run by the Indonesian national oil company Pertamina until its collapse a few years later—the result of internal mismanagement and a global recession.[20] A group of Indonesian government technocrats was given authority to broaden the scope of development to include industries that would generate more exports and employment opportunities,[21] and Batam was thus declared a bonded economic zone as imports and exports became exempt from duties and tariffs. More generally, there was a shift in development strategy from competition to cooperation with Singapore. A new master plan projected a population of seven hundred thousand by 2004, identifying in detail—in keeping with the ideals of modernist planning—different zones for housing, commercial activities, and industry. BIDA was given the right to manage all land on the island, which allowed the forcible acquisition of land from local residents for as little as little as two U.S. cents, or fifty rupiah, per square meter.[22]

In 1978 B. J. Habibie, later Indonesia's president—invited back from Germany to become Suharto's minister of research and technology—took over as head of BIDA. Habibie opposed the technocrats' vision of transforming Batam into an export-processing zone for foreign interests; instead, he argued for creating a competitive advantage by focusing on "high technology."[23] Through the 1980s Habibie initiated a series of major infrastructure projects on Batam—including an airport, telecommunications facilities, a power station, an extensive network of roads, and a series of spectacular bridges that would eventually connect Batam with neighboring islands— as the island's population officially grew from three thousand to over ninety thousand between 1973 and 1989. Despite Habibie's pretensions of becoming a competitor to Singapore—which was in line with Suharto's dream—through the 1980s economic development on Batam remained, as one commentator put it, "sluggish at best" (*Far Eastern Economic Review,* November 30, 1989). The nationalist strategy that created laws requiring shared foreign ownership with Indonesian companies appeared contrary to Singaporean interests and led to limited foreign investment. As Singapore and Malaysia boomed through the 1980s, Batam remained a backwater.

PRODUCING NEW FRONTIERS

The investment delegation that left for Batam island one bleary Tuesday morning a fortnight ago looked nothing like the pioneers of the old Wild West. No horse and wagon loaded with possessions, no bush clearing implements, no farming utensils. . . . Romantic notions of what pioneers actually look like aside, this ferry full of briefcase toting, shirt and tie business men were the real thing.

Article from *Singapore Straits Times,* 1989

In 1965, two years after Singapore merged with Malaysia, the union proved untenable and the city became an independent nation-state. Under the leadership of Lee Kuan Yew and the People's Action Party (PAP), the

Singaporean government pushed political opposition aside and disman-
tled labor unions. Turning to manufacturing industries in the late 1960s,
Singapore developed rapidly, becoming, like Hong Kong and Taiwan, a
"production platform" for low-cost manufacturing in the new international
division of labor. In the 1970s Singapore also became the regional center for
oil refining because of its strategic location and long history as an entrepôt;
by the late 1980s it was the world's busiest port, as the production platform
economy reached its peak with the global electronics boom (Perry, Kong,
and Yeoh 1997, 119).

Through the nineteenth and the first half of the twentieth centuries
Singapore had developed not only into a center of economic and political power, but also a chaotic frontier town—an ideal location for smugglers who moved easily outside of the gaze and grasp of the colonial state,
as well as a center for Chinese and Japanese prostitution.[24] Even in the
mid-1960s over half of Singapore's inhabitants were living in poverty, but
within two decades the city was transformed into a booming city-state with
low unemployment rates and extensive public housing. Singapore exemplified the Asian economic miracle. By the mid-1980s, however, with the
global recession, rising manufacturing costs led to a government attempt
to reinvent Singapore as a financial hub (Rodan 1997), and within a matter
of years the combination of financial and business services overtook manufacturing as the largest part of the economy (S. Macleod 1995, 171). This
meant, however, that certain industries had to be moved to neighboring
countries with lower labor and production costs.

In 1990 a handshake between Singaporean prime minister Lee Kuan
Yew and Indonesian president Suharto on Batam symbolized not only the
emergence of an international Growth Triangle between Singapore, Indonesia, and Malaysia, but also the shift of Singapore's economy into "post
industrial world city mode" (Macleod and McGee 1996, 438). Suharto's
and Habibie's vision of turning Batam into an economic power in its own
right quickly faded in practice. Instead, Batam was transformed into an
export-processing zone where Singaporean capital and inexpensive Indonesian labor would create a comparative advantage within close proximity to
Singapore,[25] thereby overtaking a role that Johor had played on the Malaysian side of the border.

The new regional capitalist logic of flexible accumulation, which
demanded less rigid and more mobile forms of labor processes, production, and consumption, redefined Singapore as the center and places like

Batam as the periphery in the Growth Triangle's "segmentation of production" (Van Grunsven 1998, 194). By all accounts, economic development took off on Batam as a result of the agreement. Increasing investments, migration, and tourism transformed Batam from a backwater into a booming frontier area. Approved foreign investment increased fivefold between 1988 and 1990, and the value of exports increased by almost fifty times between 1989 and 1995 (Smith 1997).

Population growth on Batam demanded new forms of governance, and BIDA's strict focus on economic development led to the creation of a Riau Local Government (Pemerintah Daerah Riau, hereafter Pemda) in 1983. According to the master plan, BIDA's mandate was to focus attention on developing industrial areas; the local government was to deal primarily with social, cultural, and political aspects of life on Batam and other issues such as the processing of identity cards (Smith 1996, 158–159).[26] Struggles over resources and political power between BIDA and the local government have been an enduring theme on Batam. BIDA yielded far more power than Pemda until the end of the 1990s,[27] enjoying direct links to the center of political power in Jakarta; this was particularly obvious during the twenty years that Habibie doubled as the head of BIDA and as the minister of research and technology. BIDA's power, however, diminished after the Asian economic crisis and the fall of Suharto, as the Batam mayor's office and the local government gained influence in the process of political decentralization around Indonesia (Aspinall and Fealy 2003).[28]

THE EFFECTS OF "BORDERLESSNESS"

The development of Batam illustrates broader transformations in the global economy. This includes a dramatic increase in transnational corporations during the late 1970s and improvements in international transportation and communications technologies. With these changes Indonesia was repositioned as a source of inexpensive labor, rather than primarily of exports such as oil, timber, and other cash crops (Douglass 1997, 130). Batam pushes these transformations to an extreme. In the early 1970s, as a logistics base for Pertamina, it functioned as a state within a state before becoming a site where inexpensive labor and international capital converged. The Batamindo Industrial Park, the subject of the next chapter, and the flagship of development on Batam exemplifies these processes whereby labor and production that previously would have been located in Singapore have been moved across the border.

These changes in the formal industrial sector have been matched by those in the informal sector. When the PAP and Lee Kuan Yew came to power in the late 1950s, Singapore's position as a regional center for prostitution was threatened as the new government initially banned prostitution through the "anti-yellow culture" drive, before shifting to a strategy of containment in the mid-1960s (Lian 1991, 64–67; J. Ong 1993, 246–247). Prostitution has since come to inhabit an ambivalent space in Singaporean society; although legal, major constraints control its practice.[29] As will become evident in chapters 3 and 4, these constraints have become an important reason for Singaporean men to cross the border to buy sex on Batam. In contrast to Singapore, the extent of prostitution was relatively limited in Riau during the colonial era. It was first after Konfrontasi and the development of Batam that prostitution began to flourish, before booming with the advent of the Growth Triangle.

The growing ease by which various forms of capital and foreign citizens have been able to move into Batam, however, has been matched by the increasing regulation of the Singaporean border to Indonesian citizens through tighter immigration controls as the transnational mobility of labor and capital have moved in opposite directions. As during the colonial era, state strategies of regulating borders have formed and expanded in tandem with the transgression of these same borders (Tagliacozzo 2005). Most notably, since the 1970s economic growth and higher salaries in Singapore and Malaysia have made it increasingly lucrative for Indonesians to cross the Straits of Malacca in search of wage labor.

In this process, Batam and neighboring islands have become key transit points for crossing the border either legally, with a passport through immigration controls, or illegally, usually smuggled across the border at night (see chap. 5). Since the early 1990s, however, it has become far more difficult to enter Singapore illegally because of the relatively short coastline, increasing surveillance, and harsher punishments for smugglers. The length of peninsular Malaysia's coastline makes illegal entry far easier, with crossing points from Aceh in North Sumatra to Batam, but periodic deportation campaigns and amnesties keep Indonesians on the move. More generally, the regional economic networks that for centuries connected Riau with Singapore have been reinvented in the guise of the Growth Triangle, but in contrast to the contemporary rhetoric of "borderlessness," the unbounded

Singaporean colonial entrepôt has been transformed into a bounded and regulated global city.

THE APPEARANCE OF DISORDER

James Scott (1998) has argued that as the modern state emerged, new forms of "state simplification"—types of classification ranging from standards for taxation to notions of citizenship—were developed to help the state "see" its territory and subjects. In Indonesia, what Scott more generally calls "state projects of legibility" (1998, 80) are made most explicit through discourses and practices surrounding "development," or *pembangunan*.[30] *Pembangunan* encompasses not only economic change, but also the transformation of its citizens, thus pointing to the need for careful guidance, a process of engineering, including development programs ranging from the national lingua franca to family planning (Heryanto 1988).[31]

However, in the gap between development (or planning, more generally) and implementation—in this case, between *pembangunan* and *implementasi*—state projects of legibility inevitably produce their own forms of disorder (cf. Mitchell 1988, 79–80; Lefebvre 1991, 23; Roy 2005). For instance, in his ethnographic study of Brasília, the planned capital of Brazil, James Holston (1989) has described how, despite its egalitarian pretensions, disorder and inequality were inscribed in the city through squatter communities even as it was being built. The planned city is always "thin" and lacks the complexity of local life and neighborhoods.[32] It needs the "thick" unplanned city in order to sustain it (Scott 1998, 130), a "disorderly" city that makes the official city work (1998, 261).

On Batam these forms of disorder are made explicit in relation to the *liar,* the "wild," which has a history that is intimately connected with the development of Batam and the Growth Triangle.[33] In 1990 it was possible to claim, as one Indonesian newspaper did, that "Batam is a portrait of the future of Indonesian technology" (*Suara Karya,* August 30, 1990). But with economic development and demographic change *liar* squatter houses rapidly expanded. In 1994, when an estimated fifteen thousand *liar* houses existed in about sixty locations around the island, the Jakarta-based newspaper *Kompas* recognized the local nature of the *liar:* "*Ruli* [an acronym for *rumah liar*]," they revealed to their readers, "is not the name of a man but one that is familiar to the ear of Batam's inhabitants as squatter housing" (*Kompas,* September 9, 1994).

The source of the *liar* is to be found in the opposition between the Dutch colonial state and the society that it aimed to govern[34] before being appropriated by the Indonesian state, as the *rakyat,* the people and one collective body of the nation, was replaced by two bodies, the "privileged" and the "underclass." While the former emerged in the "family" form as the basic building block of the Indonesian nation (Brenner 1998, 237–241; Boellstorff 1999, 491), the latter remained "on the streets" as a threat to the nation's well-being[35]—corresponding directly to Hildred Geertz's (1963) distinction between the new metropolitan superculture of bureaucrats and skilled workers and the growing urban proletariat who remained bound to their rural villages (see introduction).

The emergence of the *liar* should be related to this split, in which the primary problem for the state was the appearance of disorder in the process of urbanization (Kusno 2000, 117–118). In contemporary Indonesia, however, *kampung*—which means both "village" and "home"— and slum can

Migrants building squatter housing. Photo by author.

both be subsumed within the *liar,* suggesting that the *liar* can be understood either as an effect of development or connected to more primordial forms of social organization.[36] These contradictory senses of the term suggest a starting point for considering the unstable position of the *liar*—and the migrant underclass associated with it—on Batam.[37] The *liar* is thus not disordered but rather governed by logics that are not necessarily evident a priori. For instance, understanding squatter communities as counterspaces (e.g., Shields 1991, 53–54) misses the point that *liar* housing is by no means random but can be organized along lines of more "primordial" sentiment, such as ethnicity, or other forms of social networks. Conceptualizing the *liar* thus demands ethnographic specificity.

From the position of planners the *liar* appears easy to identify but in reality has unclear boundaries and blends with "development" and modernity in unexpected ways. Consider some of the figures that we will meet later in the book: the *liar* prostitute who takes the drug Ecstasy so that she will forget her *malu* as she saves money to send to her family; the factory worker who lives in *liar* housing not only because it is less expensive, but also because the physical and social environment reminds him of his village; or the woman who lives in a *liar* marriage with a Singaporean man in one of the many gated housing estates on the island. Certainly these are only a few of the cases where the "*liar*" and "developed" blend and become indistinguishable. While we might expect that such discursive contrasts will ultimately dissolve once we turn our attention away from state representations to everyday practice, they are distinctions that individuals struggle with in their everyday lives.

FROM HOUSTON TO ROTTERDAM AND BACK AGAIN

In the early 1970s, the head of Pertamina, Ibnu Sutowo, claimed that Batam would be transformed into the "Houston of Asia," displacing Singapore as the region's oil center. A decade later, when this dream had turned sour, B. J. Habibie envisioned an Asia Port that would "*meng-Rotterdam-kan* Batam" (literally, "turn Batam into Rotterdam"). This, in turn, would make it possible to *mem-Batam-kan* other parts of Indonesia.[38] Yet Batam could not generate the competitive advantage of Habibie's dream; it could merely offer the comparative advantages of a developing country: inexpensive land and labor.

Although Houston and Rotterdam have at times been considered models of development for Batam, Singapore has been the archetype from the beginning. BIDA is modeled directly on the Singaporean Jurong Town Corporation (Smith 1996, 73); PT Persero Batam, which originally was in charge of infrastructure, customs, and the control of goods moving in and out of Batam, has copied Singapore facilities and setups "right down to the wording of its forms, and the colors of its trucks and vehicles" (Smith 1996, 113).

At the center of this process was the "self-conscious making of spectacle" (Tsing 2004, 57) that positioned Batam not at the margins, but rather at the very center of contemporary forms of economic globalization. The modern imaginary of development on the island, which circulates in media, brochures, and master plans produced by BIDA and other developers, inevitably mimics forms of modernity located elsewhere. A series of revised master plans defines how each part of the island is supposed to be developed in the future. Several of these plans present visions of the island as a new Singapore, with shopping malls and gated communities such as Palm Springs and Beverly Batam that could be imagined anywhere from Tokyo to Los Angeles.

An international airport, which remains almost strictly domestic, opened with much fanfare as a potential rival to Singapore's Changi Airport, and the Asia Port was conceived as a competitor to Singapore's harbors. The modernist vision that is produced on Batam, however, inevitably creates unanticipated spatial and social forms. Plans are constantly deferred to the future, with empty lots and half-finished buildings identified by both government officials and local residents as "not yet developed" (*belum dibangun*) or "not yet ready" (*belum siap*).

A striking sense of temporality thus surrounds the development of Batam; a future is anticipated where the island will be like "Singapore" (or "Houston" or "Rotterdam"). What some might see as failure—be it the emergence of *liar* housing or prostitution—is redefined as a problem that planning can solve, a form that "development" appears to take globally (cf. Ferguson 1994). However, temporality takes on added local dimensions when Batam is compared with the Singapore of thirty years ago. For instance, at a signing ceremony in 1980, Goh Chok Tong, then Singapore's minister for trade and industry, claimed that Batam "is better than what Singapore's Jurong industrial estate was in the sixties" (quoted in Smith 1996, 133). But while the minister was referring to the state of development projects, people like Pak Haji, a retired Singaporean living on Batam, tell me that the island reminds him of his childhood Singapore, precisely because of the *lack* of development.

The unofficial models of Batam are equally telling. The public nature of prostitution, the increasing use of drugs, the appearance of HIV and

A T-shirt from Singapore. Photo by author.

human trafficking as social problems that demand intervention, and the many squatter communities have made Batam, local residents frequently say, "like Texas,"[39] or part of "Western" or "Singaporean" culture. Batam is a place where people "forget religion" (*lupa agama*) and "don't care" (*cuek*) about their neighbors.

A T-shirt from Batam. Photo by author.

That Batam has become "like Texas" is of course also related to the comparative advantages that it offers to Singaporean men. It is not only economic incentives that lure Singaporeans across the Straits of Malacca, but also the less regulated environment on Batam, which allows for open-ended relationships with prostitutes and the use of recreational drugs, particularly Ecstasy. These differences are reflected in the popular cultural discourse that binds Singapore and Batam together. Compare, for instance, two different T-shirts commonly seen in street markets and shops in Singapore and on Batam, respectively. While the T-shirt found in Singapore claims that it is a "fine city" where acts like chewing gum and not flushing a public toilet will result in monetary fines, the one sold on Batam—created in response to the Singapore T-shirt—claims it is a "free city" where you can do most things without facing arrest, including sex and drugs. Batam has, at least from a particular perspective, "established its reputation as a liminal destination, a social as well as geographic margin, a 'place apart'" (Shields 1991, 112).

Batam has thus become a place where it is possible to imagine a wide range of futures and possibilities not only for the island's bureaucrats and planners, but also for Indonesian migrants and Singaporean tourists. These transformations have led to a growing self-consciousness that Batam is not only part of Indonesia, but also of a larger world. For people such as Pak Padil and Pak Awang Ali, this new world is largely oppressive; for others it appears to offer opportunities. As will become evident in the coming chapters, however, the various licit and illicit economies that extend throughout and beyond the Growth Triangle cannot be understood a priori, but are best considered from the perspective of the various circulating populations who bring the borderlands to life.

2

The Diluted Enclave

Batam is rapidly becoming a modern city, increasingly connected to international forces. Because of this anyone who wants to come here has to have some kind of special skill.

Batam mayor R. A. Aziz (quoted in *Suara Pembaruan,* November 20, 1995)

Wati gets off the *ojek* (motorcycle taxi), pulls a one-thousand-rupiah bill out of her pocket, and pays the driver. It is just past seven and the morning air is still cool. She has just finished a twelve-hour shift at a Singaporean electronics company in the Batamindo Industrial Park, where she is in the middle of a terminal two-year contract that began in 2002. As she exits the park through the main gate and crosses the busy street crowded with taxis, a young man, a *calo,* or tout, waves aggressively at her, trying to get her attention. For each taxi he fills the driver pays him one thousand rupiah (about ten U.S. cents). But she looks right through him, stopping at one of a long line of *liar* food stalls that crowd the other side of the street. A large billboard above them advertises a new housing estate by depicting a couple and their two children getting out of a car parked on their driveway. The caption reads, in English, "Family Dream."

Wati buys a breakfast snack and continues down the street past the wide variety of *liar* shops and stalls selling everything from food to pirated jeans and VCDs (video compact disks). After a couple hundred meters, she turns left and walks through a gateway with a sign that reads "Gampung Aceh" (Aceh Village).[1] The pavement turns to dirt as she follows a path that leads through the *liar* community, across a small bridge, before finally reaching the house where she lives with her two brothers. Wati sits down on the bench on her porch and takes off her shoes before entering the house.

Once inside she removes her *jilbab* (headscarf or veil), carefully folds it over a hanger, and changes out of her work clothes. Quickly she eats her breakfast before washing the pile of clothing that is waiting for her. Within an hour she is asleep; in eleven more she will begin her next shift.

UNRAVELING THE ENCLAVE

More than any other project, the opening of the Batamindo Industrial Park in 1991 symbolized the emergence of the Growth Triangle.[2] Located on 320 hectares of land, Batamindo houses around one hundred multinational corporations such as Philips, Sony, and Hitachi and employs around seventy thousand workers, more than 80 percent women between the ages of eighteen and twenty-four. The park is at the center of a particular imaginary of the contemporary global economy. Young women such as Wati are the "paradigmatic subject" (Sen 1998, 36) within this imaginary, a subject that takes a more specific form in the electronics industry as the "nimble-fingered" female factory worker (A. Ong 1987, 151–153; Salzinger 2003, 9–10).[3]

Batamindo is generally considered an example of an "enclave" form of development (Van Grunsven 1998, 197), "a gated and policed space

The Batamindo Industrial Park. Photo by author.

of labour control" (Phelps 2004, 212) where workers are subject to the disciplinary power of multinational corporations (A. Ong 1999, 222). In an important sense, Batamindo is self-sustaining. It has its own electricity and water plants. There is an air-conditioned mall, outdoor food courts, markets, small variety shops, telephone shops, ATMs, and health clinics, as well as restaurants catering mainly to the foreign managerial staff. A community center with a basketball court, a soccer field, table tennis, and spaces for other activities is located at the center of the park, as is a large mosque. The park is dominated by the seemingly endless rows of factories and dormitory housing surrounded by fences and divided between men and women. In order to enter each particular dormitory area one has to pass through guard posts that are often manned by security guards. The inside of the park is more reminiscent of Singapore than of Batam, with clean, tree-lined streets and functional sidewalks, something of a rarity in Indonesia. As one commentator has noted, "The aim [of Batamindo] is to offer a Singapore-type environment with cheap labor and land costs in order to make investors feel at home; to feel as if they were doing business in Singapore" (Smith 1996, 185).

The park stands in stark visual contrast to the *liar* shops and communities that surround it, named for the factories behind which they are located (Belakang Sony), or according to ethnicity (Gampung Aceh). As the number of factories and workers increased dramatically beginning the 1990s, so did the *rumah liar*.[4] For the Batamindo management and BIDA, the spatial expansion of the *liar* appears to pose a direct threat to the implementation of the island's master plan, which, in keeping with the ideals of modernist planning, divides place of residence from work. These anxieties are doubled as *liar* villages are imagined as spaces of *liar* marriages, thereby threatening the apparent control of female sexuality in the park. While there are recurring attempts to eradicate housing, shops, and stalls, the regulation of sexuality has mainly concentrated on the religious and health education of workers within the park. In both cases, however, the *liar*, or the fantasy of the *liar*, reappears.

This chapter describes how young factory workers negotiate the spatial and symbolic distinctions between the industrial park and the *liar* squatter areas and how particular moral boundaries emerge in this process. As Wati's story suggests, however, for factory workers the distinction between the developed industrial park and the *liar* spaces and practices that surround it does not map neatly onto everyday life. Workers move easily in and out of the park and become engaged in forms of life that can be reduced neither to the disciplinary power of the factory nor to an unregulated regime of the *liar*. While some migrants find *liar* housing inexpensive and practical and a type of place where a sense of community is created, others, young women in particular, avoid *liar* areas since they lack facilities such as running water and are often considered sites of immoral behavior.

It is in this context that the gendered relationship between *merantau* and *malu* becomes relevant. While the demand for economic success is essential for most migrants, for young women in particular concerns regarding sexuality are ubiquitous. The fact that over half the women working in Batamindo wear the *jilbab* suggests that religious practice and the performance of piety are one way of constituting a moral boundary to the *liar*, thereby dealing with feelings of *malu*. More generally, this chapter describes the process through which a gendered emotional economy of *merantau* takes form. The temporal aspect is critical, as I highlight the disjuncture between how migrants imagine Batam before arrival and what social life permits once there (e.g., Appadurai 1996, 54). It is through this process that *malu* becomes salient as migrants come to learn that they are part of a disposable underclass in Batam's industrial parks.

Batam is not only a place where migrants travel in search of work—where a particular type of global laborer is found—but also a place that promises new forms of consumption and a life beyond traditional structures of parental or village authority. This chapter is therefore concerned with how migrant workers negotiate labor conditions and control inside the park and social relationships and patterns of consumption outside the park (e.g., Mills 1999), showing not only how gender is embedded in global production (e.g., Gottfried 2004, 9), but also how global production is embedded in particular places and gendered forms of life. By taking the accounts and mobility of factory workers as a starting point for analysis, the chapter situates and unravels a particular global form, the "development enclave," which in practice becomes a "diluted enclave" that demands a form of analysis that moves beyond the factory floor.

ENTERING THE *RANTAU*

I always wanted to get a job at Batamindo because it seemed like the factory workers lived such an extravagant (*mewah*) life!

Salim, male factory worker at Batamindo

For six months after graduating from high school, Wati helped out at a sewing cooperative in her home village and took a computer course in a nearby town. "I tried to find work in the area," she told me. "But it's difficult there. It is difficult for high school graduates to find work opportunities. That's why it is important to get a better education or gain experience." Wati's home in the northern part of Aceh had long been affected by the armed conflict between the Free Aceh Movement and the Indonesian military, so when her brother insisted that it is was easy to find work and that she should join him there, she agreed after receiving her parents' blessing. "My brother told me that there were lots of companies on Batam, that it was like a big city, so I decided to come. But when I got here I was a bit shocked (*terkejut*). There was lots of jungle and *liar* housing. It was not what I had imagined." It was, however, easy to find work. Within a week Wati had applied for and been offered a job in a Batamindo factory.

Ella comes from the Central Javanese city of Solo. After graduating from high school, she took classes at a local school of tourism and had hopes of continuing her studies in order to gain a college degree. Her family's economic constraints made this impossible, however, and she felt great disappointment when her mother told her that she would have to find something closer to home. Angry at her mother and confused about her future, one day Ella and a friend passed an office recruiting workers for Batamindo. Together they decided to apply, though neither of them knew much about Batam. "I had seen something on television. I remembered a beach and a mall." A few weeks later they were asked to take a test, and soon afterward both were accepted. But before being hired she needed her mother to sign a letter of permission. Despite initially refusing, she finally submitted when Ella persisted. "She realized that it was better for me to work than just to spend time around the house with little hope of finding a job in the area. Actually, I didn't really want to go to Batam, but I just acted automatically (*otomatis*) without thinking. I just wanted to make money in order to become independent (*mandiri*)."

When Ella graduated from high school she had imagined higher education as a route that would allow her, much like Radjab in the previous chapter, to break free from the bonds of tradition. Her decision to enter the *rantau* was not driven by a specific desire to travel to Batam, but rather by a more generalized desire to lead a kind of life that was not available to her in Solo. Batam thus appeared not as a particularly meaningful place, but as the only available route in Ella's geography of possibilities. It is first upon arrival on Batam that her mobility acquires meaning for her.

After a workshop at the recruitment agency, Ella and the other women —all in their late teens and early twenties—who had been hired flew to Batam on a two-year contract. "I remember when we first flew over Batam it was like being in the middle of the jungle. Batamindo was not much better: it was like an island in the middle of nowhere." Together with eleven other women from Solo she was taken to a dormitory where she was given a bed. Two days later she began assembling television sets for the French company Thomson.

Chandra, whose attempt to enter Singapore opened this book, comes from a rural village in North Sumatra. After high school he was sent to Medan to continue his education, but when the military arrested his father for smuggling marijuana, Chandra was forced to drop out, and his hopes of higher education were dashed. He claims, however, that he saw no future in his village either. "After a year in the *kampung* I realized that there was nothing I could do there. There was no place to work, no factories, and I was not strong enough to work in the fields."

A friend from Chandra's village was working on Batam as a taxi driver and wrote him a letter about how easy it was to make money there. He invited him to come join him: "The main reason that I went is because I felt responsible toward my family, especially toward my younger siblings who were still in school. Even my mother encouraged me to go so that I could send her money." Chandra left for Batam after having seen most of his friends who had tried their luck in Jakarta fail, and upon arrival he experienced the familiar shock that Batam was not the advanced society he had imagined. Living in his friend's *liar* squat, he decided to apply for work at Batamindo. Together with other job seekers, he walked from factory to factory, checking lists of available jobs posted on the front gates. Although he was called to several interviews, after a couple of months he remained unemployed. According to his friend it was far more difficult for men than women to find work at Batamindo, and he would need to find *bekking* (backing), someone inside the company who would support his application. In other words, Chandra could not rely merely on his own capabilities, but would need to establish connections to others who were closer to centers of power. In the end, it turned out that one of his neighbors was a security guard at Batamindo, and he helped Chandra get a job. In return, Chandra gave him half of his first month's salary.

Wati's, Ella's, and Chandra's stories show that any understanding of *merantau* strictly in relation to economic hardship is insufficient. For all three, higher education appears as the ideal route into an economy of development and away from a traditional form of life. It is first when this is denied that Batam appears as a possibility. Before leaving home, none of them knew much about Batam except what other people—a brother, a friend, a labor recruiter—had told them or what they had seen on television. This structure of communication is constituted not only through corporate and media images, but also through the stories of other migrants. This is reminiscent of the description of Radjab in the previous chapter, who, while still in the *kampung,* could not imagine the stories of migrants who had failed.

Most striking, however, are the experiences of young women such as Ella, who, with a particular decisiveness, decide to enter the *rantau.* The transformation of these women into migrants is, as I have noted, a novel phenomenon in Indonesia. But it is difficult to find a clear explication to these changes in the words of the women themselves. Ella acts, as she puts it, *otomatis.* Beyond a demand for independence in a world beyond her family, she cannot clearly explain her own desire—a beach and a mall associated with a world of consumption—that she perhaps had sensed but not experienced in Solo.

For migrants such as Ella the factory is imagined as a site of white-collar work (cf. Elmhirst 2000, 223). But the world that she has pictured is not exactly what she finds on Batam. The shock of arrival is evident not only in relation to the physical environment, but also the actual labor in the factory. Ella described her first experience of the factory: "I wanted to cry. Apparently our job involved a lot of heavy work and the factory was dirty. I had come all this way to Batam to make money and I had to work like a coolie. At the time I regretted it." The first day that Chandra showed up at work, dressed in his best clothes and carrying a ballpoint pen, he was in for a surprise. "I thought that I would be sitting behind a desk at an office, not standing on the factory floor." Although Batam and the *rantau* are perceived as a route into the Indonesian middle class—or the forms of consumption with which it is associated—it in fact becomes a place where migrants begin to understand themselves in different terms, outside the promises of development.

ENTERING THE ENCLAVE

Batamindo provides five different types of ready-built factories for companies. Most choose to lease factory space, which allows them to move in and out of the park, Batam, and Indonesia without having to invest heavily in infrastructure. One of the park's brochures reads,

> The Park's management style and industrial infrastructure were established with emphasis on the provision of efficiency, flexibility and quality; three factors cherished by foreign investors. Batamindo Industrial Park facilitates start-up operations in the quickest possible time frame. It also offers the foreign investor a climate of ease and efficiency in terms of hassle free operation. (Batamindo Industrial Park 1992, 4)

This logic is extended to the management of workers. Investors may choose to use Tunas Karya, Batamindo's official recruitment agency, which hires workers such as Ella through their regional offices in Java and Sumatra and then manages them in the park. Workers from the same geographical area are placed in the same factories and dormitories, where they are organized according to a neighborhood system mimicking that of the Indonesian state.[5] The aim is to create a smooth transition from home to a regulated work environment. In the factory managers are generally foreigners, rarely fluent in Indonesian, but most day-to-day operations are run by male Indonesians supervisors who are in charge on the factory floor,[6] while making salaries up to five times those of the lowest-level workers on the factory floor, such as Wati, Ella, and Chandra, who are called *operator*.

I asked Wati to explain her job testing print circuit boards (PCBs) at Beyonic, a Singaporean subcontracting firm.

> Beyonic makes PCB for computer hard drives. It has two departments and I am in BN. In BN there are four kinds of processes, router, ICT, FT, and PMI. I've been placed in FT, which is functional testing. It's a test to see if the PCBs are good or not. In the company language they say "pass" or "fail." That's what I do. I have a machine that helps me. I work standing up. The line goes by, I take the goods from the line, put them into the machine where they're tested. If they pass they go on to PMI, if they fail I put them into a box for reworking. That's it.

Ella told me about her job at Thomson.

> My job is to make the tuner, the thing in the television set that helps you change the channels. Anyway, I am not sure how it works, I just put it

together. That is just on the third floor where I work. On the second floor they make hairdryers, mixers, and irons.

Wati's and Ella's descriptions are littered with technical English terms used in the factory. Ella tells me that she is not sure how the product she makes functions, and it is clear from Wati's description that she has not considered the meaning of the production process beyond the string of words and acronyms she has learned. I ask her to explain what a router is, but she cannot, telling me that "it is something that is part of a computer." Neither of them comprehends exactly what they are making, particularly since many products are not assembled until after they leave the park or even the country. Because of the widespread use of subcontracting firms, it is sometimes unclear for which company one is working. Susanti, for instance, recalled when the name of her factory suddenly changed. "All the people, the operators and the managers, remained the same, the factory was the same, and even the products were the same. It was just the name that changed."

Almost all the workers with whom I spoke complained about the monotonous nature of their labor. Wati told me that working was "a drag" (*suntuk*), particularly in the middle of the night shift. Chandra said that "the work wasn't too hard, but it only took a few days before I was bored and wished that I was somewhere else. If I wasn't cutting metal then I was using a screwdriver. After a while I saw the screwdriver in my dreams going round and round. It wasn't what I had expected before I started."[7]

This discourse of monotony is recognizable among managers as well and is used to legitimize the hiring of women. One company manager told me that women have "more dexterous fingers" (interview, December 10, 1998), while the head of the Department of Manpower on Batam argued that women "are more careful, sharper observers and are more capable of withstanding work that is monotonous" (*Sijori Pos,* August 6, 1998). Wati offered an explanation that factory managers never would: "Female workers don't do a lot of acting up. Maybe that's why the companies mainly hire women." Both explanations are common in discussions concerning factory workers around the world—arguably a transnationally produced fantasy, but a "fantasy with consequences" (Salzinger 2003, 10), which affects hiring and production decisions on particular factory floors.

The processes of subcontracting and product assemblage in self-sustained industrial parks such as Batamindo have been understood in terms of a flexible form of capitalism that allows multinational corporations to quickly enter and exit sites of production along an expanding "Taylorist frontier" (Watts 1992a, 6).[8] For workers in Batamindo, the effects of flexibility are most obvious in relation to rising and falling production targets, which translate into increasing or decreasing numbers of hours on the floor. This means that salaries potentially fluctuate dramatically, which became especially evident during the economic crisis in the late 1990s, when companies that exported the bulk of their products to Asian countries saw orders slow considerably. Many workers who earlier had been able to double their salaries through overtime work were suddenly not getting a single extra hour. If production was high, however, most of the operators continued to work as many hours a day as they were told. Wati, for example, worked from seven to seven, either all night or all day, nearly every day. In 2003 this gave her a monthly salary of one million rupiah (approximately 110 U.S. dollars), more than doubling her basic salary, based on forty hours of work per week.[9]

The transition from an agricultural peasant economy to a capitalist work organization leads to new conceptions and experiences of time (e.g., A. Ong 1987, 108–112). Time gains a value that makes it comparable to and interchangeable with money (Thompson 1967, 61; Wolf 1992, 110). But this relationship between time and money must also be situated in relation to the particular temporality of *merantau,* namely the *belum,* or "not yet," which both positions the migrant in a relationship with home—parents, siblings, husbands, or wives—that includes more or less explicit forms of debt, and in relation to new forms of desires that emerge in the city.[10] Ella expressed it in the following way as we spoke: "If I work seven to seven every day then I have a lot of money at the end of the month and I can send money to my mother and still have some left over. But it also means that I am always tired and there is no time to enjoy myself. I am twenty years old and sometimes I feel like I am wasting my best years."

This quote clarifies a critical point of tension for many migrants. Their main anxieties do not generally revolve around labor discipline on the factory floor, but rather around the effects of their labor on their lives outside of the factory. Ella wants to engage in forms of life that she could not quite imagine before she left home, as previously diffuse desires take on particular forms (e.g., Spyer 2000, 35). But she continues to feel bound to responsibility toward her mother, as she has not become quite as free as she had initially imagined.

There is a basic injustice in not being able to buy the commodities she both makes *and* desires. This is Ella again: "These products that we make can leave the country but we can't. This hi-fi speaker can go to Thailand but I can't. We often think about how these products are extremely expensive and that even though we are the ones who make them we can't afford to buy them." [11]

Harnanto, a Javanese man in his mid-twenties—more concerned with his long-term economic prospects—asked rhetorically, "How much is an operator's salary? It is just enough to survive and there is no way that we can hope to save money." It is clear that for most workers the particular trajectory that many had hoped for is not available. Chandra put it the following way: "The factories are interested in using my strength (*tenaga*), not my brains, and once my power is used up I will be thrown out. But what am I supposed to do? I don't have computer skills and I don't speak English. I can't even imagine what kind of job I might apply for."

For most migrants, therefore, factory work ultimately appears as a dead end. Changing levels of production make it difficult for workers to judge how much money they will be making, and the hiring structures within factories offer few possibilities for career advancement. Some find alternative work on the side, such as through Avon direct sales or by becoming a motorcycle taxi driver, but most are dependent on the number of hours that become available on the factory floor. The typical two-year contract, which increasingly has been shortened to one year, offers limited education or skills that would make workers attractive on a broader labor market. The nature of these contracts, and the fact that nearly all workers are migrants, makes labor organizing complicated. [12] Those who are able to save money must work long shifts and avoid the temptations of Batam, where money is easily spent.

Like most migrants I met on Batam, Chandra claimed that his goal was to save enough capital—*modal*—to start his own business and free himself from the insecurities of everyday wage labor. "*Modal*," one man told me, "is the word that I hate the most. It haunts me in my dreams." In contemporary Indonesia, the stakes of *merantau* are high, and critical in understanding the forms of life that have developed on Batam. In economic terms, of course, most people do not succeed to the degree that they had hoped, meaning that they must return to their *kampung* as they left, remain on Batam, or move on in the *rantau*.

NEGOTIATING THE *LIAR,* REGULATING *MALU*

As I walk through the gate into the dormitory area it is early evening and most of the workers on the day shift have returned home. In the
front room of Ella's one-story dormitory building, four women are intently
watching an Indonesian soap opera on a small television produced in the
factory where they work. There are no chairs in the room, and the white-
washed walls are bare except for a calendar from the company's Muslim
organization. The back of a large wooden wardrobe, covered with shiny red
gift-wrapping paper, obscures the view of the kitchen. I am invited in, and
as I sit down to wait for my sugar-saturated cup of tea, two women wearing
jilbabs return from the early evening *maghrib* prayer. As they pass through
the front room both of them glance at the television, and within minutes
of entering their bedroom they have changed, taken off their *jilbabs,* and
returned to watch the show, despite the fact that I am there. They are
quickly filled in on the latest events that have led the show's heroine to
leave her husband.

Along with the communal kitchen and bathrooms there is one large
sleeping room with six bunk beds and a few shared wardrobes. The wall
next to each woman's bed is usually plastered with photos from glossy mag-

*A living room in a women's dormitory. Photo by Jennifer Mack. Reproduced with
permission.*

azines. The room provides limited privacy, and because the women work different shifts there is always someone sleeping. Most women complain that it is difficult to get enough sleep even though most seem to appreciate the communal atmosphere (cf. Mack 2004).

The dormitory building has ten units, with twelve women living in each. The rectangular-shaped building is divided from the next building

A bedroom in a women's dormitory. Photo by Jennifer Mack. Reproduced with permission.

by a plot of grass on which a series of clotheslines are set up. In front of each unit is a bench; many are being used by couples in search of a minimal amount of privacy. For the more daring couples, Hollywood Hill (Bukit Hollywood), a small, tree-covered area just outside the park, offers more privacy.

Batamindo is well known among male migrants as a place where it is easy to find a girlfriend. On Saturday nights the park's dormitories are packed with visitors far into the early hours of the morning, despite official rules stating that guests must leave by midnight. Adi, who lives in a squatter community near the main gate, jokingly compares the women in the park with fruit—"You get three for a thousand"—reminiscent of the description of factories as "peach orchards" in Chinese Shenzhen (Pun 2005, 140). The transnationally produced fantasy of the female worker clearly has effects beyond the factory floor.

In conversations with Batamindo management and nurses in the clinic, issues of sexuality constantly arose. One manager appeared worried that many women were becoming lesbians, asking me if I had found any evidence of this, while a nurse working in the clinic claimed that there were "very few virgins here now." Similarly, local newspapers are full of stories concerning the sexual exploits and problems of female factory workers at Batamindo. It is not uncommon for articles about female workers to move easily from the industrial parks to the brothels, often suggesting that the salary from mere factory work is not enough to survive.[13] Nongovernmental organizations that work in the park warned me that the large concentration of young women meant that large-scale HIV prevention efforts were necessary. Local newspapers and everyday gossip often carry rumors of pregnancies or abortions, or even of young mothers abandoning their babies. The occasional report of a found fetus only serves to substantiate such suspicions.[14]

As a response to the threat of female sexuality, many companies include a "no pregnancy" clause in their contracts; more generally, there is strong support for religious activities at Batamindo. The convergence of state and corporate interests in relation to religion can be seen in attempts by the Department of Religious Affairs to provide premarital counseling for workers. Just a couple of years after Batamindo opened, the head of the local office explained the reasoning: "By counseling them [the workers], we hope to prevent the possibility of negative behaviors [in particular premarital sex and pregnancy out of wedlock] being manifested. . . . If these problems occur, workers' productivity could be reduced" (*Jakarta Post,* December 19, 1992). Religion appears as the solution not only to preventing immoral behavior, but also to improving worker productivity and, in turn, facilitating the development of Batam. The convergence of economic, nationalist, and religious discourses concerning young women is recognizable from other parts of Southeast Asia (e.g., A. Ong 1987, chap. 8). As Aihwa Ong has noted, the relationship between the management and self-management of women's bodies is "in tandem with the larger forces at work in the construction of the body politic" (1995, 187).

This relationship between management and self-management becomes particularly poignant in relation to veiling. In conversations with workers who veil, it was clear that most of them began to do so only after they had arrived on Batam. The typical response to my inquiries was that they had only just "become aware" (*baru sadar*). For instance, Widya, from the city of Yogyakarta in Central Java, claimed that she had always wanted to wear a *jilbab* before she came to Batam. Whereas in Java it was easy to be branded *fanatik* (cf. Brenner 1998, 232), on Batam one gained support not only from roommates, but also from the agencies and companies that recruited them. Widya continued, "One of the good things about working here is that there are a lot of religious activities. In the *kampung* it is usually only on Hari Raya [the day of celebration that breaks the Islamic fasting month] that there is anything going on."

In Batamindo, however, it is possible to take part in religious activities on a daily basis, either in the main mosque or in a wide variety of organizations that are coordinated through particular companies or by community-based groups created by workers and supported by the park management. The interests of the workers, the companies, and the state appear to converge, as the movement of workers becomes restricted to the park. In other words—and in line with the state ideology of *pembangunan,* or development—the progress of the industrial park is matched by the spiritual development of the worker. While this may be interpreted as an added instrument in the disciplining of workers, in reality it is more complicated.

Although "becoming aware" was certainly a key motif among women who wear the *jilbab,* many—away from home for the first time—readily admitted that another major reason for veiling was to avoid male attention and *malu* in the streets.[15] Wearing a *jilbab* protects women from being approached by men, or of running the risk of being identified as a *lontong* (prostitute).[16] The contexts in which the *jilbab* was used, however, varied between individuals. Widya wore the *jilbab* at all times outside of her dormitory and inside as well if there were male guests in the sitting room. Ella would wear the *jilbab* only on particular occasions—when going to the mosque or traveling outside the park, usually to the main town of Nagoya. Wati would veil only when she left her *liar* village; on several occasions I even sat alone with her in her house when she was unveiled. Shita would veil at work and when leaving Batamindo, but not when moving around the park during her free time. She was straightforward when elaborating on the reasons for this: "When I am working in the factory it is easier to take breaks for prayer if I am wearing a *jilbab*. The managers don't bother me as much. If I go to Nagoya to shop I wear a *jilbab* so that the *calos* [touts] don't bother me. But at Batamindo I don't feel like I need to wear it since I feel safe."

For Rinda, a woman from a small village just outside of the Central Javanese city of Yogyakarta, the decision to begin veiling was motivated by a particular experience. During her first year on Batam she lived in one of the dormitories inside the park, but after becoming involved with a man from North Sumatra who also worked in Batamindo, she moved out of her dormitory and into a room that he rented in Belakang Sony. Initially, they decided to get married, but when she found out that he was seeing other women she broke off the engagement. As a result she moved back to her dormitory and decided to begin veiling. "When I lived in Belakang Sony I felt as though I was living in sin (*berdosa*), but now I have decided to be good (*baik*). I prefer living in the dorms because most of the women are religious and rarely go out. In the *rumah liar* there is no one to watch over people and you can come and go as you like."

The veil, some argue, can be understood as a kind of "symbolic shelter" that allows women to enter public spaces (A. Macleod 1992). Suzanne Brenner (1996, 674) claims that this is not the case in Java, where there is no clear delineation between male and female spheres. On Batam, however, this distinction is far more problematic, since the island has a reputation as a site of prostitution and sin, making movement through public space particularly sensitive for women.[17]

In fact, this is a boundary that women themselves are often concerned with policing. For instance, female factory workers who frequent discos make clear attempts to distinguish themselves from prostitutes, both spatially and in terms of dress. Most remain on one side of the disco and are easily distinguished by their uniform of loose T-shirts and jeans.[18] Veils serve a similar purpose in creating social boundaries and formalizing identities. Sri, who comes from Central Java and works for Seagate, told me that "when I first came here I didn't wear a *jilbab,* but when I started working the night shift at Batamindo the people who owned the house where I was boarding told me that it was dangerous for women to go out alone at night on Batam. They said that it would be safer if I wore a *jilbab.*" Shita claimed that she could tell the difference between the times when she was and was not wearing a *jilbab.* "Guys would not approach me nearly as often when I wore the *jilbab.* These days I always wear it when I go out."

In Brenner's study of university-educated women who had chosen to begin veiling in Java in the early and middle 1990s, a time when it was a "marginal practice," "becoming aware" was, as on Batam, a common theme (1996, 691; see also Smith-Hefner 2007). But associated with this awareness was a sense of moral obligation, which Brenner suggests signifies a "new subjectivity" (1996, 684). Among these women, the fear of *sin* was a greater motivation for veiling than the fear of *shame.*

In Batamindo, however, it would appear that the opposite tends to be true: shame, or *malu,* is more important than the fear of sin. Certainly, religious practice can lead to the formation of new forms of subjectivity and religious enlightenment, but it is the negotiation of *malu* that is critical for female migrants. Wearing a *jilbab* protects women from men on the street and from being identified as someone who could be a *lontong.* More generally, the distinction between sin and shame can be understood in terms of class, the former emerging as a self-reflexive project in the context of an expanding middle class, the latter as an attempt to regulate moral boundaries on the "street" and the *liar* spaces and identities associated with the underclass (Kusno 2000, 117; see chap. 1).

Yet the argument is more complicated. As I have noted, *malu* connotes not only shame or embarrassment, but also piety and modesty. Wearing the *jilbab* and engaging in religious practices may thus engage with *malu* in yet another way, namely by offering a model of individual development (*kemajuan*) in a context where saving money is difficult. Beginning in the 1980s, Islamic revitalization in Indonesia has led to intensifying engagements with the Koran through recitation competitions and prayer groups (*pengajian*) (Weix 1998; Gade 2004), as well as increasing use of the *jilbab.* For women, in particular, this means that Islamic practices have increasingly become a legitimate form of *kemajuan.* Shita, for instance, told me that "even if I have not saved a lot of money or gained skills that I can use to find a better job, people at home will see that I have a learned something while I have been away, that I have been able to develop (*maju*) through religion."

The predominance of veiling in Batamindo cannot be reduced to a new form of labor discipline or even to broader forms of regulation of women in public space. The veil is flexible, allowing many women the possibility of moving through space with feelings of greater security, performing, in a sense, as "pious women" and thereby presenting an official identity in an ambiguous social context that demands clarity (e.g., Goffman 1959). This is not to deny that many women are experiencing forms of religious and spiritual development, but it is important to think critically about how these forms of personal development are emerging at a particular historical period during which Islam has become a legitimate source of middle-class engagement in Indonesia.

I am thus not primarily concerned with issues of subjectivity in relation to religious belief. Instead, I want to point out that *malu*, or being recognized as someone who should be *malu*, becomes a force that leads young migrant women to choose to begin veiling. In other words, *malu* does not necessarily lead to withdrawal from social life, but rather directs women to actively engage in it. Although this can easily be read as a sign of increasing social control, it is important to recognize that subordination forms the basis for all forms of agency (Ortner 1997; Butler 1997; Mahmood 2005). The *jilbab* thus allows women on Batam to create social boundaries and regulate *malu* while engaging in a form of personal development that has become increasingly legitimate in Indonesia.

ENTERING THE *LIAR*

Walking through Batamindo's far gate around noon, one will usually find a few touts hanging around in search of taxi passengers, though not nearly as many as at the main gate. On both sides of the driveway that leads onto the road, a few small stalls covered by green plastic tarpaulin sell cigarettes, candy, and drinks and prepare everything from West Sumatran Padang-style food to deep-fried bananas. Since they are *liar* and lack permits, they constantly run the risk of being dispersed. As one turns left up the road, the factories continue on the left-hand side into the horizon. The high concrete wall that surrounds the park makes it nearly impossible to enter without passing through one of the gates. The right-hand side of the road, however, is covered by woods and thick shrubbery, with paths visible at a few points.

Approximately three hundred meters farther down the road, a slight opening reveals a small dirt road—the same one from which Chandra emerged as I told his story in the introduction. Turning right, onto the dirt road, there are a few rows of wooden barracks that are subdivided into rooms that are rented to migrants, most of whom work at Batamindo or are job seekers. They have been built by an industrious middle-aged man from the eastern Indonesian island of Flores who also owns the electricity generator that powers the area. Moving along the curving road, full of deep potholes, one reaches Padang Service, a large repair shop for cars and trucks. On the left-hand side, the rows of shacks continue, and beyond Padang Service planks cover the road as protection against the inevitable mud during the rainy season. To the right, through the shrubs, one can see two houses, one obviously older than the other and that was used as a storage space for the rubber that was harvested before Batamindo was built. Most people call this area Belakang Sony named after the nearby factory.

The area has no obvious beginning or end, and abodes are constantly being built in new clearings that stretch farther into the woods. While the inside of the industrial park is dominated by women, men make up the majority of the population in the squatter areas that surround it. As I have already suggested, many women avoid *liar* housing precisely because it is associated with extramarital sexuality and other forms of illicit activities. All of the roughly twenty migrants living in Chandra's house and the building located next to it are associated with Sony, either directly or through a spouse, girlfriend or boyfriend, or relative. The most serious drawbacks of living there are the endemic lack of fresh water—entirely dependent on rain—and the frequent problems with the electricity from the unreliable generator. When there is no rain the inhabitants carry water in buckets from the industrial park.

Despite the lack of a functioning infrastructure, Chandra doesn't want to live in the Batamindo dormitories. "In the dorms there is not enough privacy. I can bring my girlfriend here without anyone bothering me and it also feels like a *kampung;* everyone knows everyone else. Besides that, it is inexpensive and cool because of the shade from the trees." Harnanto, who lives in the older building next to Chandra's, put it more strongly: because most of the inhabitants work at the same factory, there is "the feeling of being part of a family (*kekeluargaan*). Even though I am in the *rantau* it feels like I am living in a *kampung*."

At the opposite end of Batamindo lies Gampung Aceh, where Wati lives with her two brothers, both of whom are unemployed. She uses most of her salary to support them and herself; any money that is left over is usually sent to her parents. Wati takes care of most of the household chores, as she did when she was still at home, but she refuses to complain, despite working seventy hour weeks at the factory.

Gampung Aceh is strikingly different compared to Belakang Sony. Both represent a continuum of *liar* squatter areas around Batamindo that vary in terms of stability and organization. However, as the name suggests, Gampung Aceh is ethnically more homogenous. Effort has been placed on creating a village infrastructure, with bridges and a community center that is used for meetings and religious ceremonies. Inhabitants have invested more time and energy in building houses than in Belakang Sony—Wati's floor is made of concrete, Chandra's of dirt.

By creating administrative units on their own initiative, community leaders in Gampung Aceh are engaged in attempts to make the village legitimate within the state structure, so that it will not be destroyed, or at

A kitchen in a squatter house in Belakang Sony. Photo by author.

the very least so that the inhabitants will be offered reasonable compensation if they are forcibly evicted. This became particularly clear during the celebration of the Prophet Mohammad's birthday, Mawlid, that I attended in 2003. The village council had invited government and religious officials as guests of honor, and the community leader began his introduction welcoming the guests by stating emphatically that "although we live in a *liar* community, we are not *liar* people." The crowd of around two hundred people cheered and clapped enthusiastically.

Wati does not feel *terbuang* (exiled or displaced) in Gampung Aceh. "I pretty much do the same things here that I would at home. I speak Acehnese, I cook Achenese food, and I have my brothers." She feels comfortable because her home has been re-created. While the *liar* community is like home, it is in fact the outside area, the street, that appears as a threat. This is why her veiling is dictated primarily by the boundaries of her community—by space rather then gender.

But Batam is different. It is not her *kampung*. She traveled there in order to become something that she could not in Aceh. Wati has aspirations. She wants to study English and learn to use a computer, because, just like in the products she assembles, they appear to belong together. "Computers use English, so that is why I want to learn English first," she tells me. "After I finish working in the factory I'll go back to school and graduate after three years. I'll work, but not as an operator. I'll work in an office because I'll have a diploma and I'll be competent in computers and English."

Wati does not want to become a housewife (*ibu rumah tangga*) who merely takes care of the children. She hopes to become a *wanita karier,* a career woman, who works in an office, and she imagines herself wearing clothing from the glossy fashion magazines that she reads (but does not buy) in the mall located adjacent to Batamindo (e.g., Brenner 1999; Jones 2004). But the *kampung* that is reconstituted on Batam entails obligations. Wati has not yet been able to save money for school, since she is supporting her two brothers. The feminization of labor on Batam, which allows her to find work easily, has not given her the means to advance toward the kind of life that she hopes for. Not feeling *terbuang* also means that she remains connected to the gender structures from which she hopes to move away.

When Chandra first arrived on Batam, his goal had been to support his mother and help his younger siblings through school, but the more time that passed, the less money he sent home. He has found it increasingly difficult to motivate himself. He articulates the tension between the demands of *merantau* and his own personal development: "When I was still in my *kampung* I felt *stres* because there was no work. But there were no other demands and no responsibility. Now I have to work for others and become like my parents. I want to return home but I don't have anything to show for my time here and that makes me feel *malu*. I can't return until I have succeeded."

Wati is not *malu* since she remains directly connected to an emotional economy that binds her to her family and home. She protects herself by veiling and has hopes for the future. In contrast, Chandra expresses his anxieties about not being able to move forward (*maju*) in life. The *modal*, or capital, he aspires to is beyond his reach, and his possibilities appear limited. His attempt to enter Singapore (see the introduction) was one way of trying to break out of the structure of wage labor, as are his connections with acquaintances who might help him become a security guard within BIDA, a job that—beyond the formal salary—appears to guarantee access to an economy of bribes. But at this moment he does not know in what direction to move. He has time to contemplate his debt to his family, thus evoking feelings of *malu*. "To feel emotion," Merleau-Ponty writes, "is to be involved in a situation which one is not managing to face and from which, nevertheless, one does not want to escape" (2002, 99). Chandra remains bound to the place from whence he has come, but cannot return until he has experienced a change in status.

BECOMING *LIAR*

Three months after Ella arrived on Batam, a young man who also worked in Batamindo began flirting with her as she stood outside the post office. He bought her lunch at the food court and soon afterward started paying visits to her dorm before they eventually initiated a romantic relationship. "I thought it was pretty exciting from the beginning and I decided to go along with it. Actually," she said, pausing for a moment, "he was ugly, but I liked his motorcycle." During the first couple of months he often suggested that she spend the night at the room he rented with his cousin in a *liar* village near Belakang Sony.

It was only one night when I had been drinking *arak* [a type of inexpensive alcohol] with him and other friends that I agreed. At the time I didn't want to have sex (*berhubungan seks*) with him and afterward I felt as though I had been forced and regretted it. For the man there is no regret because once a woman has slept with someone it is difficult to find someone else. But for the man it is impossible to tell if he is still a virgin (*perawan*) or not.

However, the story became more complicated when she revealed that she had continued to have sexual intercourse with him but had not wanted to use contraceptives. She explained, "I don't want to, because if I do use something like that, the guy won't take responsibility. . . . Later if he is bored he will just leave." After a few months Ella discovered she was pregnant. Pressured by her boyfriend, she agreed to take pills that he had bought at the pharmacy to induce an abortion, but the only effect was that she became ill and vomited. "After that I was scared, especially since there was a story in the news at the time about a worker who had died getting an abortion at a *dukun* [a traditional healer]. So finally we just got married, but I was *malu* and afraid (*takut*) to tell my mother." When Ella finally did call to tell her the news, her mother was furious not only because of the pregnancy, but also because Ella had two older sisters who were not yet married. But there was nothing that could be done.

Because of factory regulations forbidding both marriage and pregnancy, Ella did not tell her supervisor, and she did not dare visit the Batamindo health clinic. Fortunately, no one but her closest friends at the factory found out, since the work uniform at her company was loose and her abdomen remained relatively small. However, in the late stages of the pregnancy she finally revealed her plight to a friendly Javanese supervisor who kept her secret and gave her lighter work. A couple of weeks before she was to give birth she took a leave of absence, and her new mother-in-law came to help. When the baby was only two weeks old her mother-in-law took him to her home in Aceh, and since then Ella has seen the child only sporadically during holidays when her mother-in-law comes to Batam. "It feels strange to hold him because we rarely meet," she tells me. "He doesn't seem to recognize me."

Although Ella is still married, she rarely sees her husband, since she works the day shift and he the night shift. For a while they lived together, but she was unhappy and moved back to be with her friends because she, like Wati, "didn't want to be like a housewife." She also has seen him together with other women and has heard rumors that he has several girlfriends, but she is *malu* to approach him about it. According to her, "Women should not go to visit a man's house, the man should always come to the woman's house." One of the main reasons she does not want to live with him is her fear that she will become pregnant again. When I asked why she would not use contraceptives, her initial answer was merely that she did not want to. However, she finally revealed that her main fear was that contraceptives makes one fat, and she did not want that to happen.[19] "If I become fat my husband will not want me anymore and will leave me. That is why I don't want to use contraceptives [*pil KB,* or *keluarga berencana;* literally "family-planning pill"]."

For Ella, Batam and her work in the factory are not what she had hoped for: the island is still rural, she is "treated like a coolie," and the products that she makes are worth more than her labor. But *merantau* also offers freedoms: to spend time with friends, have a boyfriend, and not have anyone tell where you are going. These freedoms, however, led to Ella's unwelcome pregnancy and marriage. Ironically, while she wishes to be free and avoid obligations and the life of a "housewife," cultural discourses surrounding female sexuality and her attempt to regulate her *malu* led her down a path where she preferred the risk of pregnancy.

Despite the fact that the Islamic regulation of *zina* (illicit or forbidden sex) applies both to men and women, the contradictory gendered ideals concerning sex in Indonesia are widely acknowledged (e.g., Murray 1991; Suryakusuma 1996; Bennett 2005). Often considered a sign of masculinity for men, for women premarital and extramarital sex signify immorality. For men, *zina* is less a potential source of *malu* than the economic burden that comes with a relationship and the anticipated role as a "provider" in the context of the nuclear family.

The men I knew who drank alcohol, consumed drugs, or engaged in premarital sex readily admitted that they sinned, but these activities did not trouble them in everyday life or generally evoke feelings of *malu*. In contrast to the women I have discussed, it is striking that almost none of my male informants were involved in religious activities inside or outside the park. Many would visit mosques on major religious holidays, but few would attend on a weekly basis, or even pray regularly. When I asked why this was the case, most would reply that they were *malas,* or lazy.

On Batam, men have less to gain by becoming involved in religious activities than women. First, they do not face the same moral ambiguity in public space as women and thus have less need to perform piety through dress and public action. Second, men cannot claim increased religious knowledge as a legitimate source of personal development (*kemajuan*) upon return from Batam to the same degree as women, unless they have spent time at a *pesantrian,* an Islamic boarding school. Batam is not a place that men travel to in order to learn about Islam.

At the time of my main period of fieldwork, Chandra was having a relationship with Sri, a woman from Central Java who worked in Batamindo. Although she officially lived in a dorm inside the park, she would spend most of her nights in his room. At one point, when Sri returned to her home village for a month, however, Chandra had an affair with another woman working at Batamindo. When Sri returned she soon found out about his new girlfriend from another woman at the factory and broke off their relationship. Although Chandra appeared to regret his actions, he also said the following.

> I am still fooling around. I don't have the money to get married and all the women I meet are just for *happy* and to get rid of the boredom that I feel. I work all the time and this gives me *stres.*[20] I don't have any other entertainment, I don't have anything, so this is all I have. . . . It is sort of the same thing with my mother. Now I tell her that I can't send her money all the time because the cost of living on Batam is extremely high. I also sometimes want to buy something for myself, like a new shirt, and not just send all my money home.

Like many of the male migrants living in and around Batamindo, Chandra frequents a nearby low-charge brothel. He claims that from a strictly economic perspective it is cheaper to go to a prostitute every now and then than to have a girlfriend. "If I have a romantic relationship (*berpacaran*), I need money all the time, but at Kampung Flores [the brothel area] all I need is a bit of money one day." Similarly, the possibility of marriage is complicated by a lack of funds more than a lack of desire to marry. Chandra thus claims that marriage is not an option since he has no way of supporting a wife and children. While perhaps this statement should not be taken at face value, he is certainly plagued by the hegemonic image of the middle-class *bapak* (man or father) in contemporary Indonesia.

When I spoke with Sri, she was clearly of a different opinion, claiming that Chandra was irresponsible. "You can't trust men on Batam," she told me adamantly.

I always felt that I was sinning (*berdosa*) when I was with Chandra, especially in relation to the other women who came from my part of Java. But
I thought that in the end we would get married and it wouldn't matter,
no one would know. I should never have begun to stay there [in his room];
it was a bad influence on me.

Sri expressed her regret in spatial terms: she claimed it was easier to be
immoral in the squatter communities, where there were no forms of surveillance. On the other hand, she argued that the fact that most of the
women in her dormitory were pious Muslims and wore a *jilbab* created a
kind of moral community that protected against the *liar*. But as should
be clear, the reverse is also true. For Wati, Gampung Aceh was precisely a
moral community where she felt safe and therefore did not veil. It is therefore reasonable that few people lived in *liar* marriages, since they, in an
important sense, had never left home.

CONCLUSION: MOVING BEYOND THE ENCLAVE

For migrants living and working in and around Batamindo, the major
paradox of *merantau* is that development does not offer what they initially
had imagined. While Batam—and especially Batamindo—is presented
as the "locomotive" of Indonesian economic development, most migrants
quickly discover that they are outside of this world, that the white-collar
work they had expected and the possibilities they have in "developing" or
"advancing" (*maju*) are relatively limited. The structure of employment in
Batamindo does not offer migrants a way forward.

It is in this process of realization that *malu* gains a particular force for
migrants. For men who must live up to the ideal of the "provider" in order
to become a *bapak,* or father, of the Indonesian middle class and nation, success is measured in terms of *modal* that will lead to independence from the
labor market. This is clear in Chandra's case and will become increasingly
so in the next chapter. For young women, it is common to send money to
parents or siblings, but it is expected that they will eventually marry and be
supported by a husband. Instead, other forms of interaction and actions—
most notably relationships with men and premarital sex—become sources
of *malu*.

The nuclear family—inflected by patriarchy and Islam—is the ideological building block of the Indonesian nation-state (Sears 1996; Brenner 1998). With women's intensifying engagement with the market and increasing independence through migration, however, their sexuality appears as a threat to both the nuclear family and the nation-state. Nowhere in Indonesia do these anxieties become as obvious as in and around Batamindo, where young women dominate the labor force. The embeddedness of gender in global production thus has effects beyond the factory floor and the industrial park, and the transnational fantasy of the "nimble-fingered" female factory worker creates other forms of fantasies and desires. In this context, religion offers a form of personal development (*kemajuan*) for women while protecting against the dangers of *liar* sexuality. William Reddy (1997, 347) points out that shame "derives from thoughts about how one is seen by others. . . . Thus, shame can lead to withdrawal coupled with action aimed at managing appearances." Women can constitute themselves as "pious," suggesting that they have accumulated new forms of knowledge, that they have become someone different, thereby dealing with the balance of *malu,* which ranges from shame to modesty.

Distinctions between the "developed" and the "*liar*" are, however, not stable. For some, like Wati, community becomes constituted through the *liar,* while for others like Sri, they become spaces that should be avoided because there is, as she puts it, "no one to watch over you," but perhaps more important, because there are people there from her home region who see that she has become *liar* and thus someone who should be *malu.* In other words, there are particular forms of regulation within the *liar* that point toward the power of the *kampung,* or neighborhood, as an extension of the state. This illustrates a particular relationship in Indonesia between community and state on the village level. There is an attempt by the state and village members alike to "disguise" the difference between *kampung* as community and as administrative unit (Sullivan 1986, 63). The naming of villages as *liar* defines a gap between state and community and, more specifically, that another form of community exists outside of the state. That members of Gampung Aceh attempt to bridge this gap is a sign of the power of the state to rule indirectly (cf. Barker 1998).

But the *liar* is a site of instability, suggesting both the possibility of community and of transgression. Outside the gates of the industrial park, migrants engage with the contradictions of modernity. Chandra develops plans to enter Singapore, Wati balances her familial responsibilities with hopes for the future, and Ella becomes involved in a relationship that she most likely never would have had she remained in Solo. It remains unclear what direction their lives will take, but Batamindo is not an endpoint for any of them.

While Gampung Aceh has continued to endure, Belakang Sony existed for only a few years as I described it and was destroyed when the area was flooded by a nearby dam that BIDA had opened. Most people in the area speculated that this was a strategy to displace the squatters. One woman from North Sumatra noted sarcastically that this was a refined (*halus*) way of getting rid of people. "It's the Javanese way of doing things."[21] Whether or not this was the case, people were eventually forced to move, and the houses along the road beyond Padang Service were abandoned. The house that Chandra, Harnanto, and others had occupied was taken apart and rebuilt a few hundred meters down the road. As the flooding subsided near the old houses, new ones appeared within a matter of weeks. Six months later, half a dozen new houses had been built in the area and a new *kampung* had begun to emerge. A couple of years after that, in 2005, it had expanded further. I asked around, but there was no longer anyone there whom I knew.

3

The Economy of the Night

If you *merantau* to Batam you need to have some kind of skill or education. If not, then you will end up like me, working as a prostitute or not working at all. But compared to the *kampung* at least I can make a bit of money, and they don't have to know what I do here.

Lidya, twenty-year-old prostitute

It is nearly midnight as I reach the bottom of the hill leading up to Ozon, the largest disco on Batam. Along the busy road a series of small stalls sells everything from noodle soup to cigarettes and condoms. At the top of the hill outside the club the road is packed with taxis and *ojek* (motorcycle taxis) waiting for passengers who will pay exorbitant fares as they come out of the club. As usual, Aryo is leaning against the side of his taxi waiting for his Singaporean clients who are inside. He is one of the lucky ones who has a *tamu* (client or guest) who comes every weekend. Creating these stable patron-client relationships is crucial in order to maintain a steady income in the face of intense competition.

Passing the bouncer and the admissions booth, one is hit by a wall of sound upon entering the club. The air smells of clove cigarettes and air conditioning. On a good night, Ozon is nearly filled to its capacity of two thousand people by 11:00 p.m., and tonight this is certainly the case. To the right, at the back of the disco, the disc jockey is playing techno versions of Indonesian and Western songs, but only a few people are on the small dance floor in the middle of the club. In contrast, the high tables and barstools that surround the dance floor are packed with people who can afford to buy drinks. The majority are conspicuously moving their heads back and forth to the beat of the music—in most cases, such people are *tripping* on

Ecstasy, the popular term for MDMA (3,4-methylenedioxymethamphet-amine). Behind the disc jockey, and at the entrance to the toilets, young men are selling drugs, mainly Ecstasy or marijuana, offering their goods to anyone who looks their way. Drugs can also be ordered directly from the waiters for a slightly higher price. At the other end of the club, at the bar, waiters are busy picking up drinks for customers. One floor up, booths with a view of the dance floor and a number of private karaoke rooms are available for hourly rental.

Since the mid-1990s Ecstasy has become the drug of choice in night-clubs throughout Indonesia.[1] John, a Singaporean man who frequents Ozon, has his own theory about the composition of people at the disco and how Ecstasy circulates there: "You can take nine people. Three will be Singapor-eans looking for women. They *book*[2] three women who are given Ecstasy; two of them take the drug and the third hands it over to a *preman* [a thug or gangster], who sells it to another person who just wants to be by himself. The final person is lost because he thinks he is at a regular disco."

John's comment suggests that we can understand the social organiza-tion of the disco in relation to the circulation of Ecstasy. It suggests that there is an economy at work. Ecstasy is a key element of this economy, yet differently situated actors engage with the drug in alternative ways: in Ozon the drug is bought, given away, consumed, hidden, passed on, sold, and, for that "final person" on John's list, perhaps invisible. This economy stretches far beyond the nightclubs of Nagoya, generating revenue for gov-ernment officials, hotels, taxis, restaurants, stores, and middlemen (*calo*) who act as escorts, guards, or touts.

In the dark area in the corner next to the bar, Kartika and her friend Yasmin, both in their early twenties from West Java, are sitting, obvi-ously bored, with a group of other women. An older woman, their madam (*mami*), comes and goes, occasionally speaking into the ear of one of the women, who then goes off with a waiting man. Kartika has yet to be *dibook-ing* (booked) by a *tamu* (client or guest), and Yasmin is waiting for her *tamu tetap* (regular client or guest), who comes from Singapore every Saturday night. To pass the time, they chain-smoke menthol clove cigarettes.

Dewi, a thirty-two-year-old woman from the city of Palembang in South Sumatra, dressed in blue jeans and a white T-shirt, stands alone, obviously uncomfortable, at the front of the bar near a group of Western men. She is hoping that one of them will approach her. Lidya, a twenty-year-old Javanese woman, and her friends have specific areas where they usu-

Inside Ozon. Photo by Rama Surya. Reproduced with permission of Rama Surya and Latitudes.

ally stand and search for clients. All of them are nervously looking around, trying to find a client who will give them their initial goal, Ecstasy. These women are all *liar* prostitutes, freelance without pimps. Finding a *tamu,* usually a Singaporean, and being booked guarantees money and, usually, Ecstasy. One can either be booked at an hourly rate to sit down (*booking duduk*) together in a public space in the disco or leave the premises with the client (*booking keluar*), though this is generally not decided beforehand. For Kartika, Yasmin, and other women who have a *mami,* prices are fixed and the women receive only a percentage afterward, often in conjunction with a tip directly from the client. *Liar* prostitutes, however, must themselves initiate contact and negotiate prices, which may therefore fluctuate considerably. Furthermore, if a woman is booked out it can be for the whole night or *short-time;* prices vary accordingly.[3]

UNRAVELING THE ECONOMY OF THE NIGHT

The ethnographic starting point for this chapter is a space that is generally understood as a global type, namely the "disco." As in my earlier discussion of the "development enclave," I am not primarily interested in how local manifestations of this type might be used to critique overly general claims about the nature of globalization. I am, rather, concerned with what a particular disco, Ozon, can reveal about processes that shape the lives of Indonesian migrants and, more generally, a particular form of transnational economy. As I have already suggested, this perspective shows that the economy of the night stretches far beyond Ozon, illuminating processes that are by no means local.

Although I am consciously juxtaposing what I call the economy of the "night" with the "day," it is once again important to point out that both depend primarily on the labor of young women. Despite their differences, in this book I want to highlight common themes.[4] In particular, migrants involved in the economy of the day and the night are related through a common emotional economy of *merantau.* While the female factory worker wearing the *jilbab* was a key figure in the previous chapter, in this chapter the female *liar* prostitute and the *bronces,* the man who lives off the earnings of women, personify the cultural anxieties of prostitution, the feminization of labor, and the reversal of gender roles on Batam. Since *liar* prostitutes work outside of closed institutions (such as brothels or karaoke bars) and are not controlled by pimps, these women are unlicensed and interstitial figures in relation to the Indonesian state, thereby appearing as threats to the regulation of prostitution.[5]

In this chapter I am interested in how this form of ambiguity becomes evident and is negotiated in a number of ways beyond the direct regulation of the state. In Ozon women consume Ecstasy in order to deal with feelings of *malu*—particularly in relation to Islamic prohibitions and the fear that family members will find out they work as prostitutes—and thus more easily engage in prostitution with Singaporean clients. Outside of Ozon relationships with boyfriends, children, and other family members are transformed, as women become the main breadwinners and men are increasingly marginalized. Through this process both female prostitutes and their male Indonesian partners come to recognize themselves as *liar,* outside the promises of the Indonesian nation and part of the underclass.

CONTROLLING CONTAGION, REGULATING TRANSACTIONS

Prostitution on Batam and surrounding islands is diverse and often changing, but it can be divided into several categories. There are two quasi-official *lokalisasi,* or brothel areas, and as many as five other unsanctioned brothel villages catering almost exclusively to Indonesian migrant workers.[6] Both female and transvestite streetwalkers can be found in various places around the island, while male prostitutes catering to men are less common, but they often *nongkrong* (hang out) in particular spots such as bus stops around Nagoya. To add to the complexity, a large number of female and transvestite prostitutes frequently move between Batam and Singapore or Malaysia (see chap. 5). The most conspicuous spaces for prostitution, however, are the handful of discos and the dozens of karaoke bars concentrated in Nagoya.

On Batam the Department of Social Affairs—the government agency that deals most directly with prostitution—distinguishes between different types of prostitutes. As in the rest of Indonesia, women in *lokalisasi* are identified as WTS (*wanita tuna sila*), or literally "woman without morals," while those working in karaoke bars are called *pramuria,* more akin to "entertainers." Prostitutes not controlled by pimps are, as I already have noted, considered *liar.* These women are identified as the main problem by officials in the creation of an "ordered" (*teratur*) environment.[7]

Raids, or *operasi,* are the most common instruments for localizing prostitutes on Batam.[8] Jones and his colleagues (1995, 13) write that in Indonesia the "pressure on streetwalkers . . . drives lower-class women workers into brothel complexes, where they are controlled by pimps, procurers and the local government and police, but generally tolerated by society."[9] This follows Kusno's (2000) argument (see chap. 1) that "the street" emerged as a site of disorder and menace during the New Order, in relation to the "ordered," privileged space of the nation, namely "the family." In the regulationist tradition of the colonial state (Abalahin 2003) prostitution is tolerated and confined to particular places in an attempt to organize debauchery and, more generally, the "street" and the underclass that inhabits this space.[10]

But the localization of prostitutes in the name of public order, or increasingly in the name of Islam, not only aims to control disease and keep prostitution out of sight, but also creates spaces for economic transactions. In other words, logics of governance and economics converge when prostitutes are confined to a particular space. This is certainly the case on Batam, where not only managers of low-charge brothels but also of discos and karaoke bars make payments to various groups within the government, especially the police. In response to this, as we shall see, many women work as *liar* prostitutes so that they can control economic transactions themselves.

ENTERING THE *RANTAU*

From my experience I can tell you that most of the women who tell you that they were tricked into prostitution are lying. They are just *malu* to admit that they knew from the beginning.

Government official at a regional HIV prevention meeting on Batam, May 2000

I knew that Batam was famous for prostitution and that I couldn't really make as much as they promised me. But would it have been better to stay in the *kampung* and marry another man who can't take care of me and my children?

Twenty-five-year-old woman working as a prostitute on Batam

Dewi was born in the city of Palembang in South Sumatra, the second of six children. She married her boyfriend after graduating from high school, and a year later they had their first child. Her husband had difficulty finding steady work, however, and when one of his cousins returned from Batam for Idul Fitri, the celebration that breaks the fast after Ramadan, he was invited to join them on the trip back. He quickly agreed, and Dewi and their baby remained in the village. "We had all heard about Batam," she told me. "I had my doubts about him going away, but I thought that if he worked there for a few years we would have enough money to build our own house."

After only a few months, she heard rumors from migrants returning from Batam that her husband was not working, but spending what little money he made on women and alcohol. She decided to go see for herself and found him unemployed and living in a *liar* settlement near one of the main ports. Dewi stayed on while their child remained in Palembang with her parents, and she quickly found work in one of the electronics factories nearby. For three years she assembled television sets and telephones while her husband found only odd jobs. "On Batam," she explained, "there are lots of companies that need female labor. For men it is much more difficult."

Through a friend her husband was finally hired as a driver at a factory in a nearby industrial park. By that time Dewi had given birth to a second son and quit her job to take care of the children. They moved away from the *liar* settlement to one of the company houses, but when she caught her husband having an affair with another woman she finally left him. She returned with her children to Palembang and began trading: buying electronic goods on Batam and selling them in Palembang, and returning with garlic to sell on Batam.

It seemed promising at first, but after six months or so it was obvious that there was too much competition. I couldn't return home because there was nothing for me to do there, and I was too old to work in a factory again,[11] so I took a job as a hostess in one of the gambling halls. I met a Singaporean guy there who was a manager in one of the factories, and we started having a relationship, and finally he asked me to live with him. He was good to me even though we couldn't really speak the same language with each other, and I had enough money to send home. When his contract ended six months later, I knew where to go to meet men. That's how it started. But I only go out to look for clients when I really need the money. Sometimes I don't even go to a bar for two months or so.

Most of the time Dewi sells *pempek,* South Sumatran fish cake, on the street outside the house where she lives. Too old to continue working in an electronics factory, she has turned to prostitution when her other business fails her. More recently, especially since the economic crisis, this has become her predominant source of income, part of a broader "advancement strategy" (Brennan 2004, 23–24) when other moneymaking opportunities do not bear fruit.

> I didn't want to work in a way that was immoral (*tidak betul*), but I kept thinking that I had two children who I am responsible for. So it is better that I sacrifice myself rather than knowing that they are suffering. But I refuse to call myself a prostitute (*anak malam*). If someone asks me I tell them that I am factory worker just trying to make some extra money.

Dewi's story suggests that her path toward Batam began with a series of constraints and choices that cannot be disconnected from one another, and any attempt to identify her as a "prostitute" is problematic, in large part because she avoids this form of self-presentation herself. Dewi therefore remains *liar,* outside the control of pimps or any kind of formal sector.

Lidya, whom I will introduce in the next section, is twenty years old. She worked as a prostitute in the city of Medan in North Sumatra before she came to Batam. She ran away from home with a cousin at age fifteen when her mother died suddenly and she was left with an abusive and alcoholic father. In a matter-of-fact-manner, she summarized her route into prostitution in just a few sentences: "There wasn't really much else I could do in Medan, and when I ended up at the bus station, this guy took me to a brothel area where I lost my virginity on the first day. I stayed there for about a year, and when one of my friends there told me about Batam I decided right away to join her. That's how I got here." Together with her boyfriend and their daughter, Lidya lives in a rented room in the heart of Nagoya.

A KIND OF HOME

As Efran, Umar, Fikri, and I sit on the floor in the hallway, Diana is putting her baby to sleep, while Lidya is burning incense and reading a prayer so that she will be certain to get a client that evening. The women have already showered, dressed, and put on their makeup and are ready to go. It is 11:00 p.m. on Thursday, Ladies Night at all the discos in town, which guarantees free entrance for all women. Diana still looks pale from the close call she had that morning when she came home and breastfed her one-month-old baby boy despite having taken Ecstasy the night before. Umar, her boyfriend and the father of the child, describes the incident in a mix of excitement and horror: the baby's body started trembling and small black spots appeared on his skin. Shaking his head, he is in awe that the baby survived and seems to be doing fine. Lidya comments loudly from inside her room that she took Ecstasy every other day when she was pregnant, and her two-year-old daughter, Tika, is doing fine. Efran, her boyfriend, smiles at me as he tries to keep Tika from grabbing the ashtray on the floor between us. As Diana and Lidya step past us, Rosa, who is five months pregnant, comes out of her room and follows them down the hall. We all turn our heads and watch as they disappear down the steps. Soon we hear Lidya outside calling for an *ojek* that will take her to Ozon, less than a kilometer away.

Efran rarely goes out these days. He spends most of his time in a room that he rents with Lidya and their daughter, or sitting out in the hallway smoking clove cigarettes and playing cards. Born in 1977 in a village about an hour's drive from the West Sumatran city of Padang, he came to Batam when he was seventeen years old. He has never held a steady job but used to drive an *ojek,* and occasionally he makes some money as a tattoo artist. However, since the economic crisis it has become difficult to rent a motorcycle for a reasonable price, and no one has asked for a tattoo for over a month. Most often he and Umar, who lives in the next room over with Diana and their baby, try to concoct schemes to make money. Usually, these involve acting as middlemen (*calo*) in sales of cell phones, television sets, motorcycles, cars, marijuana, and anything else on the market, but usually the plans fail and they merely spend money and energy looking for buyers and sellers.

James Siegel writes that the "ability to make connections" (2002, 213) is crucial in order to "enter the so called economy of development and to take a full part in Indonesian life" (218; see also Hugo 1985, 75). For most unskilled male migrants who come to Batam, however, this ability is often beyond reach. Ethnic or kinship networks provide one possibility and education another, but they are far from being guarantees. None of the male migrants I discuss in this chapter have graduated from high school or are part of any kind of useful social network. This means that they are not even able to apply for factory work. Instead they tend to find odd jobs, and becoming a *calo* appears to be the only form of connection within reach. There are, however, always too many *calo,* too many people seeking connections in this way. One is often *ditipu* (tricked) by people who are more powerful and who are impossible to touch, or by people who simply disappear. On Batam, it is said, one cannot trust people.

Umar comes from the North Sumatran city of Medan. He claims that he used to work on an oil tanker and says he has traveled to Singapore, Cambodia, Vietnam, and other countries throughout Asia, but no one actually believes him. He is well known for borrowing money that he never repays, and few people trust him. A few weeks before his son was born, he disappeared for two weeks, suddenly returning without explanation just days before Diana gave birth. During that time she had frantically looked for him all over town, and most people living on the floor speculated that he had run off because he could not deal with the pressure of becoming a father.

Fikri has been on Batam for only a few months and listens intently as Efran and Umar tell him about life on the island. Fikri is sharing a room with his girlfriend Rosa, who came with him from Medan. Efran and Lidya say that the baby she is carrying in her stomach is giving her luck and that she has been getting clients every night. Umar tells Fikri that he needs to get an identity card (KTP: *kartu tanda penduduk*) in order to find a job, but to get one from corrupt government authorities, who are said to be doing a thriving business,[12] one must pay several hundred thousand rupiah. Efran adds that since neither he nor Lidya have gotten around to getting identity cards, Tika doesn't even have a birth certificate. The identity card system forms a boundary between the *warga,* the citizen, and those who are *liar,* outside of the national community (Strassler 2003, 207). As in the case of squatter housing, the *liar* follows from processes of formalization, thereby naming the marginal. Tika was thus not only born outside of a legitimate family form, but is, in fact, not even an Indonesian citizen.

They live in a three-story building, a *ruko* (*rumah toko,* literally "store building"), the most typical style of building found throughout the town of Nagoya. Located behind a large hotel, the building is owned by a Chinese family who also runs the restaurant on the ground floor. After passing through the restaurant and the rat-infested kitchen, the stairs lead up to the second and then the third floor, where Efran and Lidya have lived for two years. The floor has been subdivided by gypsum board into eight small cubicles that are approximately eight square meters each. Green mosquito nets continue where the walls end and reach up to the roof, creating an environment where sound travels easily. At the far end of the linoleum-covered, concrete hallway there is one bathroom that all occupants share, but as the plumbing rarely works, water has to be brought up in buckets from the kitchen two floors down. At the other end of the hallway is a large window from which one can gaze down onto the street. In the house across the street is a hair salon that appears to be nothing more than a front for a brothel, and next door is a karaoke bar that does not seem to be doing very well.

The turnover rate for these cubicles is very high, and during the three-year period that I visited this building, between 1998 and 2001, every one of them had been emptied at least once. Efran and Lidya lived there the longest, but few others remained for more than six months. Unlike *kost* rooms that are rented in residential areas, these rooms are rarely home to factory workers. A young junior high school teacher lived in one of the rooms for a month or so, but quickly moved once he realized that most of the women on the floor worked as prostitutes. Many people stay in *ruko* because of the freedom it offers and its location in the middle of the city. The rent for such cubicles ranges from 150,000 to 300,000 rupiah (between 17 and 33 U.S. dollars) per month, about the same one would pay for a room in a residential house, but much more than the 50,000 rupiah that it generally costs to rent a room in a squatter area. Renting a room alone would be far too expensive for most.

Just down the street, Dewi shares a room in another *ruko,* similar to the building where Lidya and Efran live, together with another woman from Palembang. The room is sparsely furnished with two mattresses on the floor, a wooden wardrobe in the corner, and a portable gas burner next to a transparent plastic box with kitchen utensils. Dewi and her roommate used to share a television set, but they sold it one month when they were short on rent. A pencil drawing of a mosque hangs next to a mirror, above a BCA Bank calendar from the year before. Underneath the drawing she has written: "Plan: in two more years I will return home."

Dewi prefers to spend time with people from her own *kampung* who speak her own language. All of them are, however, involved in some form of prostitution, and outside this group she is unwilling to admit that she is from Palembang. Her worst fear is that she will meet someone from her home village and that her parents will find out what she is doing on Batam.

"If I am face to face (*berhadapan*) with someone from my *kampung* I feel *malu* at once. That's why I don't want people to know what I do or where I am from. It's not because I am a hypocrite, I am just *malu*." Dewi's statement captures the complexity of *malu* not only as a negative, but also as a positive emotion. To be seen as a "prostitute" by someone to whom one is related or with whom one shares a *kampung* is to recognize oneself as a person who has crossed a moral boundary. But this also means that Dewi's concern with this boundary is explicitly moral since she aims to protect the reputation of her family and community so that they do not have to experience the *malu* that she does. The reason Dewi is *liar* is thus precisely to be able to retain an ambiguous position that allows her to be able to say: "I am not a prostitute."

THE ECONOMY OF PLEASURE

James Farrer has argued that—as a global sociological form—the disco should be described as a superculture rather than a subculture. In Shanghai, he claims, the disco is primarily a site for youth wishing to engage with global culture (Farrer 1999, 149). At first sight this would appear to be the case at Ozon as well. The name of the disco, the recognizable beat of the music, the availability of foreign beers and cocktails all suggest a relationship with the "global" and with the various forms of pleasure that organize contemporary forms of consumerism. Much of the vocabulary associated with Ecstasy on Batam is in English. Words like *tripping, on, enjoy, happy,* and *refreshing* are commonly used and are understood even by Indonesians who do not use Ecstasy or frequent discos on the island.[13] Titanic, Superman, Mickey Mouse, Honda, and Butterfly are among the most popular kinds of Ecstasy. Ozon, therefore, appears to offer at least a fleeting engagement with the promises of global capitalism.

However, all is not as it seems. On Batam a Long Island iced tea is half iced tea, half vodka, while the Ecstasy is often of uncertain quality.[14] Overdoses are common, as it is often difficult to judge the quality of the drug beforehand. The price of entering the disco and of buying Ecstasy makes Ozon, and the cosmopolitan culture it mimics, a site of social distinction. Ladies Night allows women to enter free of charge two nights a week, but most Indonesian men must pay the cover charge, which is twenty thousand rupiah (more than two U.S. dollars), an average salary for a day's work on Batam. Foreign men usually do not pay; once inside, they are at the center of an economy that will generate more value for the owners of the disco. In other words, the gate-keeping principles of Ozon are tied to gendered and national distinctions. Singaporean women and Indonesian men do not fit into this world as easily.

Although Ozon must be considered in transnational terms, understanding the disco as a "global form" or "superculture" prioritizes choice and pleasure. In contrast, Ozon should be understood as a postmodern example of what Pratt calls a "contact zone": "a space in which peoples geographically and historically separated come into contact and establish ongoing relations, usually involving conditions of coercion, radical inequality, and intractable conflict" (1992,6). But while Pratt's concern with "coercion," "inequality," and "conflict" highlights both the historical origins and economic dimensions of Ozon, she draws our attention away from the role that pleasure plays in situations of inequality and how "feeling good" is put to work within the political economy of the disco. Pleasure and coercion should thus be considered as emerging in tandem, taking specific forms in particular places.

Researchers who have studied sex tourism from Western countries to Southeast Asia have pointed out that the condition of inequality inherent in the relationship between client and prostitute should ideally (from the client's perspective, in particular) be denied by both parties in the context of their interaction, so it can be presented as primarily a source of pleasure (Bishop and Robinson 1998, 164–165; Kruhse-Mount Burton 1995; Oppermann 1998). This denial is necessary because many men are looking not only for sexual satisfaction, but also for "romance" or, most generally, companionship, particularly in "open-ended" (Cohen 1993) or, in this context, *liar* prostitution. Outside closed institutions such as brothels, the monetary transaction involved in "booking" can more easily be transformed so that neither party presents it as the primary reason for engaging in the relationship. As will become evident in the next chapter, one of the main reasons that Singaporean men buy sex on Batam is that in Singapore prostitution is both spatially and temporally regulated, making it difficult to deny the monetary nature of the transaction.[15] On Batam, however, open-ended prostitution is common and presents the possibility of transforming strictly sexual interactions into more extensive relationships. The client is called a *tamu,* which also means guest. These connotations suggest the potential for the inscription of other, more domestic forms of inequality in the relationship.[16]

In Ozon and other discos, the drug Ecstasy is crucial in forming a space where people may, at least temporarily, transform their subjectivities so that relationships of inequality may be presented as relationships of pleasure. Ecstasy allows women to transgress culturally powerful modes of bodily control and instead perform as prostitutes. Unlike drugs like marijuana, Ecstasy use is restricted to those who can either pay one hundred thousand rupiah (eleven U.S. dollars) or do not have to pay (for instance, drug dealers and prostitutes who are given the drug).[17] Disc jockeys in the main discos in Nagoya play the kinds of songs that they know work well with Ecstasy, while taxi drivers who shuttle people between discos and hotels do the same, as clients are shielded from the un-*happy* outside world.

Arjun Appadurai has argued that pleasure is the organizing principle and driving force in modern forms of consumerism. More specifically, he claims an aesthetic of ephemerality drives this process (1996, 83–84). Few objects are as ephemeral and as concerned with the production of pleasure as Ecstasy. One clinical study claims that Ecstasy produces "an affective state of enhanced mood, well-being, and increased emotional sensitiveness, little anxiety, but no hallucinations or panic reactions" (Vollenweider et al. 1998, 241). Conversations with men and women who frequently take the drug suggest that this is generally accurate. Furthermore, while opium is considered "primitive" and heroin is an isolationist drug, throughout contemporary Southeast Asia amphetamine-type stimulants such as Ecstasy are generally associated with mobility, modernity, and an entrepreneurial spirit (Lyttleton 2004).

In the Ozon disco—a place that constitutes itself as a global cultural form—Ecstasy produces not only pleasure, but also subjects who more readily engage in other types of economic transactions, most notably prostitution. In this way, the circulation of Ecstasy lubricates an emergent transnational economy.[18] This is in contrast to Philippe Bourgois' influential study, *In Search of Respect* (1995), in which he maps the economy of crack cocaine in New York's Spanish Harlem. Drugs per se are not, however, Bourgois' primary interest. Instead, he claims that drug use is "the epiphenomenal expression of deeper, structural dilemmas" (1995, 319), most notably the racial and class divides that plague the United States. Here,

I modify Bourgois' position, asking how drugs might be understood as a productive starting point for analysis, rather than merely epiphenomenal and a symptom of other social forces.

BECOMING *LIAR*

Lidya's initial goal when she enters Ozon is to get Ecstasy. Because of the high price she rarely buys it herself, but instead attempts to find a potential client who will give her a pill. Most of the prostitutes who work in discos use Ecstasy on a regular basis, many of them nearly every day. Lidya tells me, "I like taking Ecstasy because I am not as scared to approach a potential client. If I don't take Ecstasy, I feel inferior (*minder*) and *malu* towards the clients. Ecstasy makes me feel brave."

Cindi, another *liar* prostitute who frequents Ozon, feels the same way: "If I have not taken Ecstasy I feel *malu* if I try to pick up (*merayu*) a client. I don't know what to say or how to act. It feels strange to touch a client if I am not *on*." To be successful, women must violate Islamic (or Christian) prohibitions against alcohol, drugs, and promiscuity and learn behaviors that are the opposite of those they were taught in childhood and adolescence. Rather than avoid speaking to men they do not know, they must be aggressive and talkative. They must act as though they do not know *malu*.

Most women claim that the use of Ecstasy makes the actual sexual encounter easier and more pleasurable. This is something that both clients and the *mami* recognize. For instance, Kartika first tried Ecstasy because her *mami* forced her to. The Singaporean client wanted to book a woman who was *on* so that she would be sexually excited. Though Kartika had promised herself that she would not try Ecstasy, after that first time she could not do without it. "Now if I am at the disco and I don't take it I feel confused and I can't stand the music. I just keep asking myself why I am here. It is easier to act (*main*) in a *seksi* way."

For Lidya, Cindi, and Kartika, Ecstasy has become necessary for them to perform as prostitutes through "distancing emotion" (Scheff 1977), thus creating the very possibility for transgressing religious prohibitions and commodifying their own bodies. It allows them to become the kind of woman that a client will desire—or at least to engage in that mode of interpretation—a transformative potential that, as Kartika's story suggests,

Singaporean men play into. Ecstasy allows for the production of an ephemeral subject that, for a time, clarifies a particular form of identity within an economy.

In this context women learn a whole repertoire of actions through practical mimesis: to dance in a manner that is *seksi,* or be flirtatious without appearing overly aggressive, or change attitudes depending on the client. The most successful *liar* prostitutes are not necessarily those who are considered most beautiful, but rather those who have mastered this repertoire. For instance, Cindi, who rarely had problems finding a client, argued that her success was based on her ability to make clients feel comfortable, "like we were boyfriend and girlfriend." More generally, impersonation becomes the key to distinction (Appadurai 1996, 84).

For those women who know enough about the particular effects of drugs, it is also possible to transform the relationship with the client and create certain forms of advantages. Reni explained that "if I find the client unattractive and he wants me to buy Ecstasy for him, then I always try to get a drug that will not let him get an erection. Of course, this doesn't work on the clients who have been around for a while. But if I really like the guy [starts laughing] then I get one that will give him one all night." In other words, Ecstasy has different uses within Ozon's economy, and pills have various values depending on who uses them, both in terms of consumption and distribution. There is a local science of drug use, as different pills affect the body in particular ways.[19] The primary point, however, is that Ecstasy distances emotions of *malu,* thereby facilitating economic transactions for freelance prostitutes. Unlike brothel areas, which are "closed institutions" (Cohen 1993), Lidya and other *liar* prostitutes must, to a greater degree, enter a less structured space and perform.

Ecstasy is thus a technology that is located at the very center of a transnational economy of pleasure. In an important sense, this is reminiscent of the young women I described in the previous chapter who veil in order to protect themselves from the *liar.* Though the performance of prostitution may appear as an inversion of the performance of piety, in fact they are both crystallizations of particular gendered styles.[20] While women who wear the veil aim to "develop" (*maju*) themselves through religion, or at least present an identity of themselves as such, prostitutes can sometimes experience a similar passage by entering the *liar* before exiting with economic capital.

Although there are certainly varying degrees of reflexivity involved in these acts, in all situations the primary problem is not self-identity, but rather avoiding being identified as someone who does not belong. It is important, however, to highlight the reflexive nature of this process; Batam is a place that not only produces new kinds of power relations, but also offers new forms of freedom and agency for migrants, many of whom are away from the *kampung* for the first time. As I showed in the previous chapter, in the context of *merantau, malu* is an emotion that leads women to engage with, rather than withdraw from, a new kind of world and its contradictions; it is a process that does not, however, necessarily guarantee success. For both the factory worker and the prostitute, it is the avoidance of *malu* upon returning to the *kampung* that is at the heart of the emotional economy of migration. In this context, economic success and religious insight are two different models of "development" (*kemajuan*) that can be presented upon return, as various forms of an aesthetic of display is employed by returning migrants.

LEARNING TO LABOR

As night turns to morning it becomes increasingly difficult to find a client. If Ozon is quiet, Lidya may try her luck at other discos in Nagoya, but there is no guarantee of success. Some women who have been on Batam for a decade or more remember the early 1990s as the "golden days": there were clients for everyone, and Singapore dollars were the standard of payment. "Now," one woman complained, "the Singaporeans know the value of the rupiah. They are not stupid anymore. There is increasing competition among women and you have to fight for your clients." Among prostitutes and others who depend on the presence of Singaporean, the ebb and flow of tourists is an endless source of discussion. If there is a holiday in Singapore, everyone knows and the nightclubs are packed.

If Lidya gets a booking out of Ozon she can earn anywhere from 200,000 to 500,000 rupiah (22 to 56 U.S. dollars) for a night. In comparison, the basic salary of a factory worker hovers around 500,000 rupiah per month; with overtime and housing benefits it rarely exceeds one million rupiah.[21] Lidya has been working as a prostitute for three years on Batam, and she recalls how she learned to negotiate.

Before I would just sit and wait until someone came up to me. He would ask, "Do you have a *tamu*," and I would say, "No." Then he would ask me to come and sit with him and I would. Usually he would ask if I wanted to be booked, and I would ask, "How much?" My friend taught me that I should always ask the price and then ask where we would be sleeping. He would say 150,000, and I would say, "Add a little, make it 200," and he would say, "Okay."

However, after a few years of experience she has learned to be more active and perform in relation to the client whom she approaches.

Now when I look for a client I try and figure out what kind of person he is, and how he wants me to be. Some men like it if you touch them at once while others don't. Some like you to be aggressive and others that you just sit politely. Often it is difficult to figure out.

Although Lidya is still young, only twenty years old, and is generally considered attractive, the number of clients she gets and the amount of money she earns during a month can fluctuate dramatically.[22] Sometimes she will have several a week, while during other periods she will get only a few per month—hardly enough to support her boyfriend and daughter.[23]

Many of the prostitutes I knew had already built houses in their home villages with the money they had made, all of them planning to return in some distant future. Dewi sent most of the money she made to her mother in Palembang, while she remained in a constant state of poverty. Kartika showed me her savings from two years on Batam, which amounted to nearly five thousand Singapore dollars (approximately three thousand U.S. dollars), neatly stacked in a shoebox that she kept hidden in her closet, since she does not trust banks. Others, however, had little sense of how much money they made and had great difficulty saving. Lidya, for instance, was drawn into shopping sprees as soon as she had the chance.

Women who have Singaporean or Western clients tend to be better off than those who mainly have Indonesian clients. Lidya, for instance, claims that about 90 percent of her clients are Singaporean, most of whom speak some form of Indonesian. She tries to avoid Indonesians, since she doesn't trust them to pay her, and Westerners, since she doesn't speak English. Dewi, on the other hand, prefers Westerners, whom she claims treat her better, pay her more, and are *romantis*. They also allow her to use a far from universal asset: a fair command of English. Her relationship to prostitution is, however, as I have noted, extremely ambivalent. This can be seen in her style; she refuses to dress "like a prostitute" and does not let men kiss her in public. She is passive in bars and discos and waits until she is approached. "If you look at prostitutes (*anak malam*), they usually wear high-heeled shoes, short skirts, and tight shirts that show their breasts. But I don't like wearing clothing that is too *seksi,* so usually I wear regular clothing: pants and shoes with no heels."

Dewi is far less successful in finding clients than Lidya and other women, largely because of her refusal to perform. She is primarily interested in finding a *tamu tetap,* a regular client. Indeed, most women say having a *tamu tetap* is far superior to having to look for a new *tamu* each night since, at least for a time, he guarantees a steady source of income. Along with this comes the added benefit of, as one woman put it, "knowing what you get" and, for Dewi at least, not having to deal with the *malu* of being seen in a public space associated with prostitution.

Most women who work as prostitutes have had a *tamu tetap* in one form or another. Throughout the two years that I have known her, Lidya has had several, on occasion two at once. This usually entails meeting regularly whenever the client comes to Batam from Singapore, sometimes once a month and at other times up to twice a week. Another way of organizing the relationship is by becoming a *piaraan,* or mistress. This usually means living in a room or house that the client rents and receiving a monthly allowance. Many of my informants had at least for a time lived in such a relationship, usually with a Singaporean, claiming that the domesticity of the situation often displaced experiences of sin, retaining a feeling of propriety, thus keeping *malu* in balance. In fact, in an Islamic society that allows for male polygamy, this allows many women to consider themselves "second wives."

Kartika, on the other hand, has a *mami* who acts as an initial mediator. The structure of the situation means that neither performance nor having a regular client is as important as they are for Lidya. However, she also has less control over the economic transaction and the choice of clients than does Lidya. Kartika told me that she broke down crying several times when she was booked to a client she found unattractive or threatening. Similar forms of control by the *mami* are obvious in everyday life, since women living in her house are not allowed to go out by themselves for fear that they will visit their own clients.

In his discussion of social relations in complex societies, Eric Wolf (2001) makes ideal-type distinctions between emotional friendship, instrumental friendship, and patron-client relations. In instrumental friendships, access to resources is vital to the relationship, and each member may be linked to other people outside of the relationship, unlike emotional friendship, which is dyadic in nature. However, in the context of instrumental friendship, a "minimal element of affect" (2001, 177) remains crucial to the relationship, and if "it is not present, it must be feigned" (177). Patron-client relationships, on the other hand, are examples of "lopsided friendship" (Pitt-Rivers, in Wolf 2001, 179), where the relations of power are clear.

Open-ended prostitution works along a similar continuum; it tends to begin in the context of instrumental friendship.[24] Again, both parties ideally deny the economic nature of the transaction and primarily identify it in terms of mutual sexual attraction, in a sense parading as emotional friendship. As will become clear in the next chapter, this appears to break down most frequently with the emergence of a domestic sphere in relationships in which the *tamu* rents a house or room and pays the woman an allowance. If the initial encounter is transformed into a more sustained relationship, tensions often arise when the "lopsidedness" of the relationship cannot be displaced, or when it becomes clear that the man and the woman have different expectations from the relationship.

TURNING GENDER ON ITS HEAD

While they would all deny it, Umar, Efran, Fikri, and Tirta, who live on the same floor, could readily be described as *bronces,* men who live on the income of women. The stereotypical image of the *bronces* is an attractive young man whose girlfriend is a prostitute. While the woman searches for customers by night, the lazy and irresponsible man uses her as a source of money and sex without meeting any kind of obligation to her. In many other parts of Indonesia, the *preman,* more akin to a thug, would be a more common figure (Ryter 1998). On Batam, however, these men are transformed into sexual predators, reflecting the cultural anxieties that I elaborated upon earlier.

For these men connections are made to women, who in turn make connections to a *bapak* (man or father), be he Indonesian or Singaporean. While Efran would agree that Lidya makes all of their money, he does not consider himself irresponsible, since he claims there is nothing else they can do to survive. "Of course," he says, "I feel heartbroken (*sakit hati*) and *malu* when

I know that Lidya is going out to sleep with men while I sit here. But what else can I do? I am sick of looking for work, and no one will hire me. We have to think of our daughter, and someone has to take care of her." Efran first came to Batam when his older sister enticed him with stories of high salaries on an island of twenty-four-hour activity and constant entertainment. This form of communication creates anticipation, desire, and hope. Without a high school diploma, however, it proved difficult to find work, and he was turned away at Batamindo and other factory estates since he lacked the proper connections. After four months he gave up and decided to return home, where he knew he could find work. However, upon arrival he learned the meaning of *malu* when his older brother, who had never been in the *rantau,* teased him about coming back so quickly with nothing to show for his time away. After only a week in the *kampung* Efran decided to return to Batam.

This situation exemplifies the feelings of entrapment that *merantau* generates: the *malu* that keeps Efran from returning to his home in West Sumatra is stronger than the *malu* that he feels with regard to Lidya working as a prostitute. *Malu* and the thoughts of home become the force that drives the *rantau.* Despite this, Efran has hopes for the future: "Once we are married it won't be possible for Lidya to do this kind of work. I will definitely be the one who works. Once we have enough money (*modal*), maybe we will return to Padang, get married, and never come back here again." Efran reveals his desire to make things right again so that he, the man, will be the breadwinner, while Lidya is at home with the children. Once they are married, once they become a "family"—thereby part of the Indonesian nation and ready to engage directly with Islam—Lidya cannot continue to be a prostitute. But more important, there is the recognition that they are not a "family," that they are still *liar,* since the money that supports them is from prostitution and the man has not yet become a *bapak.*

In the matrilineal West Sumatran Minangkabau heartland, men are guests in the homes of their wives. Historically, the *rantau* thus became a space where the father gained more power than he could in the matrilineal heartland (Mrázek 1994, 10–11). For Efran this possibility has been closed, and a strange reversal has taken place. He is *malu* here and *malu* there. There is no space for him, except the hallway where he sits and smokes. This is the plight of the Indonesian migrant underclass.

Lidya claims that she wants the same things in life as Efran, but she is more pessimistic. "I don't know what to do about my situation. I feel all this *stres* but I don't know what to do about it. I don't want to work like this any longer, but how are we going to get enough money so that we can move to Efran's *kampung?* I really want a house, kitchen, and a garden where our daughter can play." Lidya's desires are reminiscent of the representations of an ideal middle-class life so evident in Indonesian popular culture (Sears 1996; Brenner 1999; C. Jones 2004). The house she imagines is not drawn from the reality of the village where she grew up. It is an image that might be found in women's magazines such as *Femina* or in descriptions of middle-class life on Indonesian television, the same image that is consumed by factory workers like Wati in the previous chapter. Lidya's own relationship with Efran is an aberration from this form. That they live so far from the ideal is clearly a source of anxiety for both of them.

In this context it is critical to ask not what the "family" fails to do, but what it actually *does* (Ferguson 1999, chap. 5). In the Zambian Copperbelt, Ferguson claims that constant reference to "the fiction of the modern family" (1999, 205) effectively obscures more basic political struggles between men and women and between generations. In Indonesia, however, the family ideal produces a gap between the underclass and middle class. Siegel has pointed out that in Indonesia the family is no longer a source of legitimacy.

> At one time law inhered in the construction of the family. When the nation declared itself to be the source of law, the family became mere custom. The traditional family is now merely customary while the Indonesian family is an effect of the nation, deriving its legitimacy and its form from outside itself. From that perspective, the household is no longer the place one goes to find someone who knows how the family should operate. That knowledge rests with the enlightened nationalists. The family is a site of potential disruption. (1998, 87)

Efran and Lidya both see their current situation—as a disrupted family—as their own fault. The hegemonic force of the Indonesian nation becomes most evident through the individualization of *malu*, as many blame themselves for not living up to the ideals associated with the middle class. In fact, however, they are not only hindered by their own *malu*, but also by the economic transactions that the state demands for identity cards and marriage certificates, and an ideology that positions women in the household and men as workers. On Batam these gender positions are turned on their heads in a context where women can make money far more easily than men.

These gendered tensions can also take more violent forms. Efran is relatively quiet compared to Lidya, who is loud and often considered obnoxious by others living on their floor; however, Fikri, Umar, and Tirta more often engage in open conflict with their girlfriends. For instance, one day when I came over to visit, Reni had a black eye; Tirta had once again hit her when she came home from Ozon *on* without any money with her. At the time Reni complained to me that Tirta "always gets mad if I come back without any money even though it sometimes is difficult to get a client."

> If he had any sense of responsibility (*bertangungjawab*), I wouldn't have to work like this, but he always says that it is difficult for men to find work on Batam. What I really want is to be a housewife and have children, but if he keeps hitting me I will leave him since I am the only one making any money.

Tirta, of course, had a slightly different story; he had become increasingly angry at Reni since she frequently came home *tripping* on Ecstasy but without any money. However, he claimed that the first time he hit her was when she had actually brought a client back. Everyone else on the floor was shocked at this, and it made Tirta furious.

> It's bad enough that she has to work as a prostitute for us to survive, but she doesn't have to make me even more *malu* by bringing this guy back. Now she also seems more interested in taking drugs than she is in making money. All I do is sit here and wait for her all night, and when she returns she is *tripping* and has no money! I wish that I had never come to Batam. I had a good job before in Medan [North Sumatra], but I just wanted too much and now I am stuck here. I would rather die than return home *malu* without any money.

Both Fikri and Efran accept that their partners are selling sex. But Efran makes it clear that he sees a difference between looking for "clients" (*tamu*) and "guys" (*cowok*), the latter carrying the connotation of a boyfriend or romantic relationship in which pleasure is more important than the economic transaction. This distinction may be one that makes life bearable: the commodification of the body, and the spaces where this is allowed, are distinguished from personal relationships and the space of home.[25]

Occasionally, Lidya will bring some Ecstasy home to Efran. Whenever he takes it he feels *happy* and forgets how bored he is. "When I take Ecstasy in the house I feel good (*sehat*). All the thoughts in my head disappear, and my affection (*sayang*) toward my daughter increases. She wears me down (*pusing*) if I am not taking the drug." Fikri, across the hall, also likes to take Ecstasy; he enjoys cleaning his room whenever he is *on,* and this helps him get rid of his *stres.*

The *bronces* is a stereotype that reveals the basic contradictions in Batam's cultural economy. While the *bronces* is identified as an aberration, as an Other, the figure is located at the very center of a series of tensions and paradoxes that are played out in everyday life on Batam. Interestingly, a similar kind of female figure, the *perek* (*perempuan eksperimentel*), or "experimental girl," who had sex "just for fun," was widely discussed in the Jakarta media during the late 1980s (Murray 1991, 119–120). On Batam, however, I was frequently told that there are no *perek* since everyone is there to make money.

It is informative to compare the different forms of exchange that the *perek* and the *bronces* are engaged in since they illuminate the different contexts of Jakarta and Batam. *Perek* are typically understood as well-off girls or women who are just looking for fun, while *bronces* are poor men in search of money. While the *perek* represents the anxieties of a world where cultural values are threatened—exchanging her body for fun, thereby challenging the ideal of sexual relations within the context of marriage—the *bronces* emerges in a political economy where the transformation of gender roles is the primary anxiety, with the man using or selling his body to the female breadwinner.[26]

These representations are of men who are socioeconomically at the bottom of society and cannot live up to the official representations of masculinity that identify them as reasonable (*akal*) (cf. Peletz 1996). What is crucial to grasp is that gender representations are connected with political economy, with blame ultimately being placed on those who are most marginalized. The failures of Efran and the others in this chapter to live up to the ideal of men as breadwinners should be understood within a similar framework. None of the men that I have discussed graduated from high school, and few have held steady jobs. They often grow long hair and make tattoos that they understand as signs of resistance to societal norms. However, for most other observers these signs merely suggest that they are *bronces,* and thus their resistance reinforces their marginalization (cf. Willis 1977).

CONCLUSION: SPHERES OF TRANSACTION

All forms of economic systems, Bloch and Parry have argued, "make—indeed *have* to make—some ideological space within which individual acquisition is a legitimate and even laudable goal; but . . . such activities are consigned to a separate sphere which is ideologically articulated with, and subordinated to, a sphere of activity concerned with the cycle of long-term reproduction" (Bloch and Parry 1989, 26; italics in original). In other words, reproducing the long-term order depends on individual short-term endeavors; more important for our purposes, the short-term order is often morally undetermined, in contrast to the explicit morality of the long-term social order. While this model can be used to understand *merantau,* more generally it is particularly obvious in the context of prostitution, in which becoming *liar* and engaging in labor that is explicitly immoral is a way of transgressing experiences of *malu* in order to reproduce a long-term moral order.

Throughout this chapter, however, I have shown that it is precisely the distinction between the short-term and long-term that is constantly threatened. Many prostitutes become *liar* not only as a more efficient means to live up to the monetary demands of *merantau,* but also as a way of negotiating other forms of moral boundaries. The drug Ecstasy is, I have argued, a critical technology in this regard.

Most of the female prostitutes I met on Batam would agree that extramarital sex is sinful, but they frequently justified their actions in terms of responsibilities toward children and family members, often in the context of an absent or divorced husband. In fact, most women I talked with claimed that they were divorced and had children and family members to whom they were sending money. To a certain degree having a child thus legitimates the practice of prostitution. For instance, when I first met Mega, a woman in her mid-twenties who mainly worked in the discos in Nagoya, she told me that she was divorced and had a child who was living with her mother on the island of Bangka. However, after I had known her for almost a year it became clear after a conversation with her sister that she neither had a child nor had ever been married. She was noticeably *malu* as she admitted that she had lied, because she now lacked any acceptable moral reason for being a prostitute.

There are also clear spatial distinctions between the short term and the long term, which corresponds to the distinction between the developed and the *liar*. For instance, Sri, who has worked as a *liar* prostitute on Batam since the early 1990s and lives in a squatter community with her two children, was extremely embarrassed when I came to visit her once when she was wearing only shorts and a T-shirt. "Don't come in! I am hardly dressed!" she shrieked. But I had seen her wearing a short mini-skirt and a revealing top many other nights; later she explained, "If you see me like that in the bar it's fine, but in my own house I feel *malu.*" A similar point can be made about the fight between Tirta and Reni described above. Reni brought home a client, efficiently disturbing the spatial distinction between the long term and the short term.

This spatial distinction is dependent on what each person identifies as "home" and, thus, the threshold where the long-term moral order begins. This effectively disturbs the distinction between *kampung* as the space of long-term moral order and *rantau* as that of the morally undecided short-term order. For Sri home was, in an important sense, defined by the place where she lived with her children. Similarly, Tirta sensed that the place where he lived with Reni should not be part of the short-term sphere. These cases make it particularly evident that people who are engaged in what the state identifies as *liar* marriages are most certainly concerned with moral order.

For many women, their greatest fear is that rumors of their work as prostitutes will spread back to the *kampung*. In the *rantau* the *kampung* potentially reappears; this is, for instance, a source of Dewi's *malu*. What haunts her is not primarily the violation of religious norms—"Whatever work I do," she tells me, "the Lord will be just"—but rather being recognized by members of her own community as abnormal, thereby destroying her family's reputation. Dewi says that for her father, "*malu* is worse then death," making explicit an emotional and moral economy that she must constantly respect. This is why she has become *liar* and refuses to localize herself as a prostitute. This is also why she sells fish cake on the street; it gives her an identity that she can present to people who do not know that she works as a prostitute.

Like most other migrants on Batam, Dewi claims that when she has saved enough money she will stop being a prostitute and return home in order to open a small shop or business. Twenty million rupiah (about twenty-two hundred U.S. dollars), she suggested, seemed like a reasonable amount. But when I last saw her in 2005 this goal appeared to be far off, and she still did not have a bank account after more than a decade on Batam. What little she can save each month she sends to her parents, who care for her children. Without this money she cannot return home, since she has to prove to her parents and to people in her village that she can succeed in the *rantau*. This *malu,* she tells me, is more powerful than the *malu* she experiences as a prostitute. This is the emotional double-bind that places Dewi and many other migrants on Batam in a perpetual state of liminality—a liminality that positions them in the underclass, outside the promises of development.

4

Fantasy Island

It is Friday night and Andi is taking his weekly forty-minute ferry ride from the World Trade Center in Singapore across the border to the Indonesian island of Batam. He has just gotten off work at one of Singapore's docks, where he loads containers that will be shipped around the world. Upon arrival and after passing through immigration and customs, Andi is surrounded by *calos* (touts), but in the crowd he quickly finds his usual taxi driver, who takes him straight to the main town of Nagoya, where Sri, his Indonesian girlfriend, is waiting for him. Andi has rented a room for Sri in a three-story *ruko* building, which is at the higher end of the scale in terms of price and quality, with solid walls and clean, white tile floors. The room is simply furnished with a king-size mattress, a small plastic table, a television set, a refrigerator, and a few posters of Sri's favorite Indonesian pop stars on the wall.

Andi used to travel to the Malaysian border town of Johor, which has provided opportunities for similar forms of excursions in the past. Increasing prices, overcrowding, and the Malaysian state's regulation of "sin," however, have made Batam and neighboring islands a new frontier for prostitution and drug use. These days Andi comes to Batam once or twice a week and stays as long as he can, whether a couple days or only a few hours. Often he just spends time in the small room he rents for Sri, watching TV and chatting with other people on the same floor, among them a Chinese Singaporean man who occasionally visits his mistress.

On this particular evening Andi showers and takes Sri out for dinner at one of the town's many food courts, packed with Singaporeans who have come to Batam for the weekend. His Manchester United soccer jersey, baggy jeans, and red Adidas shoes mark him as Singaporean. Just before midnight they take a taxi to Ozon, where they consume Ecstasy together. Andi usually has Sri buy the drug for him and they split one pill between them. He doesn't approach the dealers himself. "I like for it to be placed in my hand so that I can just put in my mouth."

On Batam Andi experiences, as he puts it, "total enjoyment," which means "doing Ecstasy, listening to good music, and having a woman," all of which would be more expensive and dangerous in Singapore. Batam, he says, "is like fantasy, Fantasy Island, while Singapore is like reality." Taking Ecstasy in particular allows him to forget about the pressures of everyday life in Singapore and to avoid thinking about the future. "Ecstasy," he tells me, "clears my head of all the stress that I feel at home."

This chapter shifts attention away from Indonesian migrants who come to Batam in search of a better life, and toward transitory Singaporean men such as Andi.[1] As Singapore has become increasingly prosperous in relation to neighboring countries, a growing number of its citizens can both afford and desire to leave the country as tourists. They do not have to look far. The Growth Triangle includes an efficient transportation infrastructure, as ferries run from Singapore's World Trade Center to Batam approximately every fifteen minutes between 7:00 a.m. and 10:00 p.m. The number of tourists, the majority of them Singaporeans staying only a day or two, has increased dramatically since 1990, making Batam the third most popular tourist destination in Indonesia.

A billboard advertisement for Southlinks Country Club. Photo by author.

Lonely Planet's widely read guidebook to Indonesia recommends to its largely Western readership that "there is no reason to pause [on Batam] longer than it takes to catch a boat out" (P. Turner 2000, 602). But Singaporeans such as Andi do not read such books. They learn from friends and acquaintances. If they do read about Batam, it is on low-tech Internet sites such as the Batam/Riau Entertainment Update,[2] where one can ask advice about how to deal with prostitutes and avoid scams (Lindquist 2008). Their movement is typically concentrated not to places of formal tourist development, but rather in the spaces and relationships that the Indonesian state identify as *liar,* or "wild," "undomesticated," "unlicensed." Andi, who is in his late twenties, has a *liar* relationship with an Indonesian woman; Suleiman and Ibrahim, two men in their mid-twenties, come to Batam nearly every week to take Ecstasy at Ozon; Pak Haji, a retired customs officer, has chosen to live in a *liar* squatter community on Batam because it reminds him of the Singapore of his youth.

The stories in this chapter are all of ethnically Malay working-class men, increasingly marginalized in Singapore but who experience a cultural, linguistic, and religious connection with Batam and other islands in the Riau Archipelago. ("You know," Pak Haji told me, "Singapore and Batam used to be the land of the Malays [Taman Melayu]. I have more right to be here than all the migrants on Batam!") Some might call them "post-tourists" (Rojek 1993, 133–134; Lash and Urry 1994, 274), these men who travel to Batam to escape, at least temporarily, from what is experienced as an overly regulated and expensive society. The transformation of Singapore has not only led to intensifying alienation, but also the means of more easily crossing the border to Batam, which offers a "Malay" environment beyond the Singapore theme parks.[3] Like the Indonesian migrants I have discussed in previous chapters, the meaning of these men's mobility can be described in terms of emotion, namely the displacement of the "stress" that Andi associates with everyday life in Singapore.

This chapter uses these men and their engagements with the *liar* as an ethnographic vantage point from where it becomes possible to offer new kinds perspectives on Singapore, Batam, and the Growth Triangle. More directly, conceptualizing the *liar* from the perspective of the Singaporean tourist highlights the multiplicity and overlapping forms of life that characterize contemporary forms of globalization (cf. Hardt and Negri 2004, 126–127). The *liar* is not to be located outside of, but rather should be conceptualized as an integral part of, the organization of development, capitalism, and modernity. As should be evident from the preceding chapters, the squatter housing, prostitution, and tourism with which I am concerned in this book can by no means be excluded from these processes. The modernist attempt to develop Batam, or any place for that matter, through processes of "state simplification" (Scott 1998) inevitably creates "disorder," the *liar* being the form that is specific to Batam.

By replacing Aihwa Ong's (1999, 2003) "flexible citizen"—the model citizen of the Growth Triangle, best represented by the middle-class Singaporean manager who works at the Batamindo Industrial Park (chap. 2)—with working-class "flexible tourists" such as Andi, I continue to problematize the standard story of Singapore as a global city and Batam as an offshore site for post-Fordist capitalism. Instead, I consider the global city from its periphery, through the stories of working-class men who experience marginalization in Singapore and who gain new forms of power and agency on Batam not through the formal processes of offshore capitalism, but through the possibilities of the *liar*.

ORGANIZING MODERNITY, CREATING DIFFERENCE

Rem Koolhaas (1998) has described Singapore as a "Petri dish" reflecting a "pure ecology of the contemporary." In this spirit, the radical transformation of Singapore's built environment during the last thirty years has been matched by a carefully engineered effort to produce a national cultural identity. In an explicit attempt to downplay the racial differences between the Chinese majority and the Indian and Malay minorities following the race riots of the 1950s and 1960s, "industrial modernity" became the metanarrative of Singaporean development during the early years of Lee Kuan Yew and the People's Action Party (PAP), eventually being replaced by a discourse of "Asian values" in the 1990s (C. J. Wee 1996, 501; 1997, 84).

In forming a discourse of "Asian values," the PAP has explicitly attempted to promote "communitarian" values identified as "Asian," in direct juxtaposition to "Western" liberalism and the social ills associated with it: unemployment, divorce, drug use, and a weak work ethic, to name a few. Singapore's three official Asian cultural traditions—Chinese, Malay, and Indian—share a set of "values" in which collective welfare takes precedence over individual rights (e.g., Chua 1997).[4] The fundamental difference between "Asia" and the "West" in this context is the primacy of the family vis-à-vis the individual in Eastern societies (C. J. Wee 1997, 80). As in Indonesia, this "family" is explicitly patriarchal and has even been referred to as a "state fatherhood" (Heng and Devan 1995). "Asian values" are not merely produced through discourse, however, but are also implemented through a series of techniques, ranging from the creation of public housing as a tool for ethnic integration (Tremewan 1994), to offering cash awards to middle-class women as incentives to have more children (Heng and Devan 1995); from the use of caning as punishment for crimes such as vandalism (Tay 1997), to stiff jail sentences for the consumption of illegal drugs (e.g., *Straits Times,* November 16, 1999).

Noting that "almost all of Singapore is less than 30 years old," Koolhaas argues that "the city represents the ideological production of the past three decades in its pure form, uncontaminated by surviving contextual remnants. It is managed by a regime that has excluded randomness: even its nature is entirely remade. It is pure intention: if there is chaos it is *authored* chaos; if it is ugly, it is *designed* ugliness; if it is absurd, it is *willed* absurdity" (1998, 1011; italics in original). The form of urban planning and public policy described by Koolhaas has been constituted in tandem with the transformation of Singapore from a chaotic but dynamic city characterized by widespread poverty into a financial hub with an extensive system of social welfare with low rates of unemployment (see chap. 1).

"Asian values" identifies a particular model citizen who will function efficiently within Singapore's "Next Lap," with its intensifying focus on higher education and skilled labor in the context of contemporary forms of global capitalism (A. Ong 1999; C. J. Wee 1996). But as unskilled migrants are brought into the country and factories are relocated throughout East and Southeast Asia, members of the Singaporean working class become—and experience themselves as—increasingly peripheral to the transformation of the economy and society (e.g., Rodan 1997, 165). Ethnic Malays, who make up 14 percent of Singapore's population, have been particularly affected in this process: doubly marginalized, culturally in relation to the dominant Chinese, and economically in relation to the forms of inequality that become prevalent in the new economy (Rahim 1998). In this process there has been an increasingly explicit politics of distinction. In a National Day Rally speech, for instance, the Singaporean prime minister claimed that the nation could be divided into elite "cosmopolitans" and working-class "heartlanders," the bus drivers and factory workers who populate the city's public housing estates (Chua 2003, 8).

More specifically, this has led many working-class Singaporean men to experience a particular crisis of masculinity—recognizable globally in this era of "millenial capitalism" (cf. Comaroff and Comaroff 2000)—as their decreasing economic power has affected their status as breadwinners within the Singaporean family. Andi, for instance, tells me that "in Singapore women won't even look at me. They can sense that I don't have a future." However, the shifts in the Singaporean economy that have led to the constitution of a discourse of Asian values and the demand for new international frontiers have also literally—some might claim ironically—created the space and incentive for the transgression of these values by the very men who feel oppressed by them in Singapore.

TRIPPING

Like Andi, whose story opened this chapter, Suleiman and Ibrahim, two Malay-Singaporean men in their mid-twenties, travel from Singapore to Batam nearly every Friday evening. Before leaving Singapore they page Agus, a taxi driver also in his mid-twenties from Padang in West Sumatra who is their chauffeur each time they come to Batam. Ibrahim claims that he has "become like a brother" to them and accompanies them everywhere they go on Batam. "When the time is right," he says, "we plan to get him a passport so that he can come over and visit us in Singapore." The border economy allows for the emergence of patron-client relationships that—in typical fashion—masquerade as kinship or friendship. Agus is waiting for them in the car that he rents by the month and regularly uses as a taxi. He takes them straight to their usual hotel in Nagoya, where they shower, drink a few beers, and smoke the marijuana that Agus has bought for them. Suleiman has his portable CD player and speakers with him, and together they sit and listen to music as they talk.

Suleiman and Ibrahim grew up together in neighboring apartment blocks in Geylang, Singapore's predominant Malay area. Both graduated from high school, but neither had adequate grades or enough money to go on to college. For the past few years Suleiman has worked in his uncle's plumbing business while Ibrahim has a temporary job at a large multinational record store in the city's main shopping area, Orchard Road. They both avidly follow the latest clothing and music fashions, familiar not only in Singapore, but also in Europe and the United States. But neither of them likes to talk about their lives in Singapore when they are on Batam. In fact, they don't even dare tell their parents that they travel to Batam because of its reputation as an "island of sin." "Enough!" says Ibrahim when I ask him to elaborate on how he feels about living in Singapore. "Now we're here, let's just enjoy."

By 11:00 p.m. they are ready for the short drive up the hill to Ozon. Agus drops them at the door, and as they wait for him to park and join them they chat with the bouncer, who knows them by name. Once inside, a waiter takes them to their seats in a booth overlooking the dance floor, and within minutes another waiter, whom they have met on previous visits, approaches and tells them what kinds of Ecstasy are available. They order beer and Ecstasy, and within fifteen minutes of consumption the drug has taken effect and they start shaking their heads back and forth to the beat of the techno music. They smoke a marijuana cigarette in order to intensify the effect of the Ecstasy. Occasionally they stop to say a few words to each other, have a drink, or go to the toilet, but most of the time they continue moving their heads to the beat until early morning, past the early morning Muslim prayer (*subuh*). Later they tell me that they don't like to hear the call to prayer when they leave the disco. In their movement on the island thus far, Ibrahim and Suleiman have been protected by middlemen from experiences that might threaten their engagement with pleasure. Fantasy remains intact.

Suleiman rarely takes Ecstasy at nightclubs in Singapore, but if he does he claims that the experience is different. Since the penalties for drug use are stiff in Singapore and because he suspects that there are police everywhere, he has to control his body so that no one can tell that he is taking Ecstasy. Suleiman claims that "if you take drugs in Singapore and get into the music everyone will turn and look at you. There are police everywhere." The specter of the state is present, affecting the bodily, phenomenological, and psychic experience of drug use. This is the familiar logic of Bentham's panopticon, where the constant possibility of being under surveillance leads to self-surveillance (Foucault 2000, 58–59).

Although it is frequently suggested that Indonesian undercover police officers (*intel*) frequent Ozon, what makes these spaces appear relatively safe is that the primary interest of Indonesian state actors is to transform power into money, rather than law enforcement per se (cf. Barker 1999b, chap. 4).[5] The frequent spectacles of police destroying confiscated drugs for the media is often viewed by the public with cynicism (1999a, 224–226).

Managers at discos on Batam report a steady flow of government officials who show up to pick up their "envelopes" (*amplop*).

The Indonesian state thus appears as the very opposite of its Singaporean counterpart.[6] On Batam, one can expect that "envelopes" will resolve problems that they cannot in Singapore precisely because the state is imagined as a homogeneous sovereign form. In Ozon, Suleiman can therefore let the drug take over his body without fearing punishment and, like Andi, "release" his stress. Indeed, one of the most common reasons Singaporeans I talked with gave for taking Ecstasy was to get rid of "stress," which Chua (1995, 236) has identified as a key metaphor in relation to anxieties about modernization in Singapore.

These forms of self-presentation suggest that taking Ecstasy on Batam, a place that is not Singapore, initially releases a burden in which geographical and subjective borderlessness emerge together. In other words, while Ecstasy for the Indonesian women I described in the previous chapter is productive by displacing feelings of *malu* (shame or embarrassment) and inferiority—making women, as Lidya put it, "brave"—for Singaporean men Ecstasy gets rid of "stress" and the fear that one is potentially under state surveillance and its associated punitive effects. For many prostitutes and their clients the production of pleasure through drug use is of primary importance, and sexual and economic transactions take place later, after they leave the club. In a broader economic context, Ecstasy is one of the primary attractions of Batam; therefore, for a large number of people it generates revenue that stricter law enforcement would destroy. Ecstasy is thus functional, albeit in a fragile sense, as a lubricant that allows for the constitution of a gendered transnational economy.

Carl Trocki (1990) has described how in nineteenth-century Singapore opium was an instrument for controlling labor through addiction. In contemporary Batam, Ecstasy has a similar function as it helps create a zone of fantasy (in Andi's term), thus becoming a technology for temporarily displacing stress and easing asymmetrical relations. Unlike opium, which is considered "primitive," and heroin, which is an isolationist drug, throughout contemporary Southeast Asia amphetamine-type stimulants such as Ecstasy are—as I noted in the previous chapter—generally associated with mobility, modernity, and an entrepreneurial spirit. More specifically, Ecstasy should be understood in relation to the self-conscious concern with pleasure associated with modern forms of consumerism (Lyttleton 2004).

THE LIMITS OF FANTASY

When Ibrahim and Suleiman first began to travel to Batam they primarily had drugs in mind. "We didn't really plan to go there to *book* women," Ibrahim told me. "Andi and I just headed over to Batam one weekend to see what it was like. We wanted to do Ecstasy because we knew that it was cheaper and safer there than in Singapore." They tried different discos before they eventually settled on Ozon. Ibrahim told me that "in the beginning I was sort of put off by the prostitution. There were all these beautiful women approaching us, but I wasn't interested. I didn't like the idea that I had to pay for sex. But then I started talking to them and one time this woman asked me if I would buy her some Ecstasy. She told me she wanted *thin lady*. So I thought, 'I might as well.'"

After taking Ecstasy with her, Ibrahaim booked the woman for the night. This was repeated as he and Suleiman continued to return to Batam nearly every weekend. "It became easier and finally I didn't even think about it," Ibrahim told me. When I asked him to specify if it was the drugs that had made it easier, he agreed. "Yeah, you forget about things when you are doing Ecstasy and then once you have paid the woman, it feels different the next time, like you already know her. Then it is easier to meet her again." In other words, a bond has been created that is not merely sustained by money.

Eventually Ibrahim and Suleiman developed more extensive relationships with two women for whom they rented a house on Batam. Within a matter of months, however, they discovered that both women were seeing other Singaporean men whenever they returned home. "One morning," Suleiman told me, "I decided to come over to Batam spontaneously, without calling first, and neither of the girls were at home. That was what first made me suspicious." Since then they claim to have made a conscious decision to stay away from Indonesian women because, as Suleiman put it, "you cannot trust them." Now they just come for the drugs.

When Andi first traveled to Batam he mainly frequented a karaoke bar near the main port, where he would choose a woman from the "fish tank" and sing a few songs before booking her out for the night. Usually they would go to a disco to take Ecstasy and then to a hotel room for the night. During the first couple of years he booked a different woman each time, but eventually he began regularly to choose Sri, a Javanese woman in her mid-twenties. After booking her out almost every week for a year he decided to settle her debt at the bar and set her up in the rented room I described at the beginning of the chapter.

Sri wants to visit him in Singapore, but Andi tries to explain to her that he has to maintain a separation between the two places—in his words, between "fantasy" and "reality." Life in Singapore, he tells her, is much more boring and difficult than she imagines. Sri says that she cares about him, but he complains that she seems to be more interested in the money. He tests her sometimes by not bringing any, and this makes her angry. Once she threw his cell phone out the window so that it shattered on the street below; another time he almost left her because he found out that she had a Javanese boyfriend on the sly, meeting him whenever Andi was gone.

He also doubts her history. She claims that before coming to Batam she had never been a prostitute, but her sexual prowess makes him believe otherwise. Nevertheless, Andi says he enjoys his role of being her *tamu* (guest or client) and that he might consider marrying her if he ever determines whether or not her feelings for him are true. Suggesting that he has accepted his own marginalization and the limits of "reality," he claims that "in Singapore I am too poor, have a dead-end job, and am already too old to change my life."

For working-class Malays, Batam is in many ways a recognizable space. Linguistically, and to a certain degree culturally, Andi, Ibrahim, and Suleiman blend in. With salaries that do not get them far in Singapore—a constant theme in our conversations—on Batam they can rent their own room or house, or stay in a hotel. On Batam these men establish relationships in which sex and respect are offered in exchange for money, though the basis for this exchange is not always recognized as such.

The forms of pleasure that drive contemporary forms of capitalism are ephemeral (Appadurai 1996, 83–84). Ultimately, however, the ephemeral does not sustain Andi. He has become concerned with creating a life based on a long-term moral order not unlike those of the Indonesian men and women I discussed in the previous chapter. In order to move beyond the short-term engagements with pleasure that Ecstasy and prostitution entail, the formation of patron-client relationships becomes critical. Suleiman and Ibrahim's relationship with Agus, the taxi driver, is one example; Andi's with Sri is another. An Indonesian manager at Ozon told me, with slight disdain, "Most Singaporean *tamu* who come here are taxi drivers or something like that. Here they can be like kings, bosses. They give my staff cell phones and have beautiful women. Over there, they are nothing."

As I noted in the previous chapter, however, these relationships tend to be framed in terms of friendship, kinship, or romance. The ideals of freedom and trust upon which modern forms of romantic relationships are based and which come to define their authenticity are thus threatened when the economic basis of the relationship becomes explicit. Much like the Indonesian migrants described in the previous chapters, and the story of Radjab in chapter 1, these Singaporean men thus struggle with the tensions between traditional and modern social forms of relationships, the latter ideally based on economic power and the former on ideals of romantic love and trust.

FANTASY PRODUCTION

Along with the opening of industrial estates such as Batamindo, in the early 1990s Singaporeans rapidly moved into the Batam real estate market, buying houses and shop units and joining golf and country clubs. Gated communities such as Lucky View and country clubs such as Batam Fantasy Resort quickly sold out as many Singaporeans took the opportunity to buy houses or join clubs that they could never have afforded at home. It soon became clear, however, that many of the developers did not deliver what they had promised, with housing estates becoming ruins before they were even inhabited. "Dream of Batam Home Turns Sour," read the headline of one article, which described how one man had invested 40,000 Singapore dollars (about 24,000 U.S. dollars) in a house that was never finished (*Straits Times,* July 18, 1994). Similarly, Waterfront City, the $600 million (in U.S. dollars) tourism project that became a $1.2 billion dollar project, met a similar fate. A Singapore newspaper described it in the following way in the early 1990s: "The new city could well be the Caribbean of the East—a heady mix of Florida-style resort living, Bali beach casual chic, Queensland Gold Coast excitement, ancient Japanese charm and Indonesian cultural heritage" (Quoted in *Singapore Business Times,* June 23–24, 1990).

Once home to Southeast Asia's largest indoor ski slope—fittingly destroyed in a fire—in its extended contemporary moment, Waterfront City, together with a series of housing estates and country clubs, stands as an expensive failure, on most days a ghost town with few visitors. It is not surprising, therefore, that the majority of the Singaporeans who enter Batam as tourists desire experiences located outside of the gated communities, country clubs, golf courses, and entertainment centers identified as sites for "tourist development" within the framework of BIDA's Master Plan. Just as Batam could not become like "Rotterdam," neither could it successfully mimic the Caribbean. Instead, for most Singaporeans, usually men, it is the undisciplined "Texas" that has beckoned. But along with the sale of sex and drugs that many Indonesians associate with Singapore, other forms of life have become possible on Batam.

MODERNITY'S DISCONTENTS

All the new housing, accommodated in high-rises, close together,
entirely devoid of the centrifugal vectors of modernism, obscuring both
sky and horizon, precludes any notion of escape. In Singapore, each
perspective is blocked by good intentions.

    Rem Koolhaas, *Small, Medium, Large, Extra-Large*

I could usually find Pak Haji sitting on his porch smoking Dunhill cigarettes. On the dirt path leading up to the community's mosque he would watch his chickens and geese wander about. Leaning back in his chair he would tell me, "In Singapore I could never do this, sit without a shirt, throw my cigarette on the ground and wait for the rain to wash it away, or let these chickens run around. Nothing there is authentic; everything is planned."

Pak Haji is a retired Malay Singaporean customs officer who made the pilgrimage to Mecca in the mid-1980s. He first came to Batam in the early 1990s with friends looking for business opportunities. At once disillusioned by the modern lifestyle in Singapore and proud of his role in its success, he felt immediately at home on Batam, which seemed, as he put it, "like Singapore was thirty years ago." Increasingly estranged from his wife and her desire to be modern and have her own career, he decided to marry again, this time to a Javanese woman whom he met on Batam and who would take care of the household and fulfill his wishes for a more "traditional" wife. In Singapore, he says, women have too many rights vis-à-vis their husbands.

Unhappy in Singaporean public housing and not interested in gated communities, Pak Haji has built an inconspicuous house in a squatter settlement for one thousand Singapore dollars, a freshwater well his only luxury ("in Singapore I could never even build a toilet for that kind of money").

Unlike his neighbors, it was not economic constraints that led Pak Haji to choose the settlement, but rather a sense of nostalgia for the *kampung* life he remembered from his childhood in Singapore. "I am trying to regain something I have lost. When I was young I loved my *kampung,* but within a matter of years it was lost, wiped out by Singapore development. Now it's just flats. You can't even see the stars because of the lights."

Many older Singaporeans have a sense of ambivalence about the success of development, as social life and the physical environment have been radically transformed. The main object of this discontent has been the expansion of public housing, which is organized in a ring of urban satellite "new towns" characterized by high-rise apartment buildings. By the 1990s more than 80 percent of the population lived in public housing (Perry, Kong, and Yeoh 1997, 10).[7] In this context the *kampung* has become one of the key public tropes that offers a critique of contemporary Singapore (Chua 1995, 236). The eradication of the last *kampung* in 1993 was widely publicized and provided a forum for commentary on the loss of community in Singapore (Seet 1995). In 1980 one observer wrote, "Nearly gone are . . . the familiar *atap* and timber houses nestled among the lush vegetation of the rural districts. Instead [one] would be confronted by a horizon crowded with glistening high-rise blocks where the populace, their swelling precluding the horizontal spread once so much a part of their way of life, live in flats stacked layer upon layer" (quoted in Sequerah 1995, 186).

In his discussion of the nostalgia surrounding *kampung* life in Singapore, Chua claims that "the central defining quality of this 'memorialized' *kampung* is one of a 'relaxed' pace of life, communitarian cooperation and happy days in spite of material privation" (1995, 226). The nostalgia in relation to this transformation of everyday life is one of the great themes of modernity—new flats represent anonymity while the *kampung* suggests intimacy and community. The quote from Sequerah (1995) above gives the "glistening" flats an almost industrial quality that is easily juxtaposed with the "lush vegetation" of the *kampung.* This form of juxtaposition is made equally evident as Pak Haji reflects on his own life: "On Batam my head is not filled with unnecessary thoughts and I don't need a lot of money like I do in Singapore. Here I know all my neighbors and everyone living in the *kampung,* while in Singapore people close their doors and sit and watch television. In Singapore all I do is sit in my flat and feel bored."

Since Pak Haji is the only *haji* in the *kampung,* he has also become the *imam,* the religious leader of the community, thereby gaining a sense of respect that he does not have in Singapore. He complains that "Singapore has lost its religious feel, it is too modern. Here I can still wake to hear the call to prayer from the mosque." Along with donating substantial amounts of money to build the local mosque, on Hari Raya, the day of celebration after the fasting month, he is always one of the main contributors when the community leaders pool money to buy goats to sacrifice in front of the mosque; the goats are then distributed throughout the community. In Singapore these forms of public sacrifice are illegal, leading many Muslim Singaporeans to cross the border on religious holidays.

Although Pak Haji is married to his Indonesian wife, the religious ceremony was not conducted under the auspices of the Indonesian or the Singaporean state. With more than a hint of pride, he comments that he is located somewhere "in between" those two governments. If he married in Singapore he would be charged with bigamy, and if he decided to marry within the framework of the Indonesian state (where bigamy is legal for Muslims) he would encounter other problems, primarily in the form of bribes. Since he comes to Batam each time on a tourist visa, he remains in a liminal state that he finds empowering.

But the Indonesian authorities know that he lives there and occasionally he has been called to the police station to pay bribes. According to his own story, one officer told him, "I don't want to touch you because you are a powerful Singaporean. If I touch you I will lose my job. But this woman [pointing to Pak Haji's wife, who had come along] is an Indonesian under my jurisdiction and could be fined for harboring a foreigner." Smiling, he told me that the officer had wanted 5 million rupiah, but he bartered the bribe down to 1.5 million. Once again, envelopes solve problems.

Although Batam is considered dangerous for Singaporeans, Pak Haji claims that he is not afraid. "If I go anywhere I always dress in well-worn clothing and put my money in my sock so that no one will suspect that I am a Singaporean." Despite the fact that his house has been burglarized he still feels safe in the *kampung*, since everyone knows him. But after I had gotten to know him he began to complain about the perceived jealousy in the area. "Some people feel that I am arrogant and others that I should not be an *imam* since I am a foreign citizen." Still others attempt to deny him access to the informal village council. In response, he has waited for people to come to him for financial support rather than offering it himself. This is the way of the patron. More generally, as I noted in the previous chapter, this suggests that the *liar* is not only a site of community formation, but also *potentially* of moral regulation and indirect forms of state rule that exclude and destroy that which is foreign (cf. Siegel 2006).

For Pak Haji, one of the many Singaporeans who lived in the *kampung* as a child, a whole series of spaces and experiences have been lost in the process of development. On Batam the *kampung* is—almost miraculously, it seems—rediscovered. Recalling Koolhaas' quote at the beginning of this section, a "notion of escape," or to use Deleuze and Guattari's (1987) term, a "line of escape," apparently become possible through the Growth Triangle. Thus Pak Haji can lead a *kampung* life, but still return to Singapore to pick up his retirement check, all while enjoying the high status of an *imam.* All he has lost is the material privation of his childhood *kampung,* something he certainly can live without. The fact that the village is *liar* converges with Pak Haji's own interests; it is this type of area that he desires, precisely as the state defines it, and not the gated communities that mimic Singapore. In Singapore everything is "too planned," and it is the seemingly organic nature of change and growth in the *kampung* that appeals to him. For Pak Haji, Batam's *liar* social landscape appears *unauthored,* thereby re-inscribing *authority* in his own life.

These days, he goes back to Singapore only once a month to retrieve his pension check and supplies unavailable on Batam, as well as to visit his children. In the future he is planning to move to his wife's village on Java, which he prefers to Batam. But for the time being Batam will do; it is very practical being so close to Singapore. Though presenting himself initially as exceedingly self-confident, he showed signs of ambivalence about his lifestyle after I came to know him. "Am I crazy," he asked, "to live in this simple world, while Singapore is just half an hour away?"

THE PLEASURE OF INEQUALITY

In her discussion of the South China border with Hong Kong, Aihwa Ong (1999, 154) notes, in relation to many Hong Kong working-class men who have Chinese mistresses or second families across the border, that "it is one of the many ironies of late capitalism that premodern family forms and female exploitation, which the communist state had largely erased in the cities are being resurrected" (see also Hobson and Heung 1998). In the relationship between Singapore and Batam, and in many other border areas that have "opened up" as capitalist frontiers, there are similar processes at work. Yet the skepticism that is inherent in the irony that Ong expresses with regard to renewed forms of exploitation demands ethnographic specificity.

In her work on male heterosexual clients and commercial sexual exchange in the United States, Bernstein notes that the transformation of erotic life is increasingly facilitated by the marketplace. She argues that "what is unique to contemporary client narratives is the explicitly stated *preference* . . . for bounded intimated engagement over other forms" (2001, 399), "a fantasy safely contained by the bestowal of payment" (402). As she puts it, "Clients are indeed seeking a real and reciprocal erotic connection, but a precisely limited one. For these men, what is (at least ideally) being purchased is a sexual connection that is premised upon *bounded authenticity*" (402; italics in original).

As in the United States, commercial sexual exchange in and around Singapore has been restructured through a changing political economy. But while Bernstein equates "real" with "reciprocal" and connects this to "authenticity," in large parts of Southeast Asia this assumption does not hold, as it is based on an understanding of the person as an autonomous (market) actor rather than one positioned in a social hierarchy (e.g., Errington 1989). In the relationships between Indonesian women and Singaporean men I have described, the ideal patriarchal relationship is one in which "servitude" rather than "reciprocity" is desired, thus blurring the boundaries of prostitution. These types of relationships are frequently legitimized in the name of Islam, most notably in the case of Pak Haji, but have arguably also efficiently been reworked through the discourses and policies of both the Indonesian and Singaporean state (Heng and Devan 1995; Sears 1996). In Indonesia performing gendered servitude is recognizable in many different social contexts, through religious practice or more general patron-client relations.[8] On Batam this becomes evident in a transnational context and facilitates relationships between Singaporean men and Indonesian women. Working-class Singaporean men are thus able to become patrons and potentially patriarchs, and as a result regain their masculinity. The "state fatherhood" that is beyond their reach in Singapore is thereby reproduced in a space located outside of the nation-state.

In other words, and as I suggested in the previous chapter, "pleasure" and "inequality" are not mutually exclusive, but quite the opposite, mutually constitutive, something that is particularly evident in Andi's experiences. Although a particular kind of inequality is displaced through Ecstasy use—namely the economic transaction as the primary reason for the relationship—other forms of inequality are reconstituted through the reproduction of a patriarchal domestic sphere. The emergence of the Growth Triangle has therefore led to the possibility of reproducing the ideals of the Singaporean nation in a decidedly illicit and transnational form. Most directly, this highlights the force of the postcolonial state as the model of the nuclear family—fetishized in both the Indonesian and Singaporean nation-building projects—becomes a specter that haunts these men. That Ibrahim and Suleiman have stopped meeting women on Batam because they do not trust them merely reinforces this point.

Pak Haji remains married to his wife in Singapore but lives with his second wife on Batam. This marriage is recognized by neither the Singaporean nor Indonesian state, but he does not consider his marriage to be *liar,* or even primarily based on economic inequality. Instead he claims his right to have two wives within a religious moral discourse. When Ibrahim and Suleiman saw clearly that their relationships with Indonesian women were based on economic transactions, they interpreted it as a lack of trust, perhaps taking fantasy too literally, or more specifically mistaking patron-client relationships for "pure relationships" (Giddens 1991, 185–187). Andi appears more perceptive and recognizes his role as a *tamu,* the double meaning of which suggests domesticity and inequality. He plays with his position, attempting to find some proof of emotional friendship (E. Wolf 2001, 177–179; see also chap. 3) beyond monetary exchange. However, his relationship with Sri is based on the fact that he can come to Batam and she cannot come to Singapore, the central irony of this transnational economic zone. In other words, the freedom that he gains by coming to Batam depends on retaining the separation of "fantasy" and "reality," a separation that is embedded in the regulation of movement between Batam and Singapore but that constantly is threatened.

CONCLUSION: RESPONDING TO THE "BORDERLESS WORLD"

Necessarily ambiguous and oppositional in relation to "Western" individualism, Asian values and many related techniques function both as a way to discipline or manage the Singaporean population in the face of globalization and as a way to position it as a part of the Asian economy, especially in juxtaposition to Western capitalism. Aihwa Ong (1999, 201) has used the phrase "The Caring Society" to describe the form of governance that characterizes contemporary Singapore, thereby claiming particular pastoral forms of power whereby care rather than repression characterizes political relationships. She writes that "the cultural idiom of Asian values is invoked for its familiar 'traditional' appeal to articulate discourses and categories that regulate society while culturally authenticating policies that produce the social conditions desired by global business" (1999, 202). C. J. Wee (1996, 508) further points out that there is a constant attempt to position Singapore as "Asian" in order to locate it at the geographical center. In economic terms Batam is clearly part of the "Asia" that is imagined, with Singapore as the regional hub. However, in relation to the "discipline and efficiency" that Wee and Ong argue the Singaporean government wishes to instill in its citizens, the border of the state presents itself as the limit for this form of power and, in extension, as a potential problem in disciplining these citizens.

Since the early 1990s reports of Singaporean men "secretly taking second wives" on Batam have become common in the popular press. One article reports an Indonesian woman saying that she would marry an older Singaporean man so that she could live a "life of luxury" (*Straits Times,* July 7, 1991). In one of many articles published about Batam during the last decade in the Singaporean women's magazine *Her World*—similar in style to *Cosmopolitan*—a feature article titled "How Much for This Girl?" warns that on Batam there are "virgins on sale" (August 2004). Another high-profile article in the *Straits Times* (January 3, 1999) discusses the recent increase in the number of Singaporeans, particularly men, marrying foreigners. This is conceptualized as a negative effect of globalization and the growing ease with which Singaporeans can leave the country. The changing economy is presented not only as an opportunity, but also as a threat to the Singaporean family. But there have been responses.

At the end of 1999 a conspicuous story on the front page of Singapore's major daily newspaper recounted how two young Singaporeans who had been studying in Australia were tested for drug use at Changi Airport (*Straits Times,* November 16, 1999). Their urine samples showed traces of marijuana use during the previous month, and both were sentenced to two years in prison. In July 1998 the Misuse of Drugs Act was amended to allow the Central Narcotics Bureau (CNB) to charge Singaporeans and permanent residents who test positive for drug use upon returning to the country. Previously, those who tested positive only could be referred to a clinic, but after the law was passed the maximum penalty was changed to ten years in prison and a fine of twenty-thousand Singapore dollars. By November of the same year sixty people had been charged and twenty cases were pending. As the assistant director of the CNB put it at the time, "Those people who thought that they could get away with abusing drugs overseas have to think again" (*Straits Times,* November 8, 1998).

Since the mid-1990s the specter of HIV/AIDS has become a source of anxiety for the Singaporean government. Increasingly, public interventions such as advertising campaigns have been initiated,[9] and, in a more sensationalist style, men who test HIV positive after giving blood have been imprisoned, with their names and photographs published in the newspaper.[10] Official figures show that the main source of HIV infection is traveling men, infected outside of Singapore. In response, a law was passed making HIV tests compulsory for all foreigners workers[11]—significantly, on the same day as stiffer penalties for illegally smuggling migrants into the country.

The Singaporean government has thus extended its legal jurisdiction beyond national borders. It would appear that the increasing ease with which Singaporean citizens can leave the country is matched by an increasing unease on the government's part concerning people's activities abroad.[12] Through the media, the new drug laws have affected Suleiman and Ibrahim, who were worried that they would be stopped at the border. In fact, six months after I first met them they stopped coming. I could only suspect that fear was the primary reason.

Andi, Ibrahim, Suleiman, and Pak Haji's stories could be told from the perspective of marginalization. The *liar* and "not-yet-developed" spaces and relationships on Batam—as the Indonesian state defines them—appear to create an escape from Asian values, exposing them as contested and contradictory. A different reading of these stories and the Singaporean version of Asian values suggests that Batam is a place where the ideals of patriarchy and male dominance are played out more efficiently than in Singapore.[13] More generally, these men's engagements with the *liar* are not disordered, but often deeply concerned with reproducing a moral order. It is significant that for Andi, in particular, this morality has a national form that is played out in a transnational context, suggesting both the force and limits of the postcolonial nation-state. This is an ideal of the nation that exceeds the geographical boundaries of the state. From this perspective, the premodern family form that Ong sees in the Chinese borderlands in fact appears to be located at the very center of the struggle to be modern.

Whatever perspective one prefers, it is clear that Batam has become a transnational alternative to Singapore, which is now "too modern" and "too organized." Through this process, new forms of "comparative advantages" emerge, which neither Singapore nor BIDA have planned for, where *liar* spaces are re-imagined by Singaporean men as free of state control or as located in an idealized historical past. The failure of Batam to become "like Singapore" has allowed Pak Haji to become part of an environment and community that is "just like Singapore thirty years ago," thereby creating a space where he can deal with his own disenchantment with particular forms of modernity and development, but within a safe distance of Singapore. Not only is it like the *kampung* of his youth, but his wife on Batam does not embody the negative characteristics of modernity that his wife in Singapore does. In this context, the temporality the BIDA associates with the *liar,* the "not yet" (*belum*), is reframed in terms of nostalgia.

Marginal places are often constituted as the social Other in relation to dominant cultural discourses (Shields 1991). These places are, however, by no means static; instead, they have their own histories of transformation. In relation to Singaporean public culture, Batam has not only become part of an abstract industrial hinterland, but also has emerged as an "island of sin," a site of transgression for men in search of pleasure. As Hetherington (1997) reminds us, however, these transgressions are not "orderless," but must be understood in relation to processes of alternative ordering. In this particular case, this ordering is characterized by the convergence of the desires and newfound economic power of Singaporean men and the economies that have emerged in the "regulatory fractures" (Sassen 2000, 220) or "interstitial structures" (E. Wolf 2001, 167–168) of the Growth Triangle.

5

Revolving Doors of Dispossession

Lina grew up in a village in South Sumatra, a few hours' drive from the city of Palembang. The daughter of impoverished farmers, she received only a few years of schooling and, at the age of fifteen, following her parents' prompting, was married to a man twice her age. Lina moved with him to Palembang, but the marriage ended a couple of years later. Unwilling to return home with nothing and still angry with her parents, she found a job cleaning in a hotel and a year later married a man of her own choosing. They had two children before the marriage ended in divorce in 1996. Lina complained that he never worked and was often gone all night, drinking, gambling, and seeing other women. Lacking skills, she was anxious about finding a job that would help support her children and herself.

Through a friend she was introduced to a man looking for women to work as maids in Malaysia. "Think of your children," he told her. "In Malaysia you can make much more than you ever could here. Don't worry about paying for the trip. That will be taken care of." Lina could tell that he was a *preman* (thug) and that he was most likely untrustworthy. However, knowing that she had little or no chance of finding a job that would support her, much less her children, she quickly agreed, left her children with her mother-in-law, and promised to send money as soon as she received her first salary. The man brought her to an agent in the Sumatran city of Pekanbaru, where she was placed in a house with other women who were being sent to Malaysia. After one month Lina left for Peninsular Malaysia on a ferry from the Sumatran port of Dumai with her agent and twelve other women. During the first three months, she was told, her whole salary would be deducted in order to pay off her trip, her passport, and the fees of the first middleman who had brought her to the agent. Throughout the journey her passport remained in the hands of the middleman.

Upon arrival in the city of Malacca, Lina was placed with an ethnic Chinese family with six children. For two years she worked every day from 5:00 a.m. until 10:00 p.m. without getting a single day off. She was allowed beyond the grounds of the house only every other Sunday, when she would join the family on a trip to the market. During these two years she never received a salary. Instead Lina's employer promised her a lump sum when she returned to Indonesia at the end of her contract; that way, he told her, she would not waste it. While Lina claimed that her boss treated her well, his wife would often call her "pig" (*babi*) and give her pork to eat, knowing that she was a Muslim. Isolated, she had nowhere to turn.

One day in June 1998, when Lina was taking out the trash, she saw a police officer outside on the street whom she recognized as an acquaintance of her boss. He asked her to come along to the nearby police station, where she was told that they had to get in touch with the agent who had brought her to Malaysia and that she would be sent back to Indonesia. When she complained that she had not received a salary for the past two years, the officer told her that she had to wait to talk with the agent. She was put in jail for a few days before being taken to one of the detention camps where thousands of Indonesians were waiting to be deported. Lina had been caught in the Malaysian government's Operation Go Away, and although she had entered the country with a passport, it was still with her agent, and she never saw it again.[1] In order to make more money, Lina's agent had probably never processed a work permit for her, and she was therefore in the country on a tourist visa working illegally. In spite of his negligence, it was Lina who suffered the consequences. However, what outraged her most was the suspicion that her boss had set her up in order to avoid having to pay the money that he owed her.

Lina spent two weeks in the detention camp before she was deported to Dumai, the same port from where she had left Indonesia. Upon hearing her story, one of her co-passengers took pity on her and brought her along to Batam, where he said it would be easy to find work. Without any money and with nothing to show from her two years in Malaysia, Lina was *malu* to return home and decided to go along with him. As she put it, "People will ask, 'You have been gone for years. Where have you been? Where did you work? What do you have to show for it?'"

The man brought Lina to Nagoya, where he left her on her own in a dingy hotel area, a center for both prostitution and Indonesians moving in and out of Singapore and Malaysia. Within a few days the money Lina had been given was gone and she was already in debt for her hotel room. "I was already out of money and I saw that selling myself (*jual diri*) was the only way to survive. So, there was this guy who liked me and I went with him and he paid me."

I first met Lina in June 1998 along the strip of hotels and *warungs* (food stalls) where she was staying. I found that it was a place where it was easy to meet people moving across the border. When I last saw her in August 1999 she was still in the same place, trying to make money as a *liar* prostitute, still talking of returning home. Waiting in the lobby of her hotel room for clients by day or searching for them in the discos around town by night, she was making enough to survive. A year later, when I returned again, I learned she had gone back to Malaysia with her boyfriend and a passport in hand.

MOVING BEYOND THE "BORDERLESS WORLD"

The aim of this chapter is to write an ethnography of eviction that highlights the ambiguous position of Indonesian migrant labor in the Growth Triangle. More specifically, Lina's story highlights not only a process of eviction, but also a kind of revolving door of accruing dispossession. This suggests that the position of Indonesian migrant labor in the Growth Triangle should be located at the historically contingent intersections between state regimes of deportation, a gendered transnational labor market, and the emotional economy that keeps migrants on the move.

The fact that these national borders are regulated, not closed, makes the position of Indonesian labor more complicated than might first appear. First, migrant mobility in the context of state regulation is made possible by an "immigration industry" (Wong 2005) that cuts through "legal" and "illegal" forms of labor and is constituted through various forms of middlemen and documents—most notably passports—that both facilitate and constrain mobility. Second, both Malaysia and Singapore depend heavily on "illegal" Indonesian men who work for low wages in industries such as construction and plantation agriculture (in Malaysia). Identifying migrants as "illegal" is a form of de-legitimation that allows the "host" country to deport them without acknowledging any rights or entitlements (e.g., Sassen 1998; De Genova 2002). The regular cycles of amnesties and mass deportations in Malaysia and Singapore, which have tended to coincide with periods of crisis, makes this particularly clear. Third, a large number of the "legal" workers crossing the border are women who work as maids for the rapidly expanding middle classes in Malaysia and Singapore. Through the 1990s and the first years of the 2000s the distinction between "legal" and "illegal" migrants in the context of unskilled Indonesian labor migration increasingly became a gendered one. This has not, however, necessarily offered women a more livable situation, as Lina's story illustrates. Instead, it has merely guaranteed a regular flow of maids to Malaysia and Singapore. Maids, in fact, have lower salaries and are more isolated than many of the illegal male laborers, who often live and work with others in the same situation. Fourth, as Lina's story shows, there is a form of transnational exchangeability of female labor within (and beyond) the Growth Triangle. These are the gendered dynamics of inequality that have emerged in this transnational space, which position factory and sex workers on one side of the border and maids on the other. The formal and informal outsourcing of brothels and factories to the Indonesian side of the border has been matched by the dramatic increase in maids in Malaysian and Singaporean homes in the context of an emerging "care deficit" (Ehrenreich and Hochschild 2002).

Lina's story allows us to consider these groups together, not only as a gendered system of transnational labor, but also—following from earlier chapters—as part of a common emotional economy in which the relationship between *malu* and *merantau* is critical. More generally, taking the experiences of migrants seriously, and situating them historically, illustrates how state strategies and migrant tactics form part of an interconnected system that keeps people on the move in the borderlands (cf. De Certeau 1988).

HISTORICIZING BORDER CONTROL

As I described in chapter 1, at the turn of the twentieth century Singapore straddled the geographical boundary between the Dutch and English colonial empires. In terms of economic influence, however, it transgressed these boundaries as an entrepôt for colonial trade between China and India, and as a center of capitalist expansion as the production of tin and rubber fueled the industrial revolution in Europe and the United States. While Chinese and Indian migrant labor dramatically transformed Singapore into a frontier town and its surrounding regions—including Peninsular Malaysia and Riau—into sites of capitalist extraction, migrants from the Dutch

East Indies (contemporary Indonesia) found work as smallholders and merchants or worked as coolies on the Dutch side of the border in Riau.

Stricter immigration regulations were first enforced by the British colonial government during the world depression in the early 1930s, but it was first after independence in 1957 that the politics of nation building virtually stopped Chinese and Indian migration, while the flow of migrants from Indonesia slowed considerably (Spaan, van Naerssen, and Koh 2002, 165). During Konfrontasi—the defining moment in postcolonial state formation in the region—the border between Indonesia and Singapore and Malaysia was temporarily closed (Hugo 1993, 39). The long-term effects were, however, to be enduring.

Konfrontasi affected not only mobility across the border, but also much of the trade between Batam and neighboring islands and Singapore. Fishermen and farmers who had bartered and sold their goods directly in Singapore's markets increasingly handed over their goods to middlemen, signaling new forms of control over traditional trade. Beyond the transformation of economy and space, Konfrontasi also signaled emergent forms of citizenship in the postcolonial era. As one elderly informant on Batam told me, "Before they would call us the 'island people' (*orang pulau*) in Singapore but today we have become Indonesians (*orang Indonesia*). Before I would take my own boat to Singapore; today I need a passport."

In the 1970s the Malaysian and Singaporean export economies expanded rapidly. Malaysia saw its first labor shortages in rural palm oil plantations, and within a decade the same trends were evident in urban areas as foreign workers, the majority of them Indonesian, began to fill this gap (Hugo 1993, 39; Abella 1995, 125; Pillai 1995, 225). By 1997 estimates suggested that foreign workers made up a full 20 percent of the work force (Pillai 1998, 264). Similar changes were evident in Singapore. After initial restrictions during the post-independence era, immigration controls were relaxed in 1968 as a result of labor shortages. As early as 1973 foreigners with work permits made up 13 percent of the work force; by 2000 this figure had reached almost 30 percent (Yeoh 2007).

Following patterns of need and anxiety, both Singapore and Malaysia have frequently changed their policies toward foreign workers. In Malaysia, Indonesian labor has been a political issue since the recession of the mid-1980s, but policies have lacked long-term vision, being primarily reactions to short-term labor shortages (S. Jones 2000, 9–28; Gurowitz 2000). In Singapore the government has introduced levies for hiring and an explicit hierarchy that offers incentives to skilled workers (Wong 1997, 141)[2] while strictly regulating unskilled migration in gendered terms, granting the great majority of work visas to women working as domestic servants.[3]

Particularly since the Asian economic crisis that began in 1997, new regulations to control the flow of Indonesians have emerged. Punishments against undocumented migrants and over-stayers and increasing border patrols have become pervasive and are used to regulate the flow of migrants across the border (Hui 1998, 212; Pillai 1998, 271). In Malaysia recurring deportation programs have generated massive flows of Indonesians in and out of the country (Ford 2006). In Singapore a combination of strategies has been employed: raids against illegal workers and stricter punishments for smuggling or hiring illegals (*Straits Times,* July 3, 1998); sharp (though never official) increases in the required *uang tunjuk* (money to be shown at immigration), at times up to twelve hundred U.S. dollars; and shorter visas and outright denial of entry. Videos on ferries from Batam and Bintan showed police raiding worksites in Singapore (*Straits Times,* June 5, 1998); flyers and articles handed out at the World Trade Center pictured illegal workers being arrested. In the Singapore press, articles asked if the city-state would witness a similar form of "exodus" as during the 1970s, when many Vietnamese refugees arrived (*Straits Times,* March 28, 1998).

The intensifying regulation of Indonesians across the border, as well as in Malaysia and Singapore, has led to the emergence of "illegality" as a problem, much as the *liar* has emerged as an effect of "development" on Batam.[4] But illegality is also productive as a system of regulation, a kind of "revolving door (Heyman 1998; De Genova 2002, 237), that allows the state to deport (and then re-import) migrants at historical moments that are deemed appropriate. Thus while Singaporean managers who commute to Batam daily have exchanged their passports for "smart cards,"[5] which reduce the time "wasted" in immigration, for Indonesian migrants who attempt to enter Malaysia and Singapore time is not money, but rather an opportunity that must be seized in order to cross the border (cf. De Certeau 1988, xix).

BORDER KNOWLEDGE

In the 1990s Batam became a favorite exit point for Indonesians attempting to enter Malaysia and Singapore, in part because of the island's

JANGAN CUBA MASUK
SINGAPURA
TANPA IZIN

"Do not try to enter Singapore without permission." A flyer distributed at the border to Singapore.

proximity, but also because Riau province passport holders who leave from Batam are exempt from paying the exit tax that is compulsory for all other Indonesian citizens and residents (see chap. 1).[6] This has created a lucrative economy—it is common knowledge that for an extra fee immigration officers around the archipelago will provide a Riau passport under any name. Acquiring a passport is therefore more a matter of economic exchange, which allows the bearer to be identified as a person who has the right to cross the border, than a sign of an inherent identity (cf. Das and Poole 2004, 15). In this economy middlemen (*calos*), who facilitate access to bureaucratic *oknums* (bureaucrats who exercise discretion in their line of duty to bend rules) and *orang dalam* (bureaucratic insiders), become key actors.

"The contours of citizenship," Aihwa Ong (1999, 120) has noted, "are represented by the passport—the regulatory instrument of residence, travel and belonging." It is, similarly, "perhaps, the most important symbol of the *nation-state system*" (O'Byrne 2001, 403; italics in original). The passport describes a history of cross-border movement and allows immigration officers to make qualified guesses about whether or not a person has been working "illegally." For instance, many of my informants who worked in Singapore would get a two-week tourist visa the first time they entered the country. After their time was up they would go *passing*[7] to Malaysia for a day before heading back to Singapore, where their visa was renewed on arrival. In the early 1990s they generally faced few problems, but by the mid-1990s Indonesians would see their renewed visas decline from two weeks, to ten days, to a week, and so on, until they were often denied entry.

The narrative of travel that is inscribed in the passport can, however—to a certain degree, at least—be formulated by its holder. With enough money one can acquire multiple Indonesian passports with different identities, thereby creating a kind of inverse and illicit form of "flexible citizenship" that Aihwa Ong (1999) attributes to elite dual-passport holders. Other well-known tactics aim at the immigration officer's interpretive ability. Anwar, a thirty-five-year-old Acehnese man, claims that "you have to take care of your passport so that it is clean (*bersih*). It is crucial to avoid *passing* to other countries to renew your visa." Several common techniques keep the passport "clean": leave before the visa has expired, wait several weeks before crossing the border again, or carry several different passports. Sofi, a twenty-eight-year-old woman from North Sumatra who frequently entered Singapore to work as a prostitute, was refused entry on occasion and decided to bring her passport to a *dukun* (traditional healer) on Batam.

She claimed that his prayers helped her pass through immigration the next time she crossed to Singapore.

However, the passport is only the first step in entering Malaysia or Singapore legally. It is also considered important to choose the proper immigration officer: one who is Malay, because they are ethnically the "same," or ethnic Chinese, because they are considered "honest," while an ethnic Indian is to be avoided at all costs, because they appear more foreign and therefore unpredictable. By talking with other Indonesians moving in and out of Singapore, it becomes possible to piece together which immigration officers are working at particular times and who is considered particularly easygoing. The problem of *uang tunjuk,* of having money to show immigration officers, is resolved by renting money either on Batam or on the actual ferry to Singapore or Malaysia. The money is then returned to someone who is waiting outside the immigration post on the other side. The amount rented depends on what is generally considered the going rate for getting into the country.[8]

Johny, an ethnic Chinese from the island of Bintan who had been living on Batam since he was a teenager, argued that having the formal documents was only the first step in passing through immigration. Performing in the correct manner appears crucial, since even someone carrying a passport and enough money can be refused entry. Johny always wears a jacket with a tie and carries a briefcase and speaks only English, telling the immigration officer that he is on his way to a business meeting. He admitted that it was easier for ethnic Chinese to enter, but this had not prevented him from being refused entry on a couple of occasions. The reason for those failures, he suspected, was that he had been rather sloppily dressed. But some considered the tie and jacket a bad tactic. Another informant told me that he would often see men wearing ties and jackets, although it was obvious that they did not usually wear them. "The tie says that they want to go to a meeting, but their faces want to work construction. It doesn't fit (*tidak cocok*)."

Women who enter Singapore or Malaysia to work as prostitutes often wear a *jilbab.* Many argue, however, that this tactic is now so common that it does more harm than good. Sari, for instance, who traveled to Malaysia from Batam for more than five years, revealed that an immigration officer, suspecting that her *jilbab* was a facade and that she might be a prostitute, asked her, "I see that you are covered on top, but are you open from the bottom?" But in this case the officer let her through, as he could correctly identify the stereotype, but not her intentions.

Lina has realized, however, that the *jilbab* does not actually fit any of the official identities of the Growth Triangle. Despite its modernity, it reads as "tradition" and is thus located outside the market-driven economic zone. Instead she carries a cell phone and dresses like a businesswoman. Mega, a woman we met in chapter 3, said she had once been refused entry into Singapore even though she was carrying twelve hundred dollars. She believed that because she was wearing nail polish the officer suspected she was a prostitute. When we talked about it with a few of her friends, most of them agreed.

The Indonesian who performs for immigration officers does so in order to be identified as someone who should be allowed to cross the border as an official member of the Growth Triangle: the "businessman" who travels to Singapore for a meeting or the "tourist" who carries one thousand Singapore dollars to purchase goods unavailable in Indonesia. The more ambiguous woman wearing the *jilbab* presents a stereotypical religious identity that could not possibly be involved in "illegal" activities, but is positioned outside of the market-driven economy.

The local (yet transnational) forms of knowledges and sensibilities outlined above, which, like the global economy are constantly changing, are learned from friends or acquaintances and acquired through practice. These forms of performance should be understood in relation to those that I discussed in chapters 2 and 3, the "pious female factory worker" and the "female prostitute." In these cases ambiguous identities are to be avoided at all costs, and acting as though one belongs is crucial. Through experiences and discussions a number of ideal figures of border crossing are constituted, only to run the risk of collapsing as "performance" in the eyes of the officer. As we shall see later in the chapter, the failure to perform identities correctly can end violently, usually at the hands of the state.

Here it is helpful to recall De Certeau's (1988, xix) distinction between "strategy" and "tactic." In the case of border crossings, state strategies aim to circumscribe and control space, while migrant tactics depend on opportunities—on time and trickery—as they do not have a proper place. Thus the tactics of Indonesian migrants in the Growth Triangle appear as responses to state strategies that aim to regulate the environment at its disposal. The Indonesian migrant produces himself or herself as a tactician who moves through space and boundaries that are restricted but never closed. As the Malaysian and Singaporean states increasingly regulate their territorial borders and identify the individuals inside those borders as "citizens" or "noncitizens," as "legal" or "illegal," the Indonesian migrant must either play by the "proper" rules, which as we shall see are often not available or worth waiting for, or "seize the moment."[9]

Passing through immigration becomes a kind of game. As Irwan, a man in his mid-thirties from South Sumatra, put it, "The immigration officers have knowledge about psychology (*ilmu psikologi*), so you have to be able to beat them at their game." Having a feel for the game, however, also means taking it seriously and believing that one's actions can have an effect on the world.

But while the ability to pass through immigration can be read as a sign of successful tactics, it would also be underestimating the abilities of Malaysian and Singaporean immigration officers to claim that they are incapable of reading these signs.[10] From this perspective it is important to ask if the Indonesian who is crossing the border is not in fact "seizing the moment," but rather is being "given a place" by the Singaporean state that only appears to be an effect of the Indonesian's own tactics and deception. This is recognized by some Indonesians. As Handoyo, originally from the island of Lombok and a resident of Batam for ten years, argued, "It doesn't matter what we do. The immigration officials already know that we are looking for work. All they have to do is look at the number of stamps in our passports." It did not surprise me when he revealed that he had stopped trying. More generally, by claiming that the state sees everything, Handoyo's comment dissolves the distinction between "strategy" and "tactic." The state appears to control not only space but time, and the game becomes meaningless and absurd (Bourdieu 1990, 66–67).[11]

This would, however, be taking the state's self-presentation too seriously and forgetting Abrams' (1988, 81) suggestion that "the state is at most a message of domination—an ideological artifact attributing unity, morality and independence to the disunited, amoral and dependent workings of the practice of government." Migrants who choose to enter Singapore and Malaysia consume this message where it is arguably made most explicit. It is clear, however, that they take the idea of the state quite seriously, for good reason, as we shall see in the next section.

ENTERING THE GLOBAL CITY

After successfully passing through immigration at the World Trade Center in Singapore, Anwar, like most other Indonesians looking for work, would take the bus to Little India, always going straight to the same address where a network of Acehnese kept a room. "Sometimes there would be five people, other times ten. Sometimes I knew someone, other times I didn't, but the same room was always available." Others, who did not want to spend five Singapore dollars, might stay in one of the few abandoned buildings in the area, such as the infamous *rumah hantu,* or ghost house, where one would, in order to avoid police raids, enter after dark and leave before dawn. It was also well known that residence was divided along ethnic lines; for instance, the Acehnese could be found in one part of Little India and people from the city of Palembang in South Sumatra in another. Anwar put it this way: "If you are on your own in a foreign country it is someone from home who is most likely to help you."

Finding work was easy.

Early in the morning, around 6:00 a.m., we would be on *stand-by.* After we had finished drinking our coffee the bosses, the *tow kays,* would show up and ask if we wanted to work. We would ask: What kind of job is it? How many days is it for? What is the salary? If we agreed they would tell us to get into the truck. Those people need us. It is not like in Indonesia where we have to look for a job and it is not certain that we will find one. In Singapore they come looking for us and pay us well. Of course that makes us happy.

In the late 1990s the salary for undocumented, unskilled Indonesians in Singapore was around forty Singapore dollars per day, about four times the average rate in Malaysia and eight times that on Batam. The kinds of jobs available varied widely, as did the duration. For instance, Anwar had worked in construction and as a gardener, mover, plumber, and electrician, to name but a few of his positions. Some jobs lasted for only a day, while others went on indefinitely.

I first met Anwar on Batam, in one of the squatter settlements near the Batamindo Industrial Park. Using money he had made in Singapore he bought several crates of orange soda from a store that had gone out of business, and he was now peddling these to small shops and stands around the park. This was in late 1998, and it was increasingly difficult and lucrative to get into Singapore. He had already been denied entry once and was now waiting for the restrictions to be eased again. "Most days I will go down to this one cafe and ask around. There will always be someone with news about what the deal is with Singaporean immigration. Everyone wants to go now because the exchange rate is so good and opportunities for work here are so bad." This is the temporal form of the tactic, a response to changing regulations.

Like many people on Batam, Anwar moved in and out of Singapore for several years, but, unlike most, he had managed to save a fair amount of money in a bank account. "I just want to keep going for a few more years and I will have enough money to marry my girlfriend and start a small business. I have already almost finished building a house in Aceh and it all comes from Singapore dollars." Always wary of being arrested, Anwar never overstayed his visa for fear of being imprisoned or caned. He knew that if he was caught with a valid visa he would risk only deportation.

Indonesian female prostitutes who move back and forth between Singapore, Malaysia, and Batam tend to go to one of two particular areas of Singapore; the choice depends on their linguistic skills. Those who speak only Indonesian choose Geylang in the Malay part of Singapore, the best-known red-light district in the city, where hotel rooms are rented by the hour, and which sometimes is called "Batam Mini" because of the large number of prostitutes from Batam (*Riau Pos,* July 29, 2000). Many women can be found in a few of the small alleys behind the quasi-official brothels or in a couple of the Malay discos in the area. Those who speak English can find far more lucrative work in the bars along Orchard Road, Singapore's main shopping street.

As I noted in chapter 4, Singaporean men travel to Batam to buy sex not only because of the lower prices, but also for the open-ended nature of the interaction. Both in terms of time and money, a visit to a prostitute in Singapore is a much more regulated transaction, even outside the government-regulated brothel areas. This difference also affects the experiences of Indonesian prostitutes. Siti, for instance, has been going to Singapore once every other month for four years.

> Sometimes I go to a disco and other times I am on the street. It depends on how much money I have and if there are any people in the club. On the street you always have to watch out for the Anti-Vice; we call them ghosts (*hantu*). If I am on the street my heart always beats faster. Every day there are raids and you can see the women in the street running in different directions to get away.

It is important to blend in, or disappear, when Anti-Vice approaches. Compared with the men whom I have already described, female prostitutes are more vulnerable to arrest because they work in public spaces in well-defined parts of the city. For many, even the experience of sex is different in Singapore than on Batam, much less open-ended and more focused on a rapid economic transaction. If you are doing *short-time,* Siti said, "they always pay first and it is *expres.* We are frightened, even the clients, since many of them are foreigners working illegally as well, so they quickly finish their business and leave. I always charge forty [Singapore] dollars: ten for the room, two for the condom, and the rest for me."

On Batam, Siti works in one of the island's brothel complexes and says that she feels more comfortable there despite the fact that she makes far less money than in Singapore. However, while using a condom is the norm in Singapore, she uses them much less frequently on Batam, a statement that resonates with those of other women. When I asked her why that was the case she could only answer, "That is the way they do it in Singapore." Like the Singaporean men who experience Ecstasy differently in Singapore compared with Batam, the power of the state shows itself in situations that can be understood as "private" or even "intimate." In both cases power is inculcated through self-regulation, as the state makes itself felt in the lives of both citizens and foreigners (cf. Rose 1999).

Rouse (1992, 35) has described how the practices of the Immigration and Naturalization Service (INS) in the United States influence Mexican migrants' use of space. The INS commonly targets bars and illegal activities such as gambling and cock fighting; Rouse argues that this influences many migrants to confine their movements between the workplace and home. Moreover, because migrants on the street are more noticeable, and therefore are checked more frequently, if they wear cheap clothing or drive old and damaged cars, this gives many an incentive to become "good consumers" while diverting attention from themselves as potential "illegals." The fantasy of the omnipresent Singaporean state structures the experiences of Indonesians working there illegally, influencing their movement through space while leading them to form new habits and dispositions. In the Singaporean context we can see how this affects not only the way migrants walk through the city, or the fear they experience, but also how they act in what appears to be an intimate situation outside the gaze of the state.

Once in Singapore, all that matters is work. As Irwan put it,

Everything is extremely expensive and you are always afraid. There is not a single Indonesian who enjoys working in Singapore. It is not free, you are afraid of working, afraid of being caught. If your visa is alive (*hidup*) it is all right to walk down the street because if the police check you, then you are all right. But, if your visa is dead (*mati*) or if they catch you while you are working then they have got you.

Most wary and frightened are the people who have chosen to "kill" (*matikan*) their visas, remaining in the country after they have expired, which means running the risk of being imprisoned or caned. Doing so also means having to leave the country illegally again, perhaps by hitching a ride on one of the Indonesian boats that dock at the Singapore harbors, something that has become increasingly difficult since the mid-1990s. Irwan once overstayed his visa for three months and paid a man, whom he had heard about from other Indonesians in Singapore, to give him an immigration stamp in his passport so that he could leave the country legally. In immigration, however, the officer noticed that it was a counterfeit, and he was arrested and sentenced to prison for three months.

Despite his suffering Irwan appreciates the Singaporean legal system since the *tow kays,* the bosses who hire them, are punished more harshly than the workers and their names and photographs are published in the newspaper. "In Indonesia it is the other way around. The weak are punished and those with money walk away." Even Indra claimed that justice had been done in Singapore when every cent that he was carrying was returned to him after he was caned, although it left three permanent marks on his back. The pain that Indra suffered and Irwan's prison sentence are forms of "justice" that both of them accept as long as the money they have made is returned to them. Beyond any formal language of human rights, this, if anything, hints at the importance of monetary success in the *rantau.* It is a serious game indeed.

MOVING THROUGH CRISIS

Periods of crisis put into particular relief the ambivalent position of Indonesian labor within the Growth Triangle. The effects of the Asian economic crisis hit Batam months after the riots in Jakarta and the collapse of the Suharto regime in May 1998. As Malaysia and Singapore closed their borders to Indonesians, other forms of violence emerged on Batam and neighboring islands along the border. In Malaysia, in particular, Operation Go Away attempted to cleanse the country of Indonesian workers such as Lina. Channeled to camps throughout Peninsular Malaysia, many were deported to towns such as Selatpanjang and Dumai along the coast of Sumatra in Indonesia. Lured by rumors of work or perhaps hoping for another chance to enter Malaysia, many came to Batam. Meanwhile, Singapore created stricter regulations to halt the expected flood of refugees and turned away increasing numbers of Indonesians as they attempted to enter the country legally.

By mid-1998 Batam was flooded with Indonesians who had been deported from Malaysia, joining the influx of migrants from all over Indonesia who had fled economic hardship hoping to find work in Batam's booming economy. Unwilling to return to their homes in Indonesia with nothing to show for their time there, or waiting for a chance to return once things had settled down, deported Indonesians converged on Batam.

In this context, it is important to point out, as I did in chapter 1, that these effects did not represent something radically new, but merely accelerated particular processes of labor mobility and regulation that were ongoing since the 1980s and 1990s. Indeed, these mass deportations were repeated in 2002 and 2005 and have in an important sense become institutionalized. Devoid of labor rights, Indonesian migrants have in fact become the most "flexible" form of labor in the Growth Triangle.

*   *   *

Felix comes from the eastern part of the island of Flores in Eastern Indonesia, a well-known sending area for male migrants to Malaysia, where wives who remain behind are transformed into the acronym *jamal,* short for *janda Malaysia,* meaning literally "Malaysia widows." In early 1997, after spending several years working on the island of Sumbawa and in Kupang in West Timor, both in Eastern Indonesia, Felix decided to try his luck on Batam. His brother, who had returned home for the first time after many years in Malaysia, had decided to settle temporarily on Batam. He suggested that Felix join him and offered the use of his motorcycle so that he could operate an *ojek* (motorcycle taxi) at the Batamindo Industrial Park. Struggling to survive, much less saving any money, Felix found the offer too good to refuse and decided to join him. The boat they took from Flores to Tanjung

Pinang, just a half-hour from Batam, was packed; during the trip, which took a week, he quickly realized that many of his fellow passengers had Malaysia as their final destination. While some were on their own or in small groups, most were led by labor recruiters, or *tai kong,* from East Flores who had earlier worked in Malaysia.[12] By the time Felix reached Batam he had been affected by the anticipation and had already decided to travel to Malaysia. "A few people even invited me to come along right away but I decided that I wanted to see what Batam was like first."

Although he did well on Batam as a motorcycle taxi driver, Felix would hear stories about Malaysia every day in the *liar* squatter area where he lived with his brother. Most of the people in the area were from Flores, and almost all the men had been to Malaysia at one time or another. Every week someone would either be going there or coming back. However, it was primarily those who were successful who spoke. As Felix put it, "I knew that there were risks but I was so excited I didn't think about it."

Six months after he arrived Felix had saved enough money to look for a *tai kong* who would take him to Malaysia. After asking around with a friend he found a man who promised to smuggle him across once he had at least forty people, with each paying two hundred thousand rupiah,[13] which at the time was approximately two weeks' salary. For three weeks they waited in the man's house as the number of people grew, many of them also from Flores, several of them having just been thrown out but ready to return. "It seemed unreasonable to make a passport. Just getting one would have cost me more than paying the *tai kong* and even if I had one it wouldn't help me get a job in Malaysia. If I were caught in a raid there people told me it was better not to have an identity card so that the authorities wouldn't know who I was."

There is general support for Felix's opinion. One observer notes that "it is often easier and cheaper for an Indonesian illegal to be caught, detained, and deported and then come back to Malaysia illegally with the help of a *tai kong,* a smuggler, than to pay the high fees necessary to get the proper documents and avoid deportation in the first place" (S. Jones 2000, 89). Indeed, acquiring a work permit in Malaysia is a long and expensive process, and this has facilitated the increase of migrant smuggling into Malaysia from Indonesia (Pillai 1995, 230; Hugo 1995, 277). However, often no clear distinction is made between "legal" and "illegal" labor recruitment, as legal agencies and documents are often mixed with illegal ones (S. Jones 2000, 39–49). Thus many Indonesian migrants who believe that their papers are "in order" are in fact working "illegally." Lina's story offers one obvious example.

Felix took the five-hour trip to Johor with fifty other people, where they were dropped one hundred meters from land. As they waded to the beach a Malaysian middleman was waiting with a pickup truck to take them to a safe house. After two days they were taken to a coconut plantation, where they were forced to work until they had paid off the three hundred U.S. dollars they owed. After six weeks Felix had settled his debt and chose to move to another vegetable plantation. The salary was half of what he could have made working construction in the city, but he felt that it still was safer to remain in the countryside where it was easy to flee into the jungle if the police raided them. Despite this, he was always afraid. "At night when we were sleeping and someone heard a suspicious noise we got up to run and hide." For six months Felix did not leave the fields for fear of being arrested.

Most illegal migration to Malaysia is based on a system of contract labor that involves various forms of recruiters, middlemen, and contractors (e.g., Guinness 1990; Hugo 1993; S. Jones 2000). This means that the employer pays a contractor, who in turn pays the workers. The employer is thereby able to access inexpensive labor while avoiding any responsibility for the workers' welfare, and the contractor can become involved in a highly profitable industry, most often recruiting workers who have to pay them back through future salaries, while the Indonesian workers can access a network that will bring them to Malaysia (S. Jones 2000, chap. 4). This is a system of debt-bondage labor that characterizes most forms of legal and illegal transnational migration from Indonesia—ranging from plantation work to domestic service and prostitution.

By August 1997 the economic crisis had just begun to affect the Indonesian rupiah. Because his salary was paid in ringgit and therefore rapidly increasing in value compared to the Indonesian rupiah, Felix was excited to be making more than he had hoped. By this time, however, the Malaysian authorities were already beginning to crack down on foreign workers, and one night Felix was caught in a surprise raid at the plantation. "I wasn't even allowed to put on long pants, much less get the money that I had stashed in a chair. Not that it mattered because the police took the money away from those who had any."

Felix had been caught in Operation Go Away. For three weeks he was placed in a deportation camp before he was sent to the port of Dumai in

Indonesian South Sumatra. Without any money he was forced to hire a man to escort him to Batam; this man was paid three hundred thousand rupiah (about thirty-three U.S. dollars) upon arrival by his brother. With obvious anger Felix claimed that "in Dumai there are people who are like animals waiting for us. Waiting for people from Malaysia who come back with nothing so that they can make money off of them."

Felix, however, was one of the lucky ones, since he had a family member to help him when he lacked money and resources. Others, like Lina, were not so fortunate. Yahya and Amir worked on a construction site down the street from where I lived. Neither of them wanted to return to Malaysia, even when things had settled down, but they felt they could not return home with nothing. Hartanto, from Central Java, had ended up in the hotel area where Lina lived. After spending twenty years in Malaysia without a passport, and even marrying a Malaysian woman with whom he had children, he, too, was caught in Operation Go Away a few months after Felix. He was forced to wait for almost a month before a relative from Malaysia brought him enough money to buy a passport and return to what, after such a long period of time, had become "home."

It is again important to point out that these episodes were not restricted to the economic crisis but are rather associated with broader changes in the regulation of Indonesian migrants. For instance, Handoyo had been deported from Malaysia five times over a period of ten years. Nearly every time he lost all the money he had saved either because he was forced to leave it behind or hand it over to corrupt police officers.

While some "illegal" Indonesians like Hartanto became so completely integrated into society—easily adding a Malaysian dialect to their Indonesian—that they were identified as Malaysian, many others, such as Felix, remained at their workplaces and lived in constant fear of being caught. The fear was not merely limited to being deported and losing the money one had earned; there were also rumors of Malaysian police giving illegal migrants *suntik gila,* literally the "crazy shot," which made the person insane. On several occasions I saw men on Batam or other islands in the area who were obviously mentally ill. When I asked what was wrong, people would invariably reply that he had received a *suntik gila* upon being deported from Malaysia.

Importantly these fears localized Felix and others to particular spaces where they were concerned with the task at hand: working. But the same was also true of Hartanto, who avoided deportation for twenty years by becoming part of a local community. "It was only when I was in the village that I could sometimes forget that I didn't have an IC (identity card). Those few times that I traveled to the city I was always wary and careful to dress well." Once again it becomes obvious that the movement of undocumented Indonesians is structured by the fear of being arrested and deported and, more important, of losing earned money. Like Rouse's (1992, 35) discussion of Mexicans and my earlier description of Indonesians in Singapore, in Malaysia these migrants perform as model citizens of a particular form of transnational labor market.

GENDERED MOBILITY

While men dominated migration to Malaysia and Singapore during earlier periods, since the 1990s the number of transnational female migrants has been steadily increasing. Most work as documented maids and pass through various types of Indonesian labor recruitment companies that organize their passports, visas, and place of work (Rudnyckyj 2004; Silvey 2004). Agencies in Malaysia and Singapore compete by offering discounts, which eventually are taken out of the maids' own salaries—in effect, also a form of debt-bondage labor.[14] The formation of the maid industry should be understood in the context of the growth of the middle class in Malaysia and Singapore (Chin 1998; Sassen 1998). Maids thus form part of a new transnational underclass (Ehrenreich and Hochschild 2002).

While the Philippines has lobbied for maids' rights in Malaysia and Singapore, the Indonesian government has shown little interest in defending its citizens' rights abroad (Gurowitz 2000, 871). This exacerbates the vulnerable position of maids in Malaysia and Singapore, who are far removed from the public eye in their domestic workplaces (e.g., Chin 1998; Human Rights Watch 2005). Furthermore, in Singapore maids are offered limited legal protection since they are not covered by the Employment Act (Yeoh and Huang 1998, 588–589; Human Rights Watch 2005).

In both Singapore and Malaysia anxieties are obvious concerning the sexuality of female maids and their potential relationships with local citizens. In Singapore a female work-permit holder must sign a contract stating that she will not cohabit with a citizen and that any such forbidden relationship will not result in a child (Wong 1997, 161). In Malaysia women are tested three times for pregnancy and sexually transmitted diseases during a two-year contract, and a foreign maid is subject to deportation within twenty-four hours of a positive pregnancy test (Chin 1998, 110; Gurowitz 2000, 869).

In other words, work permits give the Malaysian and Singaporean governments an opportunity to enforce intimate gendered forms of bodily control that are not possible in relation to male migrants. More generally, both the distinction between "legal" and "illegal" migrants in Malaysia and Singapore and the contraction and expansion of particular labor markets in the wake of the Asian economic crisis shared common gendered dimensions.[15] I have already suggested as much through Lina's story; she worked as a maid in Malaysia before moving, with apparent ease, into the only industry expanding during the crisis that depended on female labor: prostitution.

FROM MAID TO PROSTITUTE

Putri's clothing, style, and demeanor did not really fit with many of the other women who waited for clients near the front desks or on the porches of the long row of hotels where I first met Lina. It turned out that Putri had been there for only a month. She previously had been working as a maid in Singapore, she told me, but her employers had decided to get rid of her and she was deported to Batam. I was interested in her story, but it took a month or so before I asked her to tell me what had happened. I explained that I was researching the effects that processes of globalization were having on people in the region and that I felt as though her story was one that should be told. She agreed.

Putri was born in a small village on Lombok in 1970, part of a Balinese Hindu family. Her father died when she was still a child, and since her mother couldn't afford to take care of her, she began working as a maid (*pembantu*) after just a few years of elementary school. The family for whom she worked raised her in exchange for her services, and, as she put it, "all I could do was wait for someone who would marry me." By the time she was eighteen a Balinese man was chosen as her husband, and "though I didn't like him I said nothing. I didn't dare say anything." After four years she had her first child, but by the time she was pregnant for the second time she discovered that her husband had a mistress who was also pregnant. "It broke my heart (*sakit hati*)," she said. "Never giving me any money for the household or showing any interest in me or the children was one thing, but this I could not take."

When a *tai kong* (labor recruiter) came to her village one day looking for women who wanted to work as maids in Singapore, Putri and a couple of her friends quickly decided to go together. "Rather than stay in the village and watch my husband remarry, I decided to leave and also make some money for my children." She had seen and heard people who came back from Malaysia and Singapore and built large houses, and she hoped to do the same. The *tai kong* promised her that she would also be able to make a lot of money and that passports, visas, and transportation would be covered.[16]

Along with twelve other women, Putri left for Batam, where they were "trained" to cook "Singaporean" food and use electric kitchen equipment over a six-week period. The *tai kong* who had brought them from Lombok was paid 500,000 rupiah (55 U.S. dollars) for each woman when he transferred them to the agent who ran the company. For the first four months in Singapore, they were told, they would not receive any salary in order to pay for all the preparation costs. After that they would be paid 230 Singapore dollars (135 U.S. dollars) per month.[17]

Upon arrival in Singapore it turned out that Putri would not just be cooking, as she had been told, but also cleaning, washing, and taking care of a young child and her elderly grandmother. Living in an upscale residential area in Singapore, she began work at 5:30 a.m. and was not permitted to sleep until 11:00 p.m. She slept on a mat in the living room and was strictly forbidden to use the telephone.[18]

After four months, when she was supposed to receive her first salary, Putri sent a letter to her mother telling her that she would be sending a money order. Her boss agreed to do this for her but would not let her come along to the bank, even though she tried to insist. A couple of months later, however, a letter arrived from her mother claiming that she had not received the money. When Putri confronted her boss about this he claimed that he did not know what was wrong, but he was unwilling to make any further inquiries. Distressed, she began phoning the other women in Singapore who had come from Indonesia with her and tried calling her village on Lombok. When her boss discovered her using the phone, she called the agent who was in charge of the maid company and asked to terminate her contract. One day, after seven months in Singapore, her agent arrived to pick her up. She was taken back without having been paid her salary.[19]

Putri's agent told her that she would have to "train" again on Batam before she could return to Singapore. After a month and a half of working and cleaning in different houses on Batam, Putri was paid a little more than one hundred thousand rupiah (about eleven U.S. dollars at the time), but hearing that no money had arrived in her village, she was *malu*. Her agent still could not give her a clear answer about when she would be going back to Singapore. Feeling trapped because she was working all the time, she decided to leave the agent, who had her passport and identity card, and try her chances elsewhere. "It drove me crazy to wait day after day knowing that I wasn't making any money and that my mother and children were waiting for it. Finally I couldn't take it anymore."

After receiving her first salary Putri fled from the agent with another woman from the company who had also been waiting to go to Singapore. They ended up in the hotel area where I first met her. For a few days she asked around for factory work, but with thousands of other job seekers crowding the industrial estates and her limited education, she had little hope of finding work.

It did not take long before the man working at the front desk asked if she wanted a client. Within a few days Putri had decided to sell sex. "Of course I felt *malu* at first, but it was nothing compared to the *malu* and responsibility that I felt toward my children. It didn't take long before I got used to it." It was clear that it would be difficult for Putri to make enough money to send to her children, much less return home. The economic crisis had led to a rapid increase in the number of women working as prostitutes, and competition for clients intensified. Initially, she would go to the discos around the main town of Nagoya, but she claimed that this made her *pusing* (literally "dizzy"). Like Dewi in chapter 3, she refused to "dress like a prostitute," preferring instead to wait in the hotel lobby for potential clients.

I first met Putri a few months before my main round of fieldwork ended. When I saw her six months later on a return trip she had stopped working as a prostitute and was helping out at a small food stall across the street. She was pregnant and was involved in a relationship with the child's father. Like Lina and Felix, he had been thrown out of Malaysia during Operation Go Away and was planning to return as soon as things cooled down. Putri told me with some optimism, "He is a good man and I trust him. When he goes back to Malaysia and makes some money we will get married." When I asked her if she was planning on going home to Lombok, however, she looked away and didn't answer.

CONCLUSION: CLOSED SYSTEMS

The movement of transnational Indonesian migrants in Malaysia and Singapore is formally governed by a legal distinction—increasingly gendered—between "legal" and "illegal" workers—a distinction that has become a global "generalized fact" (De Genova 2002, 419). Holston and Appadurai (1999,13) argue that these processes "render significant segments of the transnational low-income labor force illegal using the system of national boundaries to criminalize the immigrants it attracts for low-wage work." The formation of an "immigration industry" (Wong 2005), however, has made this an ambiguous distinction, one that is used or bypassed in various ways by migrants and brokers in order to facilitate cross-border mobility or by states in order to deport excess labor. This has created a more or less illicit form of flexible citizenship, quite the opposite of the elite dual passport holders that Aihwa Ong has described (1999).

Paying ethnographic attention to the transnational mobility of Indonesian migrants turns the Growth Triangle's official discourse of borderlessness on its head. Historically, in fact, the formation of the Growth Triangle has led to intensifying state attempts in the regulation of territory and citizenry, even expanding beyond its national boundaries, as in the case of Singaporeans who are tested for drug use upon return to the country (see chap. 4).

Arguably Putri and Lina represent extreme cases, but their stories help clarify certain processes at work in the Growth Triangle. One is that being a legal worker within the context of the domestic sphere does not guarantee any form of basic rights (e.g., Chin 1998). Ironically, it would seem, both of these women were more isolated and easily exploited than any of the undocumented Indonesians I described in the chapter. In the domestic sphere, the state that undocumented workers feared was nowhere to be found; this very absence allowed them to be thrown out of the country without their salaries.

One customer writing to the website for the Singaporean maid agency Noble Maids to complain about the greediness of maids indicates the historical shift that has taken place. "For the last 20 years or so when Singaporeans, Malaysians and Thais are not [*sic*] longer interested in working as domestics, my maids have come from the Philippines, Sri Lanka or Indonesia."[20] Taking a step back in history, James Warren (1986, 1993) and Carl Trocki (1990) remind us that one hundred years ago Singapore was a coolie town and a center of prostitution in Southeast Asia. Most of the women were Chinese or Japanese, a situation that many people have difficulty imagining today.

Much has changed in Indonesia as well. The days have passed when women stayed at home and the men went on *merantau* to gain experiences before returning to the village to marry. In contemporary Indonesia women travel to places like Batam or abroad to Malaysia, Saudi Arabia, and Singapore. My aim in recounting Putri's and Lina's stories is thus not to reveal "the truth" concerning the experiences of Indonesian female migrants in the Growth Triangle, nor is it to present a kind of downward-spiral type of story on the effects of the economic crisis. It is, rather, a suggestion that we bring together different worlds that are generally kept separate—most notably "domestic service" and "prostitution." This merging permits us to think about Lina and Putri not as either one type or the other, but in relation to their moral worlds (cf. Kleinman 1995, 45)—worlds that are increasingly translocal. Putri's story, in particular, describes a circuit of debt and servitude that leads from a small village in Indonesia to the Singaporean global city, and then on to Batam. This specific circuit, which comes into being through Putri's mobility, brings together practices of servitude in both Indonesia and Singapore, a changing regional economy that demands large numbers of unskilled women and the most intimate forms of experience and emotional debt.

As I have argued earlier, the links between *malu* and *merantau* are crucial in understanding what is at stake in the lives of migrants on Batam. While *malu* is a pervasive theme in narratives of Indonesians who leave Malaysia or Singapore without saving enough money, feelings of fear or isolation are often expressed by migrants who have worked there. Both fear and *malu* keep migrants on the move. The emotional economy of *merantau* demands economic success. But referring to economic success is not enough. It retains a model of analysis that is too general. Putri and others carry burdens and scars, and it is not clear if any form of success would lessen that pain. Soon she will have a new family and may well become, as Mrázek (1994, 11) has phrased it, "destitute in *rantau*."

What is most striking when we turn to stories such as the ones that Lina and Putri tell is that there is a powerful and contradictory form of emotional economy at work. The tension between the demands of migration, sending money back to their children, and the *malu* they experience when they cannot do this is one that forces them to make choices in the context of intense constraints. Putri and Lina are—needless to say—far from being "women without morals"; rather, they are intensely engaged in a moral economy in which economic success is an imperative. It is precisely this engagement, and the affect associated with it, that is missing from many accounts of globalization.

6

Between Stress Beach and Fantasy Island

Along the Batam coastline that faces the Singapore skyline is an area inhabited by *liar* bars and housing, which is surrounded by empty lots and half-finished buildings. It is an area that is—as the Batam Industrial Development Authority would phrase it—"not yet developed." Migrants call this Pantai Stres, or Stress Beach. From the shacks that serve as make-shift bars the skyline of Singapore appears to be just within reach; on a clear day one can identify specific buildings without great difficulty. As Saskia Sassen (1996, 23) has put it, the post-industrial city is the "urban form that dominates our image of today's advanced urban economy." Even for migrants who had never dreamed of crossing into Malaysia or Singapore before coming to Batam, the view of the city—which makes explicit the boundary between the "developing" and the "developed" worlds—and the stories that are constantly circulating about life there lead most to imagine what life on the other side might be like, particularly when they discover that the opportunities on Batam are not what they had hoped for.

In 2003, during a visit to Batam, I noticed an odd structure being built at the far end of the beach, near the commercial settlement of Jodoh. It had the size and shape of a cruise ship, yet was a concrete building that stood twelve stories tall, with its "bow" pointing straight at Singapore. Curious, I asked around and was informed that it was going to become a hotel and a nightclub. The name of the "ship," I was told, was "Titanic." One man living in a *liar* village near the ship suggested, with heavy sarcasm, that a better name would be "Whore Ship" (Kapal Lontong), since prostitution, drugs, and gambling would certainly be the main sources of revenue.

Intrigued, I wanted to meet the owner and see the inside. My journalist friends gave me little reason to hope for success, however, telling me that the owner, Pak Edi, never granted interviews. Indeed, the first few times I dropped by the compound to ask for a meeting, the group of uniformed guards at the gate told me that Pak Edi was not available and that I should return another time. But after a week of daily visits my persistence finally paid off and I was escorted to his makeshift office located in the row of barracks at front of the building. Pak Edi, an ethnic Chinese businessman probably in his mid-fifties, was seated at a table with his daughter, studying the blueprints for the building. He invited me to sit down and asked what he could do for me. I told him that I was making a film and writing a book about the development of Batam and that this ship appeared to be representative of the future of the island. Perhaps, I suggested, he could give me a tour and tell me about the ship. After initially deferring to his daughter, I continued to insist and finally he agreed—obviously flattered.

Originally from the island of Kundur in the Riau Archipelago, Pak Edi's family had worked for generations as small-scale rubber planters, exporting the yield directly to middlemen in Singapore until the 1960s. But as a teenager—with intensifying discrimination against ethnic Chinese (see chap. 1)—Pak Edi left Riau for Singapore in search of a different life. He ended up spending twenty years traveling the world as a seaman before returning to Batam in the late 1980s with money and Singaporean connections that were put to use in the booming economy. As he walked

Titanic. Photo by Liam Dalzell. Reproduced with permission.

me through what would become the disco, karaoke rooms, restaurants, and a conference hall, he told me, "I've loved ships since I was a child so that's why I'm building this. Sea ships are easily damaged but this one will endure! Give it a hundred years and it'll be fine."

As we climbed the stairs from floor to floor, Pak Edi—increasingly talkative—continued to comment on the possibilities that Batam offered for an entrepreneur such as himself, particularly the island's strategic location and the fact that workers did not go on strike like they did in Jakarta. Obviously fascinated by the island's proximity to Singapore, he clearly imagined himself at the crossroads of an emerging economy where he offered "entertainment" (*hiburan*) to visiting tourists and businessmen. When we reached the helicopter pad on the top floor and gazed across the straits at Singapore and down at the *liar* housing and bars located below us—waiting to be destroyed to make way for a new shopping center—I felt tempted to ask Pak Edi to stand at the bow with his arms stretched out, embracing the new world, as Leonardo DiCaprio had done in the block-buster movie. But I didn't. He laughed when I finally got up the nerve to ask if the name of the ship would be "Titanic." "No," he told me; "actually it will be called 'Ocean Palace.'"

I, of course, preferred Titanic and the multiple ironies it evoked, prob-ably—but not certainly—lost to the people who named it. The following year, in 2004, the nightclub (which in the end was named "Pacific") opened in the basement and bottom floors of the building, while the top floors of the structure remained half-finished. Within a year it had become the most popular nightclub on the island, eventually putting the disco Ozon, described in chapters 3 and 4, out of business.

Approximately forty years earlier, perhaps in a nearby location, another man was struck by the proximity of Batam to Singapore despite the fact that the skyline had not yet emerged. Batam had become an important strategic base for the Indonesian military during Konfrontasi, and at some point General Suharto—who would come to rule Indonesia for more than three decades—visited the island. According to Suharto's own account, it was at that moment he imagined that Batam could be developed to one day compete with Singapore (see chap. 1), thereby reconfiguring the regional power structures that had been constituted during the colonial era. Suharto, however, certainly could never have imagined that a "ship" such as Titanic would one day be built on Batam or even predict the path that economic development would eventually take there. Much as he misjudged the limits of his power before he was forced to step down in 1998, Batam could never be transformed into what he and the island's planners envisioned it would become.

For an outside observer it is difficult to read Titanic—at an initial stage, at least—in any other way than as a symbol for development gone awry. Much like Southeast Asia's largest indoor ski slope, destroyed in a fire at Waterfront City a decade earlier, it appears as a caricature. In many ways, however, Titanic should be taken seriously and is a perfectly reasonable way to begin the end of this book. Like the acronyms that local inhabitants create out of Batam, Pantai Stres and Titanic re-politicize the island's landscape through language, self-consciously identifying the gap between the developed and the *liar,* between migrants' desires of entering the economy of development and their actual position within this economy.

Titanic also responds to a question that one of the readers of an earlier version of this book once posed to me: "What lies between Stress Beach and Fantasy Island?" [1] While I had previously considered the question in multiple ways, here the answer literally appeared—not in terms of social theory, but rather, beyond my wildest dreams, as a material object of magnificent proportions. Yet Titanic reveals more than itself. It is a place where diverse, mobile populations come together. Chinese Indonesian entrepreneurs such as Pak Edi, Indonesian prostitutes such as Lidya (chap. 3), and Singaporean tourists such as Andi (chap. 4) come to temporarily inhabit a place that is characterized as much by inequality and exchange as it is by "stress" and "fantasy." Taking Titanic seriously in ethnographic terms, much like Batamindo or Ozon in earlier chapters, thus means that we are led to consider not only this particular building and the interactions between the people in it, but also the desires and emotions that have brought them there, as well as their connections to other places, be it the Singaporean global city, a Javanese town, or a Sumatran village.

Titanic itself divulges neither boom nor bust; much like Batam itself it suggests an undecided temporality that can potentially move in either one direction or the other. In fact, as of 2007 the building was still not finished, thriving mainly as a disco while the hotel and conference facilities had yet to open. This sense of temporality, characterized by the Indonesian term *belum,* or "not yet," is not only central to the broader process of development on Batam, in which the *liar* is de-legitimized and the island is supposed to be "finished" at some future point in time, but also in relation to the anxieties of Indonesian migrants and Singaporean tourists described throughout the book. *Belum* thus describes Batam as developing, peripheral, and unfinished—as globalization under construction.

SHIFTING TO THE VERNACULAR

Batam is imagined as a place where the promises of global capitalism may be realized. These different imaginaries—always *belum*—come to intersect in particular forms. While the Indonesian government has presented the island as the new Houston or Rotterdam of Southeast Asia—the locomotive of national development—the Singaporean government considers it part of its new Asian hinterland. While Indonesian migrants hope it is a place where they will find work and a better life, for Singaporean working-class tourists Batam appears to allow for the realization of illicit forms of desires. Singaporean men travel to Fantasy Island to get rid of the "stress" of modern life, while Indonesian migrants—deterred from returning home by their feelings of *malu*—stare at the Singapore skyline from Stress Beach as they transform Batam into acronyms that promise either success or failure.

Most observers describe globalization in terms of political economy. This book has taken a different vantage point. It has focused on a place that is exemplary in contemporary debates concerning globalization, but rather than using the Singaporean economy as a starting point for analyzing the development of Batam, it has given priority to the lives of Indonesian migrants and Singaporean tourists who inhabit and pass through the island. This has allowed me to describe globalization primarily in terms of personal relationships between individuals—as an emotional economy—rather than as sets of impersonal transactions. In this process, however, I have *not* used Batam as an example of the "local" in order to critique overly general theories of globalization, or taken the phenomenological experience of my informants as a basis for making ontological claims, but rather have attempted to develop an analytical mode of description that has emerged through ethnographic fieldwork and that can be reduced to neither individual experience, a localized culture, nor more general forms of global processes.

In this process I have used three Indonesian vernacular concepts: *merantau*, meaning circular migration; *malu*, meaning shame or embarrassment; and *liar*, meaning wild, to organize my description. Each of these concepts

implies liminal states of being and underscores the problem of belonging in a globalized marketplace. *Merantau* is about the relationship with
home while in the process of migration; *liar* is about *not* belonging; and
malu is about being in between accepted roles and emotional states. These
concepts have not neatly overlapped throughout the book (indeed, my
informants would not necessarily understand them as connected) but have
rather formed the basis for describing an open-ended—both in spatial and
temporal terms—system of human mobility that has taken shape in Southeast Asia's shifting economic and political landscape during the past few
decades. Identifying this system as open-ended means not only that it is
contingent and potentially boundless, but also that the terrain it brings to
life is highly regulated and often violent. More generally, this perspective
highlights how systems of mobility and regulation are governed by different logics—the former by emotional economies and the latter by state
simplification—that are constantly shifting in relation to one another.

MOVING BEYOND GLOBALIZATION

Engaging with a place like Batam in a long-term ethnographic project
inevitably creates frustrations, as the island is transformed and its inhabitants come and go. Indeed, a series of significant changes has affected Batam
and the broader region since the turn of the century, allowing for novel
channels of human mobility and communication, as well as new forms of
constraint and control. The emergence of budget airlines such as Air Asia
has reduced Batam's importance as a transit area for transnational labor,
while allowing Singaporean tourists to fly to places throughout Southeast
Asia for almost the same fare that it costs to take the ferry to Batam. A
new regime of labor import, in tandem with an institutionalized system
of migrant deportation in Malaysia, has led to a dramatic drop in illegal
migrants who cross the border, while new surveillance systems across the
region are making it increasingly difficult for migrants to use multiple
passports in the post-9/11 security environment. The severity of abuses
against domestic servants in Malaysia and Singapore has progressively
gained public recognition, while the growing concern with human trafficking has led to the intensifying regulation of prostitution. The widespread
availability of cell phones has facilitated communication across borders and
between *kampung* and *rantau,* while the (temporary?) ban on gambling on

Batam has been matched by the Singaporean government's development of a world-class casino. Finally, the continuing ascendance of the Chinese economy has led many multinational corporations to move their factories away from Batam to Southeast China's industrial estates.

Yet despite the importance of these changes and the transformation of Batam that I have witnessed myself, *The Anxieties of Mobility* argues that if one begins with the mobility of migrants and tourists it is possible to identify more enduring social forms made evident through the anxieties and emotional economies that I have described with *merantau, malu,* and *liar.* Together they evoke a system of mobility that adapts to the changes described above, rather than being dictated by them. In other words, the mode of description I have employed accepts that Batam, the life-worlds that I describe, as well as my own analysis, are emergent and open-ended.

Throughout this book I have described what it means to be a laborer in the global economy, both in the midst of the global city and in the industrial periphery, and I have attempted to use this as a starting point for analyzing the significance of globalization processes. This approach demands a methodology that takes the experiences of migrants and tourists seriously, paying close attention to how meaning is created in the context of dramatic political and economic change. These changes are always interpreted by people within a particular social context, and the meanings that are produced are by no means clearly bounded or homogeneous, but rather contradictory, contested, and uneven. In the preceding chapters I have highlighted this unevenness—of cultural meaning, economic development, human mobility, and gender. Positioning myself in the global periphery, I have mapped changing forms of mobility among people who hope to become part of a new middle class, but who most often learn through their actual mobility that they are part of an expanding underclass, as geographical and class mobility have become increasingly disaggregated.

This particular ethnographic approach to globalization aspires to be attentive to both the production *and* the failures of meaning in the context of uneven forms of economic and political change. The migrants and tourists I have described are part of a global underclass that struggles to make sense of the world it inhabits in different ways. These processes of sense making should be situated not only in relation to capitalist expansion and state power, but also in the context of the desires and emotions that drive migration and tourism. This calls for a form of analysis that does not attempt to reduce these observations to a "local" or a "global" perspective, or identify the subjects with whom I am concerned as "victims." Instead, the potential of this particular version of an ethnography of globalization— particularly one that is concerned with human mobility—lies precisely in its concern with tracking movement *across* various types of borders, be they between nation-states, emotions, or social scientific categories. From this perspective, *The Anxieties of Mobility* is best understood as an attempt to take mobility seriously in order not only to critique already existing forms of analysis, but more important, to begin to consider alternative modes of analysis that are not spatially or temporally bounded, but rather *belum* and under construction.

NOTES

INTRODUCTION

1. Three currencies are used throughout the book: Indonesian rupiah, Singaporean dollars, and Malaysian ringgit. After the economic crisis these currencies have remained relatively stable in relation to one another and the U.S. dollar. If not otherwise noted, one U.S. dollar is valued at 1.7 Singapore dollars, 9,000 Indonesian rupiah, and 3.8 Malaysian ringgit.

2. The Growth Triangle also incorporates several other islands in the Indonesian Riau Archipelago, most notably Bintan. It was the Singaporean deputy prime minister, Goh Chok Tong, who first suggested the "Growth Triangle" concept. The head of the Batam Industrial Development Authority, B. J. Habibie, responded by dubbing the zone Sijori, an acronym for Singapore-Johor-Riau.

3. For many years Johor had been a source of inexpensive labor and land for Singapore, but higher costs, increasingly sensitive relations with Malaysia, and overcrowding led Singapore to look toward Batam as its new hinterlands. Johor is officially part of the Growth Triangle, but in reality it engages in little or no direct cooperation with Riau, and it is "more accurate to call the triangle a growth corridor . . . [that] is driven by the Singaporean political economy" (Macleod and McGee 1996, 425).

4. Although it is impossible to be precise, the general opinion is that migrants from West Sumatra and East and Central Java make up the largest ethnic groups on Batam.

5. Aihwa Ong, for instance, argues that Batam is an example of "graduated zones of sovereignty" (1999, 2003), a place in which the regulation of particular populations and spaces are transferred to nonstate actors, primarily through the reformulation of law. This results in a "system of variegated citizenship in which populations subjected to different regimes of value enjoy different kinds of rights, discipline, caring, and security" (2003, 43). For other studies that deal with Batam, see Macleod and McGee (1996); Smith (1996, 1997); Grundy-Warr, Peachey, and Perry (1999); and Sparke et al. (2004).

6. Maurer (2003, 79) calls this the "metaphysics of 'movement.'" See McKeown (1999) for a critique of the scholarly concern with diaspora.

7. On ethnographic response, see Riles (2006).

8. Peletz (1995, 91), for instance, argues that in Malaysia *malu* is a "brake" for passion (*nafsu*) in women, while Keeler claims that learning *isin,* the Javanese equivalent to *malu,* is crucial in the emotional development of children and closely connected with learning complicated forms of linguistic and social status. He writes that "understanding the range of meanings of *isin* consists in understanding the full range of situations in which one's dignity and status are on the line" (1983, 160).

9. In Kalimantan, Anna Tsing (1993, 54, 93) has described how the Meratus, who are considered "primitives" by the Indonesian state, do "not yet have a religion" (*belum beragama*) and are "not yet ordered" (*belum diatur*).

10. Rodgers (1995, 5) defines the *rantau* as the area outside the ethnic home region. It is also the root word for *merantau,* or circular migration.

11. For a similar use of "emotional economy," see Cannell (1999, 231). On the issue of temporality in the process of gift exchange, see Mauss' classic study, *The Gift* (1954), as well as Bourdieu's (1977, 4–9) and Derrida's (1992, 1995) important—and very different—critiques of Mauss.

12 Fortun develops these ideas in her review of the second edition of *Anthropology as Cultural Critique* (Marcus and Fischer 1999). Interestingly, in the issue of *Reviews in Anthropology* that preceded Fortun's, Rutherford develops a similar ethic of openness: "Be interested in interest. Learn from confusion. . . . Contextualize and take nothing for granted, including context" (2003, 106). Beginning with these concerns, Rutherford claims that the future of anthropology in Indonesia (and in other places) may lie precisely in a renewed interest in ethnographic method (2003, 105).

13. Lubuk Baja is Nagoya's official name, but it is rarely used in everyday conversation. Rumor has it that in the early 1970s construction workers from the Japanese city with the same name were based in Nagoya as it was being built, hence the name.

14. This formation of the global city leads not only to a spatial concentration of financial elites and information technologies, but also to new gendered dynamics of inequality as the number of low-wage service workers—primarily migrant women catering to the new middle and upper classes—has increased dramatically (Sassen 1991, 1998). See Brenner and Keil (2006) for an excellent collection of essays on "the global city."

15. The methodology of the study is, therefore, closely related not to George Marcus' (1995) more widely discussed multisited ethnography, but rather to what he identifies as the "strategically situated (single-site) ethnography," which should be distinguished from more "traditional" forms of single-sited ethnographies. The strategically situated ethnography focuses attention not only on local subjects, but also on a broader system in ethnographic terms. It therefore has different concerns than traditional single-site ethnographies (Marcus 1995, 111).

16. See Castles (1967) and Jellenik (2000) for accounts of Jakarta's changing demography.

17. To a certain degree, this has to do with the coupling of "ethnicity" with "locality" in the anthropological study of Indonesia (Boellstorff 2002), which is arguably part of a more general tendency for anthropological scholarship to reinforce dominant ideologies in Indonesia (Pemberton 1994).

18. The use of young women in offshore factory locations has now become part of a corporate cultural form that is recognizable around the world. See Aihwa Ong's (1991) review article, Fernandez-Kelly (1983) for a classic study of Mexican *maquiladoras,* and Salzinger (2003) and Pun (2005) for more recent accounts of Mexico and China, respectively. For discussions on the transnational maid industry, see Constable (1997) and Chin (1998). On prostitution in Southeast Asia, see, for instance, Law (2000).

19. However, since 2005 there have been major government crackdowns on gambling in Indonesia, including Batam, while in Singapore a large-scale casino resort is expected to open in 2009.

20. Following this line of thought, the *liar* has been analyzed in relation to the forms of *kriminalitas* that emerged in Java beginning in the 1980s. This is particularly notable in discussions of *gali-gali* or *gabungan anak-anak liar* (gangs of wild kids) (Barker 1998, 11; Siegel 1998).

21. In this sense it is considered a positive sentiment, perhaps best understood as "appropriate shyness" (Collins and Bahar 2000, 39).

22. This interest in emotions both follows and diverts from the seminal work of Geertz and Rosaldo (cf. Boellstorff and Lindquist 2004). On the one hand (and here the frameworks converge), Rosaldo describes emotions as a basis for theorizing social action. Following this, I argue that emotions in general, and *malu* in particular, are an important starting point for thinking about the motivations and actions of Indonesian migrants who must negotiate both hope and frustration in the *rantau.* For migrants, propriety and shame are often at odds, and choices must be made to bring them together or, at least temporarily, keep them apart. On the other hand (and this is the main point of divergence), I am concerned with social change to a degree that Geertz and Rosaldo rarely were. Sewell, for instance, has pointed out that Geertz's notion of culture "posits a very tight fit between publicly available clusters of symbols and the moods, motivations, affects, and activities that these symbols shape" (1997, 43).

23. For similar discussions in Malaysia and Hong Kong, see Ong (1995) and Constable (1997), respectively. For a discussion of discourses surrounding women's work in Indonesia, see Ford (2003).

24. *Malu* is closely linked with sexuality. Most notably, the Indonesian word for genitals is *kemaluan.*

25. By "technology" I mean "the problem of choosing the most appropriate means for achieving given goals or ends" (Collier and Ong 2005, 8).

26. Use of the *jilbab* became increasingly common in the 1990s, during the last years of the Suharto regime, as the previous ban on veiling in schools was overturned (Hefner 2000, 18–19).

27. The word literally means "pressed rice." It is perhaps best understood within the hierarchy of rice, in which cooked white rice would be considered purest. *Lontong* is made of white rice that is "left over."

28. On the transition from the New Order, see Aspinall (2005), and on decentralization, see Erb (2005). The Ninja killings in East Java are documented and analyzed in Siegel (2006), while the conflict in the Maluku Islands, the Bali bombs, and Jemaah Islamiyah have been analyzed in a series of reports by the Sidney Jones and the International Crisis Group (see http://www.crisisgroup.org/home/index .cfm?id=2959&l=1). On Jemaah Islamiyah, see also Barton 2005.

29. For examples of books that are implicated in the production of this discourse, see *Militant Islam in Southeast Asia: Crucible of Terror* (Abuza 2003), *Jihad in Paradise: Islam and Politics in Southeast Asia* (Millard and Hall 2004), and *Second Front: Inside Asia's Most Dangerous Terrorist Network* (Conboy 2005).

CHAPTER 1: BORDERLAND FORMATIONS

Epigraph: Quote from *Singapore Straits Times* taken from Scott Macleod, "Shadows beneath the Wind: Singapore, World City and Open Region," Ph.D. dissertation, University of British Columbia, 1995, 194.

1. On the notion of the "proper" place, see De Certeau (1988), as well as Lefebvre (1991, 23).

2. For a history of Singapore that describes this process in more detail, see Turnbull (1977).

3. Equally important was the trade in opium, which generated between 40 and 60 percent of Singapore's colonial state revenue until the 1920s (Trocki 1990, 2). Indeed, Trocki argues that opium was more important than free trade to Singapore's success. Not only was opium the most crucial source of revenue for the colonial state, it was also a means of controlling migrant labor through addiction.

4. Most notably, Sri Vijaya was based in South Sumatra between the seventh and twelfth centuries, and Malacca on the Malay Peninsula emerged in the fourteenth century (Wolters 1970; Andaya and Andaya 1982).

5. See also Gellner (1983) and Anderson's (1991) seminal work on the emergence of nationalism for discussions on the lack of distinct political boundaries in the premodern era.

6. By the mid-1870s thirty thousand Chinese migrants were arriving in Singapore each year (Warren 1993, 9; Turnbull 1989, 105).

7. On labor mobility, see, for instance, Stoler (1985); Breman (1990); and

Hoerder (2002, chap. 15). On the expansion of labor migration from China, see McKeown (1999, 2001).

8. Attempts by colonial regimes to regulate the trade in human labor as part of their civilizing mission was by no means successful until the latter part of the century, when slavery and human smuggling were pushed further underground (McKeown 1999, 320; Tagliacozzo 2005, chap. 10).

9. Initially a local currency was introduced, *Uang Kepulauan Riau* (currency of the Riau Archipelago), but soon it was replaced by the rupiah (Liamsi 1989, 33). The Indonesian rupiah has been fully convertible since the mid-1960s (Winters 1996, 44).

10. By the 1870s more Chinese than ethnic Malays were living in Riau (Tagliacozzo 1999, 256; Andaya 1997, 498). They were divided into two major groups, Hokkien and Teochew (Ng 1976).

11. This was implemented through PP-10, or Peraturan Pemerintah 10 (Government Regulation 10) (Mackie 1976, 82–97). This form of discrimination had its precedent in the Dutch colonial legal system's caste distinction between "Europeans," "Chinese," and "Natives" (Rush 1990, 14) For a critical discussion of the formation of these types of distinctions in the Dutch East Indies, see Stoler (2002, chap. 2).

12. By the early 1970s almost two-thirds of the residents in Tanjung Pinang were Chinese (V. Wee 1985, 54; Ng 1976, 20). In 1971 notoriously inaccurate census figures stated that 11.7 percent of the population in the Riau Archipelago consisted of noncitizen Chinese (Andaya 1997, 503).

13. In the original Indonesian, "feeling" and "desire" refer to *rasa* and *kehendak,* respectively (Radjab 1950, 210).

14. On the Minangkabau from West Sumatra, see Naim (1973) and Kato (1982); on the Acehnese from North Sumatra, see Siegel (1969); and on the Baweanese, from the island of Bawean, two hundred kilometers off the northeast coast of Java, see Vredenbregt (1964) and Ali (1996).

15. The East being Deli, the plantation belt along the Northeast coast of Sumatra. For a seminal historical account, see Stoler (1985).

16. See, for instance, Siegel (1969); Abdullah (1971); Breman (1990); and Mrázek (1994).

17. Shiraishi aptly has termed this era *An Age in Motion* (1990).

18. For a discussion of Hamka, see Hadler (1998, 135). See also Mrázek's (1994) biography of Sutan Sjahrir, which describes Medan in similar terms.

19. This story was also confirmed to me by a high-ranking Indonesian government official (November 11, 1998). For an account of Suharto's speech, see Smith (1996, 32–34), which claims that Stephen Roszel of Ingram Contractors, Inc., an American company that serviced foreign oil companies such as Pertamina (the Indonesian national oil company), decided that Batam was a suitable location for a logistics and oil service base.

20. Initially BIDA was called BIEA (Badan Pimpinan Daerah Industri Batam, or Batam Industrial Estate Authority). Pertamina initially attempted to transform Batam into a logistics center and a location for an oil refinery. On the collapse of Pertamina, see Hill (1996, 102).

21. For a discussion of this group of neoclassically trained economists, see Schwarz (2000, 52–53).

22. In theory, only housing built before 1971, the year BIDA was formed, was supposed to be offered this minimal economic compensation. In practice, however, inhabitants on Batam whose houses were built before 1971 have been offered more money and land in order to quell discontent. For similar reasons, more recent migrants have been offered plots of land when their squatter housing has been razed. As one official told me, it is extremely difficult to distinguish between houses built before and after 1971, particularly since many of them do not differ significantly in style. This situation has created both a possibility and an economic incentive for many to claim that their houses were built before this date and thus are "legal."

23. For a discussion of the broader issues related to Habibie's program and his rise to power, see T. Shiraishi (1996). On the "high technology" strategy, see Smith (1997).

24. For descriptions of the chaotic side of Singapore during this period, see Warren (1993), which recounts the history of prostitution, and Tagliacozzo (2005), which shows how smuggling and state formation emerged in tandem.

25. New laws allowed 100 percent foreign ownership of companies on Batam. The only condition was a 5 percent divestment to an Indonesian partner within five years. This should be compared with other parts of Indonesia, where domestic ownership had to reach 51 percent within fifteen years (Smith 1996, 172–175).

26. This division of responsibilities has, however, never been clear and led to frequent conflicts between the two agencies, especially over funding. For instance, R. A. Aziz, the former mayor of Batam, stated that "we are all unclear about our authority, so I often use my personal discretion in governing" (*The Jakarta Post,* August 21, 1993). A local government was created for other reasons: as Batam gained a higher profile, the provincial Riau government complained about being left out of the development project, which was at least geographically within its jurisdiction.

27. Pemda has since changed names to Pemerintah Kota (Pemko), or Municipal (literally "City") Government.

28. A clear sign of shifting power relations in the process of political decentralization was the decision by BIDA's chairman, Ismeth Abdullah, to run for governor of the newly created province of the Riau Islands. He subsequently won the election in 2005.

29. The six "designated red-light areas" are under the surveillance of the Anti-Vice Enforcement Unit and other government agencies, which check on the ownership of brothels and the status of the women working there and conduct health checkups as well. All women working in these brothels are required to carry so-

called "yellow cards," which record their venereal disease history (J. Ong 1993, 244–248).

30. "A project of legibility is immanent in any statecraft that aims at manipulating society, but it is undermined by intrastate rivalries, technical obstacles, and, above all, the resistance of its subjects" (Scott 1998, 80).

31. At the height of Suharto's New Order, Van Langenberg described it as follows: "it is social engineering in a totalitarian sense. Economic development (*pembangunan ekonomi*) is emphatically associated with notions about 'mental,' 'moral,' and 'spiritual' development (*pembangunan mental, moril, spirituil*)" (1986: 19–20).

32. A similar discussion can be found in anthropological studies dealing with company towns. In the Indonesian context, see Robinson (1986).

33. A survey of Indonesian newspaper articles beginning in the early 1970s shows that as late as 1991 *liar* was not mentioned in discussions of squatter housing on Batam. For the first mention I found, see *Angkatan Bersenjata,* April 10, 1991.

34. See, for instance, the conflicts surrounding the "wild school ordinance" in 1932 (S. Shiraishi 1997).

35. Kusno's (2000, 107–109) main example is the transformation of Jakarta under Governor Adi Sadikin, who attempted to close the city to rural migrants and, among other things, forbade the use of the pedicab, since it was considered unmodern and unfitting in the context of the capital city.

36. In the postcolonial period, one report from 1957 described an *okupasi liar,* or "wild occupation," of land by migrants in Sumatra (Saad 1957). Another report, from 1979, described the difference between *liar* housing and "slums" (the English word was used). Significantly, the author argued that all slums are *liar* but that not all *liar* housing can be identified as slums (Tumanggor 1979).

37. The "disorder" and "problems" generated by the development of Batam and the Growth Triangle offer an analytical space that is less concerned with issues of cultural hybridity and difference (cf. Bhabha 1994) and more with the issues of spatial organization and identity that are evident in debates within cultural geography. Much of this work has, however, tended to valorize marginal spaces and identities and view them as sources of resistance, transgression, and liminality (e.g., Shields 1991; Lefebvre 1991).

38. See Smith (1996, 36, 151–152, 246) for these linguistic turns.

39. See Peachey (1998, 109, n. 37) for an example of this phrasing. The origins of this use of Texas are unclear to me, but it does turn up in other instances in Indonesia (e.g., Boellstorff 2005, 151–152). I take this usage as referring to a place that is considered uncontrolled or lawless.

CHAPTER 2: THE DILUTED ENCLAVE

1. *Gampung* is the Acehnese spelling of *kampung,* meaning "village" or "home."

2. Through state businesses Jurong Town Corporation (the premier industrial park in Singapore) and Singapore Technologies Industrial Corporation, the Singaporean government invested 350 million U.S. dollars in Batamindo in cooperation with the Indonesian Salim Group. Most of the early tenants were openly persuaded by the Singapore Economic Development Board to move their factories to Batam, while keeping their headquarters in Singapore (Macleod and McGee 1996). Batamindo has its own Master Plan that it submits to BIDA for approval, and Jurong Town Corporation is the model (interview with John Sulistiawan, general manager of Batamindo, September 2, 1998). See Batamindo's Web site: http://www.sembpark.com.sg/category.cgi?cid=13.

3. This discourse appears to have its origins in 1950s Japan, where the utilization of young Japanese women in the electronics factories "was the final piece in the puzzle of Japan's rise to post-war prosperity" (Partner 1999, 221). Interestingly, Partner notes a paradox that is central for many of the women I discuss in this chapter. "Young women in the mid-1950s were expected to work with docile subservience for minimal wages. But as Japan's consumer revolution unfolded, it became apparent that young women also had another vital role to play: as consumers" (1999, 223).

4. It is difficult to judge precisely how many people live in *liar* housing adjacent to the park. In the late 1990s my own estimate was that they numbered around twenty thousand. Five years later the numbers had dropped as factories and shopping malls were built along the periphery of the park, but new squatter areas quickly emerged in other locations.

5. The companies in the park, in turn, pay for dormitory beds and other services in Singapore dollars. In early 1999, because of the fluctuating Indonesian rupiah, companies were actually paying more for dormitory beds than for salaries. For this reason many companies have been offering cash incentives so that workers will live outside the park, and they increasingly hire locally rather than use Tunas Karya. In 2002 only 30 percent of the companies used Tunas Karya, compared to 70 percent five years earlier (Interview with Tunas Karya official, July 19, 2002).

6. Equally important, many of these managers control at least part of the hiring process for operators, supervisors, and security guards who are hired locally; this potentially gives them access to substantial bribes and the opportunity to bring in friends and relatives. Chandra's experience, described briefly above, is only one example of how money changes hands on a variety of levels in the hiring process. For one man who lived down the block from me and worked as a middle-level manager at one of the companies, his salary and added funds from hiring "assistance" allowed him to buy a new house in a middle-class area and to support his wife and two young children.

7. Resistance to work discipline would appear to be inevitable (e.g., A. Ong 1987; Wolf 1992; Pred and Watts 1992). Workers made it clear that they use a range of tactics to get an extra break or to get out of work: "foot dragging" through longer trips to the toilet, for instance, or extended periods of religious prayer.

8. See Harvey (1990, 145) and Freeman (2000, 24–30). The effects of these processes on female factory workers have been widely debated and commonly framed in binary terms of "empowerment" versus "exploitation" (McKay 2006).

9. Batam has among the highest minimum wages in Indonesia. They are government regulated and have increased substantially since the economic crisis, from around 200,000 rupiah per month in 1998 to over 600,000 in 2005.

10. As Freeman (2000, 34–37) and Mills (1999), among others, have pointed out, it is critical to consider the links between the "worker-producer" and the "citizen-consumer."

11. Stealing the products made in factories is common, and many managers identified this as a major problem. Upon leaving Batam, finished products such as stereo speakers and vacuum cleaners are taken home as gifts by workers; product components like metal wiring can be sold to middlemen or stores. Many feel they are expected to return home with commodities produced on Batam. Esti, who came from West Sumatra, made this case for her behavior: "Everyone else would take stuff so I did as well. I wasn't going to sell it, just take it back to the *kampung* when my contract ended. Even if I couldn't save any money, I would at least be able to come back with a vacuum cleaner."

12. While officials at Tunas Karya claimed that two hours of overtime per day is compulsory (*wajib*), in practice this was not generally the case. As in other parts of Indonesia, strikes and more explicit forms of organized protest were rare during Suharto's New Order. Forms of "in-house" organizing were more common than trade unions. Rather than deal with independent unions, labor issues are generally settled within the plant (Kelly 2002, 403). Since unions were legalized after 2000, strikes have become increasingly common in Batamindo, particularly in contexts where companies do not follow official regulations concerning wages or severance pay (Phelps 2004, 214–215).

13. For instance, see the articles in *Sijori Pos,* August 6, 1998, and November 24, 1998. One was titled "From Hollywood Hill to 'Free Lancer.'" "Free lancer" refers to women who work as prostitutes.

14. For one case, see *Sijori Pos,* March 10, 1998. For a Mexican example, see Salzinger (2003, 38); and for a Chinese example, see Pun (2005, 136–139).

15. Collins and Bahar (2000, 46) heard similar responses when interviewing women in the South Sumatran city of Palembang. Smith-Hefner (2007) notes that among university students in Yogyakarta, women claimed that veiling offered protection from violence during political demonstrations.

16. See Siegel's account of the Javanese city of Solo for a similar account. Women who respond to men who call out to them place themselves in the position of the "prostitute" (1986, 122).

17. Despite the direct connection made between sex, money, and nightlife in newspapers and everyday talk, I found little evidence of factory workers being involved in prostitution. During my fieldwork I met several women working as full-time prostitutes who had previously worked at Batamindo, but no one who

admitted to working as a prostitute while still at Batamindo. The opinion that factory women in export processing zones are forced to turn to prostitution is also evident in academic discourse. Aihwa Ong, for instance, claims that "low wages and vulnerability have driven many to moonlight as prostitutes in China, Malaysia, Thailand, the Philippines, and Sri Lanka" (1991, 284).

18. Many factory workers frequented a particular disco, Skyline, because there were fewer drugs and prostitutes compared to other discos. One factory worker, for instance, used a phrase I had heard in several other conversations: she goes to discos only to "get rid of stress" (*hilang stres*) or to be *happy*.

19. In rural peninsular Malaysia, Ong reports that "women taking the Pill complained of headaches, a 'bloated' appearance, and a lethargy that made them 'too lazy to work'" (A. Ong 1995, 169).

20. English words such as *happy* and *relax* are often used in everyday talk. See also chap. 3.

21. Her point was that the Javanese, who wield much of the political power in Indonesia—something that has generally caused much resentment among other ethnic groups in the country—have a reputation of avoiding direct forms of confrontation.

CHAPTER 3: THE ECONOMY OF THE NIGHT

1. Reports state that *shabu-shabu* (crystal methamphetamine) and *putauw* (heroin) may be the new drugs of distinction throughout Indonesia (e.g., *Jakarta Post,* October 1, 2000). On Batam, however, through 2005, Ecstasy remained the key drug in Batam's nightclubs.

2. To *book* refers to hiring a prostitute. Although it is an English word, it is in italics since John uses it when he speaks English or Malay.

3. For women in the discos who have a *mami,* the going rate is thirty thousand rupiah per hour for sitting with the woman in the disco and four hundred thousand rupiah for booking out all night. For freelance prostitutes prices are more flexible and depend on the prostitute's and client's bargaining abilities. In general, prices appear to be lower, but the women can keep all the money they make. These prices have remained relatively stable through 2005.

4. Academic research concerning prostitution has been plagued by debates concerning agency and structure, which, more specifically, have revolved around representations of the prostitute as "sex worker" or "victim" (e.g., Doezema 1998). Murray (1991, 108), for instance, has argued that for many lower-class women in Jakarta, becoming a prostitute is a rational choice that affords them the possibility of making more money than they could otherwise, at the same time allowing them freedom from social restraints. In this book I avoid simplistic dichotomies between "free will" and "deterministic constraints" in the context of prostitution. Instead,

I attempt to shift the terms of debates by situating factory workers and prostitutes within a common frame of analysis through descriptions of their lives, rather than beginning with a priori assumptions. For discussions along these lines, see Law (1997, 261) on Southeast Asia and Brennan's (2004, 22–25) study of the Dominican Republic. It is also informative to compare Muecke's (1992) and Lyttleton's (1994) discussions of prostitution in Thailand.

5. During my time on Batam I heard many different stories from women about how they became involved in prostitution. The motif of the middleman who finds and lures women into prostitution by promising a good job in a restaurant with a high salary and a modern lifestyle close to Singapore is a common one in arrival stories. I doubted the stories of some women, but many had certainly been lured to Batam under more or less false pretenses. More obviously, many women are bound to karaoke bars and brothels through systems of debt-bondage labor, which is generally tolerated, and perhaps supported, by the authorities.

6. Although prostitution is officially against the law, the Indonesian government policy is one of tolerance, and the act of selling sex is not subject to criminal prosecution (Sunindyo 1993, 4). Instead, the state, following the Dutch colonial tradition, has attempted to localize prostitution in brothel complexes and establish "rehabilitation centers." The regulation of prostitution is "largely determined by health and public-order rather than moral considerations" (Jones et al. 1995, 10). Some estimates put the number of prostitutes in Indonesia ca. 1993 between 140,000 and 230,000 (1995, 10). In relation to broader socioeconomic changes in Indonesia, Jones and his colleagues argue that the diminishing importance of the agricultural sector and the feminization of the *rantau,* beginning in the late 1960s and 1970s, have been important forces in the expansion of prostitution throughout Indonesia. They also suggest that the high rate of divorce on Java has facilitated the entry of women into prostitution (1995, 8–9). In the 1950s West Java—the most common geographical origin of prostitutes in *lokalisasi* around Indonesia—had among the highest rates of divorce in the world (G. Jones 1994).

7. In one case it was reported in the local newspaper that a police raid had succeeded in "putting in order 87 *liar* prostitutes." The women were given a choice: either enter one of the quasi-official *lokalisasi* or return to their place of origin (*kampung*) (*Riau Pos,* June 5, 1998).

8. For a discussion of the logics of *operasi* in Bandung, see Barker (1999a, 102–103).

9. The concern with order can also be seen in attempts to create regulations in other environments (e.g., Jones et al. 1995, 13). For instance, consider the following two regulations (from a list of ten) that government officials posted in all hotels in the town of Tanjung Balai on the nearby island of Karimun in 1999, in the wake of public protests against prostitution: 2) *Pramuria* [prostitutes] may not wear clothing that is impolite (*tidak sopan*) while in the hotel or in public spaces; and 4) *Pramuria* may not smoke while walking in public spaces.

10. In fact, Corbin's description of the *maison de tolérance* in nineteenth-century France could very well characterize the official view of prostitution in contemporary Indonesia (and Singapore). "Debauchery, defined as the abusive use of sex, of money, of oneself, sometimes invaded the home and private life. Yet it could be got rid of at the brothel; such at least was the hope and intent of the apostles of regulationism, the true creators of the registered brothel—the *maison de tolérance*" (1990, xv).

11. As noted in chapter 2, most factories have age limits for hiring new workers.

12. It is a well-known joke on Batam that the only power the local government (Pemda, now Pemko) has, at least prior to the process of political decentralization in Indonesia, is to make identity cards. See the article in *Bisnis Indonesia* (April 21, 1994) titled "The Identity Card Business, Sex and Imported Goods: Other Sides of Life on Batam."

13. The behavior associated with *tripping* has even become part of a cultural repertoire, as one frequently sees people moving their heads back and forth, simulating the experience of being on. In a particularly memorable episode in my living room, a young mother rocked her three-month-old baby so that the head moved back and forth and jokingly said that it looked like she was *tripping*. Everyone present, including the grandmother, laughed together. For another example, see Barker (1999b, 189, n. 26).

14. The basic recipe for Long Island iced tea is equal portions vodka, gin, triple sec, rum, tequila, and some cola.

15. Kruhse-Mount Burton (1995, 193) makes a similar point in relation to Southeast Asian sex tourism in Australia. There, "prostitution is often appraised by clients as deficient, in that prostitutes are criticized for being emotionally and sexually cold and for making little effort to please, or to disguise the commercial nature of the interaction. Men appear to find the latter aspect particularly demeaning since it highlights the failure to find a willing and satisfactory free partner."

16. For studies that address this issue in Southeast Asia, see Anna Tsing's chapter, "Alien Romance," in *The Realm of the Diamond Queen* (1993), and Lisa Law's chapter, "Negotiating the Bar," in *Sex Work in Southeast Asia* (2000).

17. Ecstasy is illegal in Indonesia, and police raids on discos and small-scale production units were increasingly reported in the media as it became one of the drugs of choice in discos throughout the country. On Batam arrests are usually made outside of discos (*Sijori Pos,* December 1, 1999), while transactions appear to continue uninterrupted inside. The rare arrests in Ozon and other discos are usually of Singaporeans, who express surprise since "everyone else" is using it (*Straits Times,* November 8, 1999).

18. In this context, comparisons could be made to cocoa leaves, caffeine, or sugar. See, for instance, Mintz's classic study of sugar, *Sweetness and Power* (1985).

19. In the disco Ecstasy generates distinctions between clients and prostitutes alike by becoming a sign that one is *gengsi* (hip). Not being *on,* therefore, can also become a source of *malu* in relation to other prostitutes, since it can be seen as a sign that one cannot access the drug, implying that one cannot get a client or afford to buy it. Ecstasy can also function as a kind of antidepressant outside of the disco, as many women and their male partners would take it at home.

20. Kulick (1998, 9–10) elaborates on this position in relation to Brazilian transgendered prostitutes.

21. In recent years the wages of factory work have gone up substantially compared to prostitution (see chap. 2).

22. This resonates with Cohen's (1993) study of "open-ended" prostitutes in Bangkok.

23. In their study of prostitution in Indonesia, Jones and his colleagues note that "it is difficult to give even a rough estimate of the economic significance of the sex industry, and the amount of money that changes hands over the course of year through its activities" (1995, 46). Still, they estimate that the average net monthly earnings for prostitutes range between 200,000 rupiah in the low-class sector, to 1.2 million rupiah in the middle-class sector, to 2 million rupiah in the high-class sector. This was, however, at a time when the exchange rate to the U.S. dollar hovered around 2,200 rather than 9,000. These figures, therefore, offer little guidance for understanding the current situation on Batam and probably Indonesia as a whole.

24. This logic is also obvious in the strategies of taxi drivers, such as the one I mentioned on the first page of the chapter.

25. See Day's (1990) study of female prostitutes in London and Kulick's (1998) study of transgendered prostitutes in Brazil for strikingly similar distinctions.

26. See Brennan (2004, 38) for a Dominican equivalent of the *bronces,* the *tíguere.*

CHAPTER 4: FANTASY ISLAND

Epigraph: Rem Koolhaas, *Small, Medium, Large, Extra-Large: Office for Metropolitan Architecture.* New York: Monacelli Press, 1998.

1. I first met Andi through Hari, an Indonesian man who worked as a drug dealer at Ozon. I had been having difficulties meeting Singaporeans on Batam, since most came and left quickly and were not easily approachable—protected in hotels, restaurants, discos, and taxis. I asked Hari if he could introduce me to some of his clients, and he took me to Andi, who was friendly and open from our initial meeting. Eventually he began to stop by my house whenever he came to Batam.

2. See http://batam-nightlife.hypermart.net (accessed April 15, 2002).

3. The majority of the Singaporean tourists who come to Batam are Chinese, but during fieldwork I usually found it easier to get to know Malays, perhaps because they found it curious to meet a Westerner who spoke Malay.

4. The discourse of Asian values appeared in the 1990s in international debates concerning the caning of Michael Fay, an American teenager living with his parents in Singapore who was arrested for vandalism and sentenced to caning (e.g., Tay 1997), in relation to political scientist Samuel Huntington's (1996) thesis on "the clash of civilizations," and in provocative statements by Malaysian prime minister Mahatir Mohammed and Singaporean senior minister Lee Kuan Yew, supporting an "Asian" style of economic development and governance (cf. A. Ong 1999, chap. 7).

5. Occasionally, however, a Singaporean is arrested for drug use on Batam and hung out in the press on both sides of the border. Arrests are usually made outside of discos, while transactions appear to continue uninterrupted inside. The rare arrests in Ozon and other discos are usually of Singaporeans, who express surprise, since "everyone else is doing it." For accounts in the Indonesian and Singaporean press, see *Sijori Pos,* December 1, 1999; and *Straits Times,* November 8, 1999.

6. This is the state that is located beyond critique and, in this context, produced in an explicitly binary form. Zizek (1997) calls this "ideological fantasy."

7. In keeping with Singapore's government policies, criteria for renting or owning these flats are based on the "family formation rule." Unless a woman is over forty or a man is over fifty, she or he cannot rent or purchase a flat without a "family nucleus," which consists of a husband and wife (PuruShotam 1998, 138).

8. On Islam, see, for instance, Blackwood (1995); on patron-client relationships in Southeast Asia, see Schmidt et al. (1977).

9. For instance, the following advertisement could be seen in 1999 at the World Trade Center ferry terminal near the ticket booth for Batam: a man in a business suit is pictured with a number of building blocks showing pictures of his family members. The caption below reads, "I don't want to lose everything I've built. I'll admit there are temptations when I travel or entertain, but it's not worth risking everything for AIDS—the odds are it will catch up with you."

10. For instance, in one case, a Singaporean man was sentenced to fifteen months in prison for refusing to reveal, when he donated blood, that he had unprotected sex with a prostitute on Batam (*Straits Times,* April 16, 2001).

11. The bill was passed unanimously by Parliament. Those who refuse to take the test face a fine of two thousand Singapore dollars, six months in prison, or deportation (AP, September 4, 1998).

12. Other examples show how the Singaporean government has attempted to affect regulations on Batam. In chapter 2 I discussed how statements by senior minister Lee Kuan Yew were aimed at keeping wages low on Batam. More relevant to the theme of this chapter, in the late 1980s organized gambling was halted on Batam because of Singaporean government protests (*Straits Times,* July 15, 1988).

More recently, gambling has become an issue as the closing of gambling establishments has had negative effects on tourism (*Jakarta Post,* November 18, 2005).

13. I am grateful to Don Kulick for pointing this out.

CHAPTER 5: REVOLVING DOORS OF DISPOSSESSION

1. "The biggest complaint from [Indonesian] migrants [to Malaysia] has not been their treatment by police during the raids but the fact that legal workers are too often caught in the net, either because their employers hold their passports or because the frequent change of forms and regulations leads to one part of the bureaucracy not knowing what the other is doing" (S. Jones 2000, 69).

2. Singapore distinguishes between "work permit holders" and "holders of professional passes." The former are repatriated after their permits expire and are usually not allowed to bring dependents. In contrast, holders of professional passes are those whose "skills are in high demand" and who are allowed to bring their dependents with them (Soon-Beng and Chew 1995, 197; see also Kaur 2006, 36–38). Singapore has tended to increase the levies for "work permit holders" and to decrease the levies for "holders of professional passes" (Hui 1998, 207–208), a strategy in keeping with the government's attempt to transform Singapore into a "global city." For instance, levies for maids more than doubled in the 1990s (Yeoh, Huang, and Gonzalez 1999, 117–118).

3. Indonesia is identified as a "Non-traditional Source" of labor by the government, and Indonesians are permitted to work only in the construction, marine, and domestic service sectors (Wong 1997, 150). Once again there are no official figures on the number of Indonesian men working legally in Singapore, but most sources, as well as my discussions with Indonesians who have worked in Singapore, suggest that men are rarely granted work permits.

4. In Malaysia there has been a notable shift in terminology during the last thirty years. "Irregular migrants" in the 1970s became "illegal migrants" in the 1980s and "illegals" or "aliens" in the 1990s (Healey 2000, 231).

5. "Smart cards" were developed on Batam so that foreign managers, primarily working at the Batamindo Industrial Park, could move more easily between Batam and Singapore, entering Indonesia through a special line. However, the distribution of these cards remains very limited.

6. The tax for leaving the country by plane is 1 million rupiah, or approximately 110 U.S. dollars.

7. Indonesians use the term *passing* to refer to exiting and reentering Singapore or Malaysia in order to renew visas.

8. The amount is always considerably higher for Malaysia than Singapore. It has never been a secret that money can be rented at the ports on Batam. For instance, the Jakarta daily *Kompas* had a report on the topic on January 17, 1996, claiming

that it cost between 50,000 and 100,000 rupiah to rent money; on December 12, 1998, *Sijori Pos* reported in a prominently displayed article that it cost up to 200,000 rupiah. In 2005 it could cost up to 100 Singapore dollars to rent 1,000. One man said that he had been tempted to keep the money, but "there is no point in trying to take the money and run. They copy your passport number and they know where all the Indonesians go, so it is easy for them to track you down."

9. For an alternative reading of De Certeau at the Spanish-Moroccan border, see McMurray 2001, chap. 6.

10. Immigration is a sensitive political issue in Singapore. I attempted to organize interviews on the subject with several government officials there but was refused each time.

11. The following account, from one of Mariam Ali's (1996, 136) informants who was refused entry to Malaysia, supports this position. "Look, you have to give me a reason. I am dressed well. I am wearing a Camel shirt, a [*sic*] Padini pants, I am carrying a two hundred dollar brief case, and five thousand cash and two million rupiahs. I have enough money just working in Indonesia and am not interested in working in Singapore. Why can't I enter?" The immigration officer he was talking to remained unconvinced, however, and he was turned away.

12. For discussions of the extensive networks that bring Indonesians to Malaysia, see S. Jones (2000). See also Ali's (1996) ethnographic account of how Baweanese migrants travel to Malaysia and Singapore.

13. The going rate on Batam appears to fluctuate. At the time Felix crossed, 200,000 rupiah was equivalent to 90 U.S. dollars, but at the time I got to know him it was only 20 U.S. dollars.

14. In 2000 an estimated 150,000 Indonesian maids were working in Malaysia (Hugo 2000, 108). This is compared to 585 in 1991 (S. Jones 2000, 65). In Singapore there were 20,000 Indonesian maids in 1995. There were a total of 100,000 foreign maids, which amounts to one for every eight households in the city (Yeoh, Huang, and Gonzalez 1999, 117). By 2005 there were 150,000 foreign maids in the country, of which 60,000 were Indonesians (Human Rights Watch 2005).

15. For an account of the effects of the crisis on female migrants in an export manufacturing zone in South Sulawesi, see Silvey (2000).

16. For a discussion of these middlemen, see Hugo (2002).

17. In comparison, workers in the government category "cleaners and labourers," the occupational group with the lowest gross wages in Singapore, on average made 827 U.S. dollars per month in 2000 (http://www.gov.sg/mom/manpower/manrs/wages/ows_highlight.pdf, accessed on November 19, 2001).

18. As Human Rights Watch (2005, 66–68) shows, these are within the normal working hours for domestic servants in Singapore. In fact, a widely available handbook on hiring and dealing with foreign maids in Singapore suggests that employers should expect their maids to work these long hours (Chew 2004, 68–69).

19. Indonesian maids who have problems in Singapore are often sent to Batam, since it is cheaper than paying for the ticket to return home. This is often explicitly stated in contracts that I have seen.

20. www.noblemaids.com (accessed on April 10, 2002).

CHAPTER 6: BETWEEN STRESS BEACH AND FANTASY ISLAND

1. Patsy Spyer was the external examiner for my doctoral dissertation, upon which this book is based (Lindquist 2002).

REFERENCES

Abalahin, Andrew Jimenez. 2003. "Prostitution Policy and the Project of Modernity: A Comparative Study of Colonial Indonesia and the Philippines, 1850–1940." Ph.D. dissertation, Cornell University.

Abdullah, Taufik. 1971. *Schools and Politics: The Kaum Muda Movement in West Sumatra (1927–1933).* Ithaca, N.Y.: Cornell University Southeast Asia Program Publications.

Abella, Manolo I. 1995. "Asian Labour Migration: Past, Present, and Future." *Asean Economic Bulletin* 12(2): 125–138.

Abrams, Philip. 1988. "Notes on the Difficulty of Studying the State." *Journal of Historical Sociology* 1(1): 58–89.

Abuza, Zachary. 2003. *Militant Islam in Southeast Asia: Crucible of Terror.* Boulder, Colo.: Lynne Rienner Publisher.

Ali, Mariam Mohamed. 1996. "Ethnic Hinterlands: Contested Spaces between Nations and Ethnicities in the Lives of Baweanese Labor Migrants." Ph.D. dissertation, Harvard University.

Andaya, Barbara Watson. 1997. "Recreating a Vision: *Daratan* and *Kepulauan* in Historical Context." *Bijdragen tot de Taal-, Land- en Volkenkunde* 153(4): 483–508.

Andaya, Barbara Watson, and Leonard Y. Andaya. 1982. *A History of Malaysia.* New York: St. Martin's Press.

Anderson, Benedict. 1991. *Imagined Communities: Reflections on the Origins and Spread of Nationalism,* 2nd ed. London: Verso.

Appadurai, Arjun. 1996. *Modernity at Large: Cultural Dimensions of Globalization.* Minneapolis: University of Minnesota Press.

Aspinall, Edward. 2005. *Opposing Suharto: Compromise, Resistance, and Regime Change in Indonesia.* Stanford, Calif.: Stanford University Press.

Aspinall, Edward, and Greg Fealy, eds. 2003. *Local Power and Politics in Indonesia: Decentralization and Democratization.* Singapore: Institute of Southeast Asian Studies.

Bala, Poline. 2000. "Space, Place, and Identity: Changing Meanings of the Border in Highland Borneo." Paper presented at the annual meeting for the Association for Asian Studies. San Diego, March 9–12.

Barker, Joshua. 1998. "State of Fear: Controlling the Criminal Contagion in Suharto's New Order." *Indonesia* 66: 6–43.

———. 1999a. "Surveillance and Territoriality in Bandung." In *Figures of Criminality in Indonesia, the Philippines, and Colonial Vietnam,* ed. Vicente L. Rafael. Ithaca, N.Y.: Cornell University Southeast Asia Program Publications.

———. 1999b. "The Tattoo and the Fingerprint: Crime and Security in an Indonesian City." Ph.D. dissertation, Cornell University.

Barton, Greg. 2005. *Indonesia's Struggle: Jemaah Islamiyah And the Soul of Islam.* Sydney: University of New South Wales Press.

Batamindo Industrial Park. 1992. "From Commitments to Results." Brochure.

Bennett, Linda Rae. 2005. *Women, Islam and Modernity: Single Women, Sexuality and Reproductive Health in Contemporary Indonesia.* New York: Routledge.

Bernstein, Elizabeth. 2001. "The Meaning of the Purchase: Desire, Demand, and the Commerce of Sex." *Ethnography* 2(3): 375–406.

Bhabha, Homi K. 1994. *The Location of Culture.* London: Routledge.

Bishop, Ryan, and Lillian S. Robinson. 1998. *Night Market: Sexual Cultures and the Thai Economic Miracle.* New York: Routledge.

Blackwood, Evelyn. 1995. "Senior Women, Model Mothers, and Dutiful Wives: Managing Gender Contradictions in a Minangkabau Village." In *Bewitching Women, Pious Men: Gender and Body Politics in Southeast Asia,* ed. Aihwa Ong and Michael G. Peletz. Berkeley: University of California Press.

Bloch, Maurice, and Jonathan Parry. 1989. "Introduction: Money and the Morality of Exchange." In *Money and the Morality of Exchange,* ed. Maurice Bloch and Jonathan Parry. Cambridge: Cambridge University Press.

Boellstorff, Tom. 1999. "The Perfect Path: Gay Men, Marriage, Indonesia." *GLQ* 5(4): 475–510.

———. 2002. "Ethnolocality." *The Asia Pacific Journal of Anthropology* 3(1): 24–48.

———. 2005. *The Gay Archipelago: Sexuality and Nation in Indonesia.* Princeton, N.J.: Princeton University Press.

Boellstorff, Tom, and Johan Lindquist. 2004. "Bodies of Emotion: Rethinking Culture and Emotion through Southeast Asia." *Ethnos* 69(4): 437–444.

Bourdieu, Pierre. 1977. *Outline of a Theory of Practice.* Cambridge: Cambridge University Press.

———. 1990. *The Logic of Practice.* Stanford, Calif.: Stanford University Press.

Bourgois, Philippe. 1995. *In Search of Respect: Selling Crack in El Barrio.* Cambridge: Cambridge University Press.

Breman, Jan. 1990. *Labour Migration and Rural Transformation in Colonial Asia.* Amsterdam: Free University Press.

Brennan, Denise. 2004. *What's Love Got to Do with It? Transnational Desires and Sex Tourism in the Dominican Republic.* Durham, N.C.: Duke University Press.

Brenner, Neil, and Roger Keil, eds. 2006. *The Global Cities Reader.* New York: Routledge.

Brenner, Suzanne. 1996. "Reconstructing Self and Society: Javanese Muslim Women and the Veil." *American Ethnologist* 23(4): 673–697.

———. 1998. *The Domestication of Desire: Women, Wealth, and Modernity in Java.* Princeton, N.J.: Princeton University Press.

———. 1999. "On the Public Intimacy of the New Order: Images of Women in the Popular Indonesian Print Media." *Indonesia* 67: 13–38.

Butler, Judith. 1990. *Gender Trouble: Feminism and the Subversion of Identity.* New York: Routledge.

———. 1997. *The Psychic Life of Power: Theories in Subjection.* Stanford, Calif.: Stanford University Press.

Cannell, Fenella. 1999. *Power and Intimacy in the Christian Philippines.* New York: Cambridge University Press.

Castles, Lance. 1967. "The Ethnic Profile of Djakarta." *Indonesia* 3: 153–204.

Chew, Kim Whatt. 2004. *Foreign Maids: The Complete Handbook for Employers and Maid Agencies.* Singapore: SNP Editions.

Chin, Christine B. N. 1998. *In Service and Servitude: Foreign Female Domestic Workers and the Malaysian "Modernity" Project.* New York: Columbia University Press.

Chua, Beng Huat. 1995. "That Imagined Space: The Nostalgia for the *Kampung.*" In *Portraits of Places: History, Community and Identity in Singapore,* ed. Brenda S. A. Yeoh and Lily Kong. Singapore: Times Editions.

———. 1997. "Between Economy and Race: The Asianization of Singapore." In *Space, Culture and Power: New Identities in Globalizing Cities,* ed. Ayse Öncü and Petra Weyland. London: Zed Books.

———. 2003. *Life Is Not Complete without Shopping: Consumption Culture in Singapore.* Singapore: Singapore University Press.

Cohen, Erik. 1993. "Open-ended Prostitution as a Skilful Game of Luck: Opportunity, Risk and Security among Tourist-oriented Prostitutes in a Bangkok *soi.*" In *Tourism in Southeast Asia,* ed. Michael Hitchcock, Victor T. King, and Michael J. G. Parnwell. New York: Routledge.

Collier, Stephen, and Aihwa Ong. 2005. "Introduction." In *Global Assemblages: Technology, Politics, and Ethics as Anthropological Problems,* ed. Stephen Collier and Aihwa Ong. Oxford: Blackwell.

Collins, Elizabeth, and Ernaldi Bahar. 2000. "To Know Shame: *Malu* and Its Uses in Malay Society." *Crossroads: An Interdisciplinary Journal of Southeast Asian Studies* 14(1): 35–69.

Comaroff, Jean, and John Comaroff. 2000. "Millennial Capitalism: First Thoughts on a Second Coming." *Public Culture* 12(2): 291–343.

Conboy, Ken. 2005. *Second Front: Inside Asia's Most Dangerous Terrorist Network.* London: Equinox Publishing.

Constable, Nicole. 1997. *Maid to Order in Hong Kong: Stories of Filipina Workers.* Ithaca, N.Y.: Cornell University Press.

Corbin, Alain. 1990. *Women for Hire: Prostitution and Sexuality in France after 1850.* Cambridge, Mass.: Harvard University Press.

Das, Veena, and Deborah Poole. 2004. "State and Its Margins: Comparative Ethnographies." In *Anthropology in the Margins of the State*, ed. Veena Das and Deborah Poole. Oxford: James Currey.

Day, Sophie. 1990. "Prostitute Women and the Ideology of Work in London." In *Culture and AIDS*, ed. Douglas A. Feldman. New York: Praeger.

De Certeau, Michel. 1988. *The Practice of Everyday Life*. Berkeley: University of California Press.

De Genova, Nicholas. 2002. "Migrant 'Illegality' and Deportability in Everyday Life." *Annual Review of Anthropology* 31: 419–447.

Deleuze, Gilles, and Félix Guattari. 1987. *A Thousand Plateaus: Capitalism and Schizophrenia*. Minneapolis: University of Minnesota Press.

Dirlik, Arif, ed. 1993. *What Is a Rim? Critical Reflections on the Pacific Region Idea*. Boulder, Colo.: Westview Press.

Doezema, Jo. 1998. "Forced to Choose: Beyond the Voluntary v. Forced Prostitution Dichotomy." In *Global Sex Workers: Rights, Resistance, and Redefinition*, ed. Kamala Kempadoo and Jo Doezema. London: Routledge.

Derrida, Jacques. 1992. *Given Time: I. Counterfeit Money*. Chicago: University of Chicago Press.

———. 1995. *The Gift of Death*. Chicago: University of Chicago Press.

Douglass, Mike. 1997. "Structural Change and Urbanization in Indonesia: From the 'Old' to the 'New' Division of Labour." In *Urbanization in Large Developing Countries: China, Brazil, and India*, ed. Gavin W. Jones and Pravin Visaria. Oxford: Clarendon Press.

Ehrenreich, Barbara, and Arlie Russell Hochschild. 2002. *Global Women: Nannies, Maids and Sex Workers in the New Economy*. London: Granta Books.

Elmhirst, Rebecca. 2000. "Labour Politics in Migrant Communities: Ethnicity and Women's Activism in Tangerang, Indonesia." In *Labour in Southeast Asia: Local Processes in a Globalised World*, ed. Rebecca Elmhirst and Ratna Saptari. New York: RoutledgeCurzon.

Erb, Maribeth. 2005. *Regionalism in Post-Suharto Indonesia*. London: Routledge-Curzon.

Errington, Shelly. 1989. *Meaning and Power in a Southeast Asian Realm*. Princeton, N.J.: Princeton University Press.

Farrer, James. 1999. "Disco 'Super-Culture': Consuming Foreign Sex in the Chinese Disco." *Sexualities* 2(2): 147–165.

Ferguson, James. 1994. *The Anti-Politics Machine: "Development," Depoliticization, and Bureaucratic Power in Lesotho*. Minneapolis: University of Minnesota Press.

———. 1999. *Expectations of Modernity: Myths and Meanings of Urban Life on the Zambian Copperbelt*. Berkeley: University of California Press.

Fernandez-Kelly, Maria Patricia. 1983. *For We Are Sold, I and My People: Women and Industry in Mexico's Frontier*. Albany: State University of New York Press.

Ford, Michele. 2003. "Beyond the *Femina* Fantasy: Female Industrial and Overseas Domestic Labour in Indonesian Discourses of Women's Work." *Review of Indonesian and Malaysian Affairs* 37(2): 83–113.

————. 2006. "After Nunukan: The Regulation of Indonesian Migration to Malaysia." In *Mobility, Labour Migration and Border Controls in Asia*, ed. Amarjit Kaur and Ian Metcalfe. New York: Palgrave Macmillan.

Fortun, Kim. 2003. "Ethnography In/Of/As Open Systems." *Reviews in Anthropology* 32: 171–190.

Foucault, Michel. 2000. "Truth and Juridical Forms." In *Power: Essential Works of Foucault 1954–1984, Volume 3*, ed. James D. Faubion. New York: The New Press.

Freeman, Carla. 2000. *High Tech and High Heels in the Global Economy: Women, Work, and Pink-Collar Work in the Caribbean*. Durham, N.C.: Duke University Press.

————. 2001. "Is Local : Global as Feminine : Masculine? Rethinking the Gender of Globalization." *Signs* 26 (4):1007–1037.

Gade, Anna. 2004. *Perfection Makes Practice: Learning, Emotion, and the Recited Quran in Indonesia*. Honolulu: University of Hawai'i Press.

Geertz, Clifford. 1973. *The Interpretation of Cultures*. London: Fontana Press.

Geertz, Hildred. 1963. *Indonesian Cultures and Communities: A Study Guide*. New Haven, Conn.: HRAF Press.

Gellner, Ernest. 1983. *Nations and Nationalism*. Oxford: Basil Blackwell.

Giddens, Anthony. 1991. *Modernity and Self-Identity: Self and Society in the Late Modern Age*. Oxford: Polity Press.

Goddard, Cliff. 1996. "The 'Social Emotions' of Malay (Bahasa Melayu)." *Ethos* 24(3): 426–464.

Goffman, Erving. 1959. *The Presentation of Self in Everyday Life*. Garden City, N.J.: Doubleday.

Gottfried, Heidi. 2004. "Gendering Globalization Discourses." *Critical Sociology* 30(1): 9–15.

Graves, Elizabeth. 1981. *The Minangkabau Response to Dutch Colonial Rule in the Nineteenth Century*. Ithaca, N.Y.: Cornell University Southeast Asia Program Publications.

Grundy-Warr, Carl, Karen Peachey, and Martin Perry. 1999. "Fragmented Integration in the Singapore-Indonesian Border Zone: Southeast Asia's 'Growth Triangle' against the Global Economy." *International Journal of Urban and Regional Research* 23(2): 304–328.

Guinness, Patrick. 1990. "Indonesian Migrants in Johor: An Itinerant Labour Force." *Asian Survey* 26(1): 117–131.

Gurowitz, Amy. 2000. "Migrant Rights and Activism in Malaysia: Opportunities and Constraints." *Journal of Asian Studies* 59(4): 863–888.

Hadler, Jeffrey. 1998. "Home, Fatherhood, Succession: Three Generations of Amrullahs in Twentieth-Century Indonesia." *Indonesia* 65: 122–154.

Hamka. 1962. *Merantau ke Deli*. Djakarta: Djajamurni.

Hardt, Michael, and Antonio Negri. 2004. *Multitude: War and Democracy in the Age of Empire*. New York: The Penguin Press.

Harvey, David. 1990. *The Condition of Postmodernity: An Enquiry into the Origins of Cultural Change.* Oxford: Blackwell.

Healey, Lucy. 2000. "Gender, 'Aliens,' and the National Imaginary in Contemporary Malaysia." *SOJOURN: Journal of Social Issues in Southeast Asia* 15(2): 222–254.

Hefner, Robert W. 2000. *Civil Islam: Muslims and Democratization in Indonesia.* Princeton, N.J.: Princeton University Press.

Heng, Geraldine, and Janadas Devan. 1995. "State Fatherhood: The Politics of Nationalism, Sexuality, and Race in Singapore." In *Bewitching Women, Pious Men: Gender and Body Politics in Southeast Asia,* ed. Aihwa Ong and Michael G. Peletz. Berkeley: University of California Press.

Heryanto, Ariel. 1988. "The Development of 'Development.'" *Indonesia* 46: 1–25.

Hetherington, Kevin. 1997. *The Badlands of Modernity: Heterotopia and Social Ordering.* New York: Routledge.

Heyman, Josiah M. 1998. "State Effects on Labor Exploitation: The INS and Undocumented Immigrants at the Mexico-United States Border." *Critique of Anthropology* 18(2): 157–180.

Hill, Hal. 1996. *The Indonesian Economy Since 1966: Southeast Asia's Emerging Giant.* Cambridge: Cambridge University Press.

Hobson, J. S. Perry, and Vincent Heung. 1998. "Business Travel and the Emergence of the Modern Chinese Concubine." In *Sex Tourism and Prostitution: Aspects of Leisure, Recreation, and Work,* ed. Martin Opperman. Elmsford, N.Y.: Cognizant Communications Corporation.

Hoerder, Dirk. 2002. *Cultures in Contact: World Migrations in the Second Millennium.* Durham, N.C.: Duke University Press.

Holston, James. 1989. *The Modernist City: An Anthropological Critique of Brasília.* Chicago: University of Chicago Press.

Holston, James, and Arjun Appadurai. 1999. "Introduction: Cities and Citizenship." In *Cities and Citizenship,* ed. James Holston. Durham, N.C.: Duke University Press.

Hugo, Graeme. 1985. "Structural Change and Labour Mobility in Rural Java." In *Labour Circulation and the Labour Process,* ed. Guy Standing. London: Croom Helm.

———. 1993. "Indonesian Labour Migration to Malaysia: Trends and Policy Implications." *Southeast Asian Journal of Social Science* 21(1): 36–70.

———. 1995. "Labour Export from Indonesia." *ASEAN Economic Bulletin* (12)2: 275–298.

———. 2000. "The Crisis and International Population Movement in Indonesia." *Asian and Pacific Migration Journal* 9(1): 93–129.

———. 2002. "Women's International Labour Migration." In *Women in Indonesia: Gender, Equity and Development,* ed. Kathryn Robinson and Sharon Bessell. Singapore: Institute of Southeast Asian Studies.

Hui, Weng-Tat. 1998. "The Regional Economic Crisis and Singapore: Implications and Labor Migration." *Asian and Pacific Migration Journal* 7(2–3): 187–218.

Human Rights Watch. 2005. "Maid to Order: Ending Abuses against Migrant Domestic Workers in Singapore." 17(10) C.

Huntington, Samuel P. 1996. *The Clash of Civilizations and the Remaking of World Order*. New York: Simon and Schuster.

Jellenik, Lea. 2000. "Jakarta, Indonesia: *Kampung* Culture or Consumer Culture?" In *Consuming Cities: The Urban Environment in the Global Economy after the Rio Declaration*. London: Routledge.

Jones, Carla. 2004. "Whose Stress? Emotion Work in Middle-Class Javanese Homes." *Ethnos* 69(4): 509–528.

Jones, Gavin. 1994. *Marriage and Divorce in Islamic South-East Asia*. Kuala Lumpur: Oxford University Press.

Jones, Gavin, Endang Sulistyaningsih, and Terence Hull. 1995. "Prostitution in Indonesia." Australian National University, Working Papers in Demography, no. 52.

Jones, Sidney. 2000. *Making Money off Migrants: The Indonesian Exodus to Malaysia*. Hong Kong: Asia 2000 Ltd.

Kato, Tsuyoshi. 1982. *Matriliny and Migration: Evolving Minangkabau Traditions in Indonesia*. Ithaca, N.Y.: Cornell University Press.

Kaur, Amarjit. 2006. "Order (and Disorder) at the Border: Mobility, International Labour Migration and Border Controls in Southeast Asia." In *Mobility, Labour Migration and Border Controls in Asia*, ed. Amarjit Kaur and Ian Metcalfe. New York: Palgrave Macmillan.

Keeler, Ward. 1983. "Shame and Stage Fright in Java." *Ethos* 11(3): 152–165.

Kelly, Phillip. 2002. "Spaces of Labour Control: Comparative Perspectives from Southeast Asia." *Transactions of the Institute of British Geographers* 27(4): 395–411.

Kleinman, Arthur. 1995. *Writing at the Margin: Discourse between Anthropology and Medicine*. Berkeley: University of California Press.

Koolhaas, Rem. 1998. *Small, Medium, Large, Extra-Large: Office for Metropolitan Architecture*. New York: Monacelli Press.

Kruhse-Mount Burton, Suzy. 1995. "Sex Tourism and Traditional Australian Identity." In *International Tourism: Identity and Change*, ed. Marie-Francoise Lanfant, John B. Allcock, and Edward M. Bruner. London: Sage.

Kulick, Don. 1998. *Travesti: Sex, Gender and Culture among Brazilian Transgendered Prostitutes*. Chicago: The University of Chicago Press.

Kusno, Abidin. 2000. *Behind the Postcolonial: Architecture, Urban Space and Political Cultures in Indonesia*. New York: Routledge.

Lash, Scott, and John Urry. 1994. *Economies of Signs and Space*. London: Sage Publications.

Law, Lisa. 1997. "A Matter of 'Choice': Discourses on Prostitution in the Philippines." In *Sites of Desire, Economies of Pleasure: Sexualities in Asia and the Pacific,* ed. Lenore Manderson and Margaret Jolly. Chicago: University of Chicago Press.

———. 2000. *Sex Work in Southeast Asia: The Place of Desire in a Time of AIDS.* London: Routledge.

Lefebvre, Henri. 1991. *The Production of Space.* Oxford: Blackwell.

Liamsi, Rida K. 1989. *Tanjung Pinang Kota Bestari.* Pemerintah Kotip Tanjungpinang dan Lembaga Studi Sosial Budaya (LSSB), Tanjung Pinang, Indonesia.

Lian, Connie Quah Bee. 1991. "Prostitution in Singapore Society." Master's thesis, National University of Singapore.

Lindquist, Johan. 2002. "The Anxieties of Mobility: Development, Migration, and Tourism in the Indonesian Borderlands." Ph.D. dissertation, Stockholm University.

———. 2006. "Deep Pockets: Notes on the Indonesian Cockfight in a Globalizing World." *IIAS Newsletter* 42: 7.

———. 2008. "Of Maids and Prostitutes: Indonesian Female Migrants in the New Asian Hinterlands." In *Postcolonial Disorders: Reflections on Subjectivity in the Contemporary World,* ed. Mary Jo Del Vecchio Good et al. Berkeley: University of California Press.

Lyttleton, Chris. 1994. "The Good People of Isan: Commerical Sex in Northeast Thailand." *The Australian Journal of Anthropology* 5(3): 257–279.

———. 2004. "Relative Pleasures: Drugs, Development and Modern Dependencies in Asia's Golden Triangle." *Development and Change* 35(5): 909–935.

Mack, Jennifer. 2004. "Inhabiting the Imaginary: Factory Women at Home on Batam, Indonesia." *Singapore Journal of Tropical Geography* 25(2): 156–179.

Mackie, J. A. C. 1974. *Konfrontasi: The Indonesia-Malaysia Dispute 1963–1966.* New York: Oxford University Press.

———. 1976. *The Chinese in Indonesia: Five Essays.* Honolulu: University Press of Hawai'i.

Macleod, Arlene Elowe. 1992. "Hegemonic Relations and Gender Resistance: The New Veiling as Accomodating Protest in Cairo." *Signs* 17(3): 533–557.

Macleod, Scott. 1995. "Shadows beneath the Wind: Singapore, World City and Open Region." Ph.D. dissertation, University of British Columbia.

Macleod, Scott, and Terry McGee. 1996. "The Singapore-Johor-Riau Growth Triangle: An Emerging Extended Metropolitan Region." In *Emerging World Cities in the Asia Pacific,* ed. Fu-chen Lo and Yue-man Yeung. Tokyo: United Nations Press.

Mahmood, Saba. 2005. *Politics of Piety: The Islamic Revival and the Feminist Subject.* Princeton, N.J.: Princeton University Press.

Marcus, George E. 1995. "Ethnography in/of the World System: The Emergence of Multi-Sited Ethnography." *Annual Review of Anthropology* 24: 95–117.

Marcus, George E., and Michael M. J. Fischer.1999. *Anthropology as Cultural Cri-*

tique: An Experimental Moment in the Human Sciences, 2nd ed. Chicago: University of Chicago Press.

Maurer, Bill. 2003. "International Political Economy as a Cultural Practice: The Metaphysics of Capital Mobility." In *Globalization under Construction: Governmentality, Law, Identity,* ed. Richard Warren Perry and Bill Maurer. Minneapolis: University of Minnesota Press.

Mauss, Marcel. 1954. *The Gift: Forms and Functions of Exchange in Archaic Societies.* London: Cohen and West.

McKay, Steven. 2006. *Satanic Mills or Silicon Islands? The Politics of High Tech Production in the Philippines.* Ithaca, N.Y.: Cornell University/ILR Press.

McKeown, Adam. 1999. "Conceptualizing Chinese Diasporas, 1842–1949." *Journal of Asian Studies* 58: 306–337.

———. 2001. *Chinese Migrant Networks and Cultural Change: Peru, Chicago, Hawaii, 1900–1936.* Chicago: University of Chicago Press.

McMurray, David. 2001. *In and Out of Morocco: Migration and Smuggling in a Frontier Boomtown.* Minneapolis: University of Minnesota Press.

Merleau-Ponty, Maurice. 2002 [1962]. *Phenomenology of Perception.* London: Routledge.

Millard, Mike, and Ivan Hall. 2004. *Jihad in Paradise: Islam and Politics in Southeast Asia.* Armonk: M. E. Sharpe.

Mills, Mary Beth. 1999. *Thai Women in the Global Labor Force: Consuming Desires, Contested Selves.* New Brunswick, N.J.: Rutgers University Press.

Milner, A. C. 1982. *Kerajaan: Malay Political Culture on the Eve of Colonial Rule.* Tucson: University of Arizona Press.

Mintz, Sidney. 1985. *Sweetness and Power: The Place of Sugar in Modern History.* New York: Viking.

Mitchell, Timothy. 1988. *Colonising Egypt.* Berkeley: University of California Press.

Mrázek, Rudolf. 1994. *Sjahrir: Politics and Exile in Indonesia.* Ithaca, N.Y.: Cornell Southeast Asia Program Publications.

Muecke, Marjorie M. 1992. "Mother Sold Food, Daughter Sells Her Body: The Cultural Continuity of Prostitution." *Social Science and Medicine* 35(7): 891–901.

Murray, Alison J. 1991. *No Money, No Honey: A Study of Street Traders and Prostitutes in Jakarta.* Singapore: Oxford University Press.

Naim, Mochtar. 1973. "*Merantau:* Minangkabau Voluntary Migration." Ph.D. dissertation, National University of Singapore.

Ng, Chin Keong. 1976. "The Chinese in Riau: A Community on an Unstable and Restrictive Frontier." Working Paper, Singapore: Nanyang University, Institute of Humanities and Social Sciences.

O'Byrne, Darren J. 2001. "On Passports and Border Controls." *Annals of Tourism Research* 28(2): 399–416.

Ohmae, Kenichi. 1995. *The End of the Nation State: The Rise of Regional Economies.* New York: Free Press.

Ong, Aihwa. 1987. *Spirits of Resistance and Capitalist Discipline: Factory Women in Malaysia.* Albany: State University of New York Press.

———. 1991. "The Gender and Labor Politics of Postmodernity." *Annual Review of Anthropology* 20: 279–309.

———. 1995. "State versus Islam: Malay Families, Women's Bodies, and the Body Politic in Malaysia." In *Bewitching Women, Pious Men: Gender and Body Politics in Southeast Asia,* ed. Aihwa Ong and Michael G. Peletz. Berkeley: University of California Press.

———. 1999. *Flexible Citizenship: The Cultural Logics of Transnationality.* Durham, N.C.: Duke University Press.

———. 2003. "Zones of New Sovereignty in Southeast Asia." In *Globalization under Construction: Governmentality, Law, Identity,* ed. Richard Warren Perry and Bill Maurer. Minneapolis: University of Minnesota Press.

Ong, Jin Hui. 1993. "Singapore." In *Prostitution: An International Handbook on Trends, Problems, and Policies,* ed. Nanette J. Davis. London: Greenwood Press.

Oppermann, Martin, ed. 1998. *Sex Tourism and Prostitution: Aspects of Leisure, Recreation, and Work.* New York: Cognizant Communications Corporation.

Ortner, Sherry B. 1997. "Thick Resistance: Death and the Cultural Construction of Agency in Himalayan Mountaineering." *Representations* 59: 135–162.

Partner, Simon. 1999. *Assembled in Japan: Electrical Goods and the Making of the Japanese Consumer.* Berkeley: University of California Press.

Peachey, Karen. 1998. "Where There Is Sugar, There Are Ants: Planning for People in the Development of Batam, Indonesia." Master's thesis, University of British Columbia.

Peletz, Michael. 1995. "Neither Reasonable nor Responsible: Contrasting Representations of Masculinity in a Malay Society." In *Bewitching Women, Pious Men: Gender and Body Politics in Southeast Asia,* ed. Aihwa Ong and Michael G. Peletz. Berkeley: University of California Press.

———. 1996. *Reason and Passion: Representations of Gender in a Malay Society.* Berkeley: University of California Press.

Pemberton, John. 1994. *On the Subject of "Java."* Ithaca, N.Y.: Cornell University Press.

Perry, Martin, Lily Kong, and Brenda Yeoh. 1997. *Singapore: A Developmental City State.* New York: John Wiley and Sons.

Phelps, N. A. 2004. "Archetype for an Archipelago? Batam as Anti-Model and Model of Industrializaton in *Reformasi* Indonesia." *Progress in Development Studies* 4(3): 206–229.

Pillai, Patrick. 1995. "Malaysia." *Asean Economic Bulletin* 12(2): 221–236.

———. 1998. "The Impact of the Economic Crisis on Migrant Labor in Malaysia: Policy Implications." *Asia and Pacific Migration Journal* 7(2–3): 255–280.

Pratt, Mary Louise. 1992. *Imperial Eyes: Travel Writing and Transculturation.* New York: Routledge.

Pred, Allan, and Michael John Watts. 1992. *Reworking Modernity: Capitalisms and Symbolic Discontent.* New Brunswick, N.J.: Rutgers University Press.

Pun Ngai. 2005. *Made in China: Women Factory Workers in a Global Workplace.* Durham, N.C.: Duke University Press.

PuruShotam, Nirmala. 1998. "Between Compliance and Resistance: Women and the Middle-Class Way of Life in Singapore." In *Gender and Power in Affluent Asia,* ed. Krishna Sen and Maila Stivens. London: Routledge.

Radjab, Muhamad. 1950. *Semasa Kecil di Kampung (1913–1928) (Autobiografi seorang anak minangkabau).* Djakarta: Balai Pustaka.

Radjab, Muhamad. 1995. "Semasa kecil di kampung" [Village childhood]. In Telling Lives, Telling Histories: Autobiography and Historical Imagination in Modern Indonesia, ed., trans., and introduction by Susan Rodgers. Berkeley: University of California Press.

Rahim, Lily Zubaidah. 1998. *The Singapore Dilemma: The Political and Educational Marginality of the Malay Community.* Kuala Lumpur: Oxford University Press.

Reddy, William M. 1997. "Reply." *Current Anthropology* 38(3): 346–348.

Riles, Annelise. 2006. "Introduction: In Response." In *Documents: Artifacts of Modern Knowledge,* ed. Annelise Riles. Ann Arbor: University of Michigan Press.

Robinson, Kathryn May. 1986. *Stepchildren of Progress: The Political Economy of Development in an Indonesian Mining Town.* Albany: State University of New York Press.

Rodan, Gary. 1997. *The Political Economy of South-East Asia.* Melbourne: Oxford University Press.

Rodgers, Susan. 1995. "Imagining Modern Indonesia via Autobiography." In *Telling Lives, Telling Histories: Autobiography and Historical Imagination in Modern Indonesia,* ed., trans., and introduction by Susan Rodgers. Berkeley: University of California Press.

Rojek, Chirs. 1993. *Ways of Escape: Modern Transformations in Leisure and Travel.* London: The Macmillan Press.

Rosaldo, Michelle Z. 1983. "The Shame of Headhunters and the Autonomy of Self." *Ethos* 11(3): 135–151.

———. 1984. "Toward an Anthropology of Self and Feeling." In *Culture Theory: Essays on Mind, Self, and Emotion,* ed. Richard A. Sweder and Robert A. LeVine. Cambridge: Cambridge University Press.

Rose, Nikolas. 1999. *Powers of Freedom: Reframing Political Thought.* Cambridge: Cambridge University Press.

Rouse, Roger. 1992. "Making Sense of Settlement: Class Transformation, Cultural Struggle, and Transnationalism among Mexican Migrants in the United States." In *Towards a Transnational Perspective on Migration: Race, Ethnicity, and Nationalism Reconsidered*, ed. Nina Glick Schiller, Linda Basch, and Cristina Blanc-Szanton. New York: New York Academy of Sciences.

Roy, Ananya. 2005. "Urban Informality: Toward an Epistemology of Planning." *Journal of the American Planning Association* 71(2): 147–158.

Rudnyckyj, Daromir. 2004. "Technologies of Servitude: Governmentality and Indonesian Transnational Labor Migration." *Anthropological Quarterly* 77(3): 407–434.

Rush, James. 1990. *Opium to Java: Revenue Farming and Chinese Enterprise in Colonial Indonesia, 1860–1910*. Ithaca, N.Y.: Cornell University Press.

Rutherford, Danilyn. 2002. *Raiding the Land of Foreigners: The Limits of the Nation on an Indonesian Frontier*. Princeton, N.J.: Princeton University Press.

———. 2003. "Ethnography without Culture? Modernity and Marginality in the Anthropology of Indonesia." *Reviews in Anthropology* 32: 91–108.

Ryter, Loren. 1998. "*Pemuda Pancasila:* The Last Loyalist Free Men of Suharto's Order?" *Indonesia* 66: 45–74.

Saad, Abdul Rivai. 1957. "Okupasi Liar di Sekitar Kaju Aro (Kerintji) dengan segi sosial-ekonominja." Manuscript in Kroch Library, Cornell University.

Salzinger, Leslie. 2003. *Genders in Production: Making Workers in Mexico's Global Factories*. Berkeley: University of California Press.

Sassen, Saskia. 1991. *The Global City: New York, London, Tokyo*. Princeton, N.J.: Princeton University Press.

———. 1996. "Analytic Borderlands: Race, Gender and Representation in the New City." In *Re-presenting the City: Ethnicity, Capital and Culture in the Twenty-First Century Metropolis*, ed. Anthony D. King. London: Macmillan.

———. 1998. *Globalization and Its Discontents: Essays on the New Mobility of People and Money*. New York: The Free Press.

———. 2000. "Analytic Borderlands." *Public Culture* 12(1): 215–232.

Scheff, Thomas J. 1977. "The Distancing of Emotion in Ritual." *Current Anthropology* 18(3): 483–505.

Schmidt, Steffen W. et al., eds. 1977. *Friends, Followers, and Factions: A Reader in Political Clientelism*. Berkeley: University of California Press.

Schwarz, Adam. 2000. *A Nation in Waiting: Indonesia's Search for Stability*. Boulder, Colo.: Westview.

Scott, James C. 1998. *Seeing Like a State: How Certain Schemes to Improve the Human Condition Have Failed*. New Haven, Conn.: Yale University Press.

Sears, Laurie, ed. 1996. *Fantasizing the Feminine in Indonesia*. Durham, N.C.: Duke University Press.

Seet, K. K. 1995. "Last Days at Wak Selat: The Demise of a *Kampung*." In *Portraits of Places: History, Community and Identity in Singapore*, ed. Brenda S. A. Yeoh and Lily Kong. Singapore: Times Editions.

Sen, Krishna. 1998. "Indonesian Women at Work: Reframing the Subject." In

Gender and Power in Affluent Asia, ed. Krishna Sen and Maila Stivens. London: Routledge.

Sennett, Richard. 2006. *The Culture of the New Capitalism.* New Haven, Conn.: Yale University Press.

Sequerah, Pearl. 1995. "Chong Pang Village: A Bygone Lifestyle." In *Portraits of Places: History, Community and Identity in Singapore,* ed. Brenda S. A. Yeoh and Lily Kong. Singapore: Times Editions.

Sewell, William. 1997. "Geertz, Cultural Systems, and History: From Synchrony to Transformation." *Representations* 69: 35–55.

Shields, Rob. 1991. *Places on the Margin: Alternative Geographies of Modernity.* New York: Routledge.

Shiraishi, Saya. 1997. *Young Heroes: The Indonesian Family in Politics.* Ithaca, N.Y.: Cornell University Southeast Asia Program Publications.

Shiraishi, Takashi. 1990. *An Age in Motion: Popular Radicalism in Java, 1912–1926.* Ithaca, N.Y.: Cornell University Press.

———. 1996. "Rewiring the Indonesian State." In *Making Indonesia: Essays on Modern Indonesia in Honor of George McT. Kahin,* ed. Daniel S. Lev and Ruth McVey. Ithaca, N.Y.: Cornell University Southeast Asia Program Publications.

Siegel, James T. 1969. *The Rope of God.* Berkeley: University of California Press.

———. 1986. *Solo in the New Order.* Princeton, N.J.: Princeton University Press.

———. 1997. *Fetish, Recognition, Revolution.* Princeton, N.J.: Princeton University Press.

———. 1998. *A New Criminal Type in Jakarta: Counter-Revolution Today.* Durham, N.C.: Duke University Press.

———. 2002. "The Idea of Indonesia Continues: The Middle Class Ignores Aceh." *Archipel* 64: 199–229.

———. 2006. *Naming the Witch.* Stanford, Calif.: Stanford University Press.

Silvey, Rachel M. 2000. "Stigmatized Spaces: Gender and Mobility under Crisis in South Sulawesi, Indonesia." *Gender, Place and Culture* 7(2): 143–161.

———. 2004. "Transnational Migration and the Gender Politics of Scale: Indonesian Domestic Workers in Saudi Arabia." *Singapore Journal of Tropical Geography* 25(2): 141–155.

Smith, Shannon L. D. 1996. "Developing Batam." Ph.D. dissertation, Australian National University.

———. 1997. "Batam Island and Indonesia's High-technology Strategy." In *Indonesia's Technological Challenge,* ed. Hal Hill and Thee Kian Wie. Singapore: Institute of Southeast Asian Studies.

Smith-Hefner, Nancy. 2007. "Javanese Women and the Veil in Post-Soeharto Indonesia." *Journal of Asian Studies* 66(2): 389–420.

Soon-Beng, Chew, and Rosalind Chew. 1995. "Immigration and Foreign Labour in Singapore." *ASEAN Economic Bulletin* 12(2): 191–200.

Spaan, E., T. van Naerssen, and G. Koh. 2002. "Re-imagining Borders: Malay Identity and Indonesian Migrants in Malaysia." *Tijdschrift voor Economische en Sociale Geografie* 93(2): 160–172.

Sparke, Matthew et al. 2004. "Triangulating the Borderless World: Geographies of Power in the Indonesia-Malaysia-Singapore Growth Triangle." *Transactions of the Institute of British Geographers* 29: 485–498.

Spyer, Patricia. 2000. *The Memory of Trade: Modernity's Entanglements on an Eastern Indonesian Island.* Durham, N.C.: Duke University Press.

Stoler, Ann Laura. 1985. *Capitalism and Confrontation in Sumatra's Plantation Belt, 1870–1979.* New Haven, Conn.: Yale University Press.

———. 2002. *Carnal Knowledge and Imperial Power: Race and the Intimate in Colonial Rule.* Berkeley: University of California Press.

Strassler, Karen. 2003. "Refracted Visions: Popular Photography and the Indonesian Culture of Documentation in Post-Colonial Java." Ph.D. dissertation, University of Michigan.

Strathern, Marilyn. 2000. "Afterword: Accountability . . . and Ethnography." In *Audit Cultures: Anthropological Studies in Accountability, Ethics, and the Academy,* ed. Marilyn Strathern. London: Routledge.

Sullivan, John. 1986. "Kampung and State: The Role of Government in the Development of Urban Community in Yogyakarta." *Indonesia* 41: 63–88.

Sunindyo, Saraswati. 1993. "She Who Earns: The Politics of Prostitution in Java." Ph.D. dissertation, University of Wisconsin-Madison.

Suryakusuma, Julia I. 1996. "The State and Sexuality in New Order Indonesia." In *Fantasizing the Feminine in Indonesia,* ed. Laurie J. Sears. Durham, N.C.: Duke University Press.

Tagliacozzo, Eric. 1999. "Secret Trades of the Straits: Smuggling and State-Formation along a Southeast Asian Frontier, 1870–1910." Ph.D. dissertation, Yale University.

———. 2005. *Secret Trades, Porous Borders: Smuggling and States along a Southeast Asian Frontier, 1865–1915.* New Haven, Conn.: Yale University Press.

Tay, Simon. 1997. *Alien Asian: A Singaporean in America.* Singapore: Landmark Books.

Thomas, Nicholas. 1991. "Against Ethnography." *Cultural Anthropology* 6(3): 306–322.

Thompson, E. P. 1967. "Time, Work-Discipline, and Industrial Capitalism." *Past and Present* 38: 56–97.

Tremewan, Chris. 1994. *The Political Economy of Social Control in Singapore.* Oxford: St. Martin's Press.

Trocki, Carl. 1979. *Prince of the Pirates: The Temenggongs and the Development of Johor and Singapore, 1784–1885.* Singapore: Singapore University Press.

———. 1990. *Opium and Empire.* Ithaca, N.Y.: Cornell University Press.

Tsing, Anna Lowenhaupt. 1993. *In the Realm of the Diamond Queen.* Princeton, N.J.: Princeton University Press.

———. 2000. "The Global Situation." *Cultural Anthropology* 15(3): 327–360.

———. 2004. *Friction: An Ethnography of Global Connection.* Princeton, N.J.: Princeton University Press.

Tumanggor, Rusmin. 1979. "Perumahan Liar dan Perilaku Menyimpang." Pusat Latihan Penelitian Ilmu Ilmu Sosial, Universitas Indonesia.

Turnbull, C. Mary. 1977. *A History of Singapore, 1819–1975.* New York: Oxford University Press.

———. 1989. *A History of Malaysia, Singapore, and Brunei.* Boston: Allen and Unwin.

Turner, Peter. 2000. *Lonely Planet Indonesia.* Hawthorn: Lonely Planet Publications.

Turner, Victor. 1970. *The Forest of Symbols: Aspects of Ndembu Ritual.* Ithaca, N.Y.: Cornell University Press.

Van Gennep, Arnold. 1960 [1909]. *The Rites of Passage.* Chicago: University of Chicago Press.

Van Grunsven, Leo. 1998. "The Sustainability of Urban Development in the SIJORI Growth Triangle." *TWPR* 20(2): 179–201.

Van Langenberg, Michael. 1986. "Analysing Indonesia's New Order State: A Keywords Approach." *Review of Indonesian and Malay Affairs* 20(2): 1–47.

Vollenweider, Franz X. et al. 1998. "Psychological and Cardiovascular Effects and Short-Term Sequelae of MDMA ('Ecstasy') in MDMA-Naive Healthy Volunteers." *Neuropsychopharmacology* 19(4): 241–251.

Vredenbregt, Jacob. 1964. "Bawean Migrations: Some Preliminary Notes." *Bijdragen tot de Taal-, Land- en Volkenkunde* 120(1): 109–137.

Warren, James. 1986. *Rickshaw Coolie: A People's History of Singapore, 1880–1940.* Singapore: Oxford University Press.

———. 1993. *Ah Ku and Karayuki-san: Prostitution in Singapore, 1870–1940.* Singapore: Oxford University Press.

Waterson, Roxana. 1997. *The Living House: An Anthropology of Architecture in South-East Asia.* Singapore: Thames and Hudson.

Watts, Michael. 1992a. "Capitalisms, Crises, and Cultures I: Notes Toward a Totality of Fragments." In *Reworking Modernity: Capitalisms and Symbolic Discontent,* ed. Allan Pred and Michael Watts. New Brunswick, N.J.: Rutgers University Press.

———. 1992b. "The Shock of Modernity: Petroleum, Protest, and Fast Capitalism in an Industrializing Society." In *Reworking Modernity: Capitalisms and Symbolic Discontent,* ed. Allan Pred and Michael Watts. New Brunswick, N.J.: Rutgers University Press.

Wee, C. J. W.-L. 1996. "Staging the New Asia: Singapore's Dick Lee, Pop Music, and a Counter-Modernity." *Public Culture* 8(3): 489–510.

———. 1997. "Framing the 'New' East Asia: Anti-Imperialist Discourse and Global Capitalism." In *"The Clash of Civilizations?": Asian Responses,* ed. Salim Rashid. Dhaka: University Press Limited.

Wee, Vivienne. 1985. "Melayu: Hierarchies of Being in Riau." Ph.D. dissertation, Australian National University.

Weix, G. G. 1998. "Islamic Prayer Groups in Indonesia: Local Forums and Gendered Responses." *Critique of Anthropology* 18(4): 405–420.

White, Luise. 2000. *Speaking with Vampires: Rumor and History in Colonial Africa.* Berkeley: University of California Press.

Willis, Paul. 1977. *Learning to Labour: How Working Class Kids Get Working Class Jobs.* Farnborough, U.K.: Saxon House.

Winichakul, Thongchai. 1994. *Siam Mapped: A History of the Geo-Body of a Nation.* Honolulu: University of Hawai'i Press.

Winters, Jeffrey A. 1996. *Power in Motion: Capital Mobility and the Indonesian State.* Ithaca, N.Y.: Cornell University Press.

Wolf, Diane. 1992. *Factory Daughters: Gender, Household Dynamics, and Rural Industrialization in Java.* Berkeley: University of California Press.

Wolf, Eric. 2001. *Pathways of Power: Building an Anthropology of the Modern World.* Berkeley: University of California Press.

Wolters, O. W. 1970. *The Fall of Srivijaya in Malay History.* Ithaca, N.Y.: Cornell University Press.

Wong, Diana. 1997. "Transience and Settlement: Singapore's Foreign Labor Policy." *Asian and Pacific Migration Journal* 6(2): 135–167.

———. 2005. "The Rumor of Trafficking: Border Controls, Illegal Migration, and the Sovereignty of the Nation-State." In *Illicit Flows and Criminal Things: States, Borders, and the Other Side of Globalization,* ed. Willem van Schendel and Itty Abraham. Bloomington: Indiana University Press.

Yeoh, Brenda S. A. 2007. "Singapore: Hungry for Foreign Workers at All Skill Levels." *The Migration Information Source,* http://www.migrationinformation.org/Profiles/display.cfm?ID=570 (accessed on August 5, 2007).

Yeoh, Brenda, and Shirlena Huang. 1998. "Negotiating Public Space: Strategies and Styles of Migrant Female Domestic Workers in Singapore." *Urban Studies* 35(3): 583–602.

Yeoh, Brenda S. A., Shirlena Huang, and Joaquin Gonzalez III. 1999. "Migrant Female Domestic Workers: Debating the Economic, Social and Political Impacts in Singapore." *International Migration Review* 33: 114–136.

Zizek, Slavoj. 1995. *The Sublime Object of Ideology.* London: Verso.

INDEX

Photos are listed in **bold type**. Notes are abbreviated as "n." and (in the case of multiple notes), "nn."

ABOUT THE AUTHOR

Johan Lindquist received his PhD in social anthropology in 2002
at Stockholm University, where he is presently assistant professor.
He has also been a visiting scholar at Harvard and Cornell
universities. Dr. Lindquist's research focuses on Indonesia, and
he has published on topics dealing with migration, emotions,
drug use, HIV/AIDS, globalization, and human trafficking.
His documentary film, *B.A.T.A.M.,* was awarded first prize
at the film festival of the annual meeting of the American
Anthropological Association in 2005.

OTHER VOLUMES IN THE SERIES

Production Notes for Lindquist / The Anxieties of Mobility

Series designed by Richard Hendel
with text and display in Garamond Three

Composition by Josie Herr

Printed on 60# Text White Opaque, 426 ppi

£21.50

The Anxieties
of Mobility

Southeast Asia

POLITICS, MEANING, AND MEMORY

David Chandler and Rita Smith Kipp

SERIES EDITORS